Mini Mickey

THE POCKET-SIZED
unofficial GUIDE®
ᴛᴏ Walt Disney World®

9TH EDITION

**AVAILABLE FROM JOHN WILEY & SONS, INC., AND
JOHN WILEY & SONS LTD:**

Beyond Disney: The Unofficial Guide to Universal, SeaWorld,
and the Best of Central Florida

The Unofficial Guide to Britain's Best Days Out:
Theme Parks and Attractions

The Unofficial Guide to California with Kids

The Unofficial Guide to Cruises

The Unofficial Guide to Disneyland

The Unofficial Guide to Disneyland Paris

The Unofficial Guide to Dubai

The Unofficial Guide to Las Vegas

The Unofficial Guide to Walt Disney World

The Unofficial Guide to Walt Disney World with Kids

Mini Mickey

THE POCKET-SIZED *unofficial* GUIDE®
TO Walt Disney World®*

9TH EDITION

BOB SEHLINGER *and*
RITCHEY HALPHEN

*Walt Disney World is officially known as
the Walt Disney World Resort®.

WILEY

Please note that prices fluctuate in the course of time and that travel information changes under the impact of many factors that influence the travel industry. We therefore suggest that you write or call ahead for confirmation when making your travel plans. Every effort has been made to ensure the accuracy of information throughout this book, and the contents of this publication are believed to be correct at the time of printing. Nevertheless, the publishers cannot accept responsibility for errors or omissions, for changes in details given in this guide, or for the conse- quences of any reliance on the information provided by the same. Assessments of attractions and so forth are based upon the author's own experience; therefore, descriptions given in this guide necessarily contain an element of subjective opinion, which may not reflect the publisher's opinion or dictate a reader's own experience on another occasion. Readers are invited to write the publisher with ideas, comments, and suggestions for future editions.

Published by:
John Wiley & Sons, Inc.
111 River St.
Hoboken, NJ 07030-5774

Produced by Menasha Ridge Press

Cover design by Paul Dinovo

Interior design by Vertigo Design

For information on our other products and services or to obtain technical support, please contact our Customer Care Department within the United States at 800-762- 2974, outside the United States at 317-572-3993, or by fax at 317-572-4002.

John Wiley & Sons, Inc., also publishes its books in a variety of electronic formats. Some content that appears in print may not be available in electronic formats.

ISBN 978-1-118-01232-1

Manufactured in the United States of America

5 4 3 2 1

CONTENTS

LIST *of* MAPS

SPECIAL THANKS

A BIG SALUTE TO OUR WHOLE *UNOFFICIAL* TEAM, who rendered a Herculean effort in what must have seemed like a fantasy version of Sartre's *No Exit* to the tune of "It's a Small World." We hope you all recover to tour another day.

Kudos to *Unofficial Guide* research director Len Testa; cartoonist Tami Knight; child psychologist Karen Turnbow, PhD; *Unofficial Guide* statistician Fred Hazleton; and a horde of contributors and friends too numerous to list here.

Much appreciation also to editorial and production manager Molly Merkle, typesetter Annie Long, cartographers Steve Jones and Scott McGrew, and indexer Rich Carlson.
—*Bob Sehlinger and Ritchey Halphen*

Mini Mickey

THE POCKET-SIZED
unofficial GUIDE®
ᵀᴼ Walt Disney World®

9TH EDITION

INTRODUCTION

WHY *This* POCKET GUIDE?

THE OPTIMUM STAY AT WALT DISNEY WORLD is seven days, but many visitors don't have that long to devote to Disney attractions. Some are on business, with only a day or two available for Disney's enticements. Others are en route elsewhere or want to sample additional attractions in Orlando and central Florida. For these visitors, efficient, time-effective touring is a must. They can't afford long waits in line for rides, shows, or meals. They must determine as far in advance as possible what they really want to see.

This guide distills information from the comprehensive *Unoffcial Guide to Walt Disney World* to help short-stay or last-minute visitors decide quickly how best to spend their limited hours. It will help these guests answer questions vital to their enjoyment: What are the rides and attractions that appeal to me most? Which additional rides and attractions would I like to experience if I have any time left? What am I willing to forgo?

DECLARATION OF INDEPENDENCE

THE AUTHORS AND RESEARCHERS OF THIS guide are totally independent of Walt Disney Co., Inc.; Disneyland, Inc.; Walt Disney World, Inc.; and all other members of the Disney corporate family. We represent and serve the consumer. The material in this guide originated with the authors and researchers and hasn't been reviewed or edited by the Walt Disney Co., Disneyland, or Walt Disney World. Ours is the first comprehensive *critical* appraisal of Walt Disney World.

It aims to provide the information necessary to tour Walt Disney World with the greatest efficiency and economy.

HOW THIS GUIDE WAS RESEARCHED AND WRITTEN

LITTLE WRITTEN ABOUT DISNEY WORLD has been comparative or evaluative. Many guides parrot Disney's promotional material. In preparing this guide, however, we took nothing for granted. Each theme park was visited at different times throughout the year by trained observers. They conducted detailed evaluations and rated each park, with its component rides, shows, exhibits, services, and concessions, according to a formal, pretested rating method. Interviews were conducted to determine what tourists—of all ages—enjoyed most and least during their Disney World visit.

The essence of this guide consists of individual critiques and descriptions of the Magic Kingdom, Epcot, Disney's Animal Kingdom, and Disney's Hollywood Studios, plus detailed touring plans to help you avoid bottlenecks and crowds. Also included are descriptions for Typhoon Lagoon and Blizzard Beach water parks.

WALT DISNEY WORLD:
An Overview

THERE'S NOTHING ON EARTH LIKE Walt Disney World. Incredible in its scope, genius, beauty, and imagination, it's a joy and wonder for all ages. Disney attractions are a quantum leap beyond most man-made entertainment we know. We can't understand how anyone could visit Florida and bypass Walt Disney World.

WHAT WALT DISNEY WORLD ENCOMPASSES

WALT DISNEY WORLD ENCOMPASSES 43 square miles, an area twice as large as Manhattan. In this expanse are the **Magic Kingdom, Epcot, Disney's Animal Kingdom,** and **Disney's Hollywood Studios** theme parks; 2 water parks; a sports complex; 5 golf courses; 35 hotels and a campground; more than 100 restaurants; 4 interconnected lakes; a shopping complex; 8 convention venues; a nature preserve; and a transportation system.

The formal name is Walt Disney World, but most tourists refer to the entire Florida Disney facility simply as Disney World. The Magic Kingdom, Epcot, Disney's Animal Kingdom, and Disney's Hollywood Studios are thought of as being "in" Disney World.

THE MAJOR THEME PARKS

The Magic Kingdom

Opened in 1971, this is the heart of Disney World. It's the collection of adventures, rides, and shows symbolized by the Disney cartoon characters and Cinderella Castle. The Magic Kingdom is divided into seven subareas, or "lands," six of which are arranged around a Central Plaza. First encountered is **Main Street, U.S.A.** Moving clockwise around the hub, other lands are **Adventureland, Frontierland, Liberty Square, Fantasyland,** and **Tomorrowland. Bay Lake Tower,** the **Contemporary Resort, Polynesian Resort,** and **Grand Floridian Resort & Spa** are close to the Magic Kingdom and connected to it by monorail and boat. **Shades of Green** and **Wilderness Lodge & Villas** are nearby but not served by the monorail.

Epcot

Epcot opened in October 1982. Divided into two major areas, **Future World** and **World Showcase,** it's twice as big as the Magic Kingdom. Future World consists of pavilions relating to human creativity and technological advancement. World Showcase, arranged around a 41-acre lagoon, presents the architectural, social, and cultural heritages of 11 nations, each represented by famous landmarks and local settings.

Epcot has six hotels: the **Beach Club Resort, Yacht Club Resort, Beach Club Villas, BoardWalk Inn & Villas, Swan,** and **Dolphin.** All are within a 5- to 15-minute walk of the International Gateway entrance to Epcot. The hotels are also linked by canal. The monorail links Epcot to the Magic Kingdom and its hotels.

Disney's Animal Kingdom

Opened in 1998 and more than five times the size of the Magic Kingdom, Disney's Animal Kingdom combines zoological exhibits with rides, shows, and live entertainment. A lush rain forest funnels visitors to centrally located **Discovery Island,** dominated by the 14-story-tall, hand-carved Tree of Life. The island encompasses guest services, shopping, and dining. From here you can access the themed areas of **Africa, DinoLand U.S.A., Asia,** and **Camp Minnie-Mickey.** The 100-acre Africa has herds roaming in a re-creation of the Serengeti Plain.

Animal Kingdom has its own pay parking lot and is connected to other Disney World destinations by the Disney bus system. Although the park has no hotels, the **All-Star Resorts,**

Animal Kingdom Lodge and Villas, and **Coronado Springs Resort** are nearby.

Disney's Hollywood Studios

This $300-million, 100-plus-acre attraction opened in 1989 and has two areas. The first is a theme park related to the past, present, and future of the movie and television industries. It contains movie-theme rides and shows and covers about half the complex. The remaining half consists of three soundstages, a back lot of streets and sets, and creative support services.

DHS is connected to other Disney World areas by highway and canal but not by monorail. Guests can park in the Studios lot or commute by bus. Epcot resort guests can arrive by boat.

WATER PARKS

DISNEY WORLD HAS TWO WATER THEME parks: **Typhoon Lagoon** and **Blizzard Beach.** Typhoon Lagoon has a wave pool capable of producing six-foot waves; Blizzard Beach features more slides. Typhoon Lagoon and Blizzard Beach have their own parking lots.

OTHER DISNEY WORLD VENUES

Downtown Disney

This is a large shopping, dining, and entertainment complex encompassing **Downtown Disney Marketplace** on the east and **Downtown Disney West Side** on the west. The Marketplace has the world's largest Disney-merchandise store. The West Side combines nightlife, shopping, dining, and entertainment. It includes a permanent showplace for the extraordinary Cirque du Soleil show *La Nouba;* **DisneyQuest,** a high-tech, interactive virtual-reality and electronic-games venue; and a 24-screen cinema.

You can access Downtown Disney by bus from most Disney World locations.

Disney's BoardWalk

Near Epcot, the BoardWalk is an idealized replication of an East Coast 1930s waterfront resort. Open all day, it features restaurants, shops, and galleries; a brew pub; an **ESPN Sports Bar;** a nightclub with dueling pianos; and a dance club. Clubs levy a cover charge at night. Also on-site are a 372-room deluxe hotel and a 532-unit time-share development.

The BoardWalk is within walking distance of Epcot's resorts and International Gateway. Boats link it to Disney's Hollywood Studios; buses run to other Walt Disney World locations.

ESPN Wide World of Sports Complex

The 220-acre Wide World of Sports is a competition and training facility consisting of a 9,500-seat ballpark; two field houses; and venues for baseball, softball, tennis, track and field, beach volleyball, and 27 other sports. It's the spring training home for the Atlanta Braves, and it hosts numerous professional and amateur competitions. Spectators must pay. Guests may not use the facilities unless they're in one of the competitions.

Walt Disney World

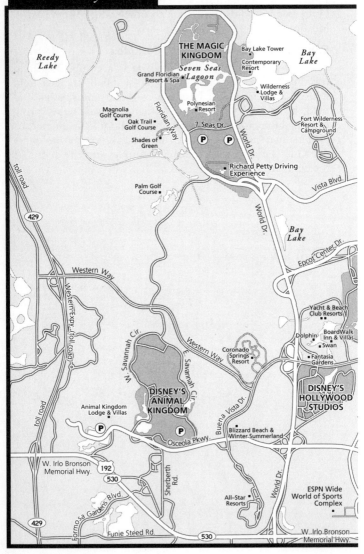

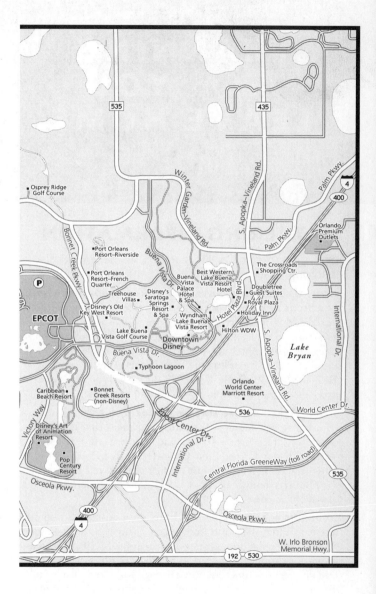

PART ONE

PLANNING *before* YOU LEAVE HOME

GATHERING INFORMATION

IN ADDITION TO THIS GUIDE, we recommend the following resources:

1. THE WALT DISNEY TRAVEL COMPANY FLORIDA VACATIONS BROCHURE AND VIDEO/DVD This resource describes Walt Disney World in its entirety, lists rates for all Disney resort hotels and campgrounds, and describes Disney World package vacations. The brochure and video/DVD are available from most travel agents or by calling the Walt Disney Travel Company at ☎ 407-828-8101 or 407-934-7639, or by visiting **disneyworld .com.** Be prepared to hold if you inquire by phone.

2. THE DISNEY CRUISE LINE BROCHURE AND DVD This brochure provides details on vacation packages that combine a cruise on the Disney Cruise Line with a stay at Disney World. Disney Cruise Line also offers a free DVD that tells all you need to know about Disney cruises and then some. To obtain a copy, call ☎ 800-951-3532 or order online at **disneycruise.com.**

3. TOURING PLANS.COM Our website offers more than 140 different touring plans and updates on changes at Walt Disney World. Our most popular new feature for subscribers is **Lines,** a mobile application that provides continuous real-time updates on wait times at Walt Disney World and Disneyland. Touring plans are also available. The app is free to touring plans.com subscribers for the Apple iPhone and iPad at the iTunes Store (search for "TouringPlans"; requires iOS 3.0 or later) and for Android OS–based phones at Android Market;

owners of other phones can use the Web-based version at **m.touringplans.com.**

4. ORLANDO MAGICARD If you're considering lodging outside Walt Disney World or if you think you might patronize attractions and restaurants outside of Disney World, it's worthwhile to obtain an Orlando Magicard, a Vacation Planner, and the Orlando Official Vacation Guide (all free) from the Orlando Official Visitor Center. The card can be conveniently downloaded from **orlandoinfo.com/magicard.** To order the accommodations guide, call ☎ 800-643-9492. For more information and materials, call ☎ 407-363-5872 or go to **visitorlando.com.** Phones are staffed during weekday business hours and 9 a.m.–3 p.m. EST weekends.

5. FLORIDA ROOMSAVER GUIDE Another good source of discounts on lodging, restaurants, and attractions statewide is *Florida RoomSaver.* You can sign-up at **roomsaver.com** to have a free monthly guide sent to you by e-mail, or you can view the guide online. You can request a hard copy by calling ☎ 800-222-3948 Monday–Friday, 8 a.m.–5 p.m. Eastern time. To order by mail, write to 13709 Progress Blvd., Box 14, Alachua, FL 32615. The guide is free, but you pay $3 for handling ($5 if shipped to Canada).

6. KISSIMMEE VISITOR'S GUIDE This full-color guide is one of the most complete available and is of particular interest to those who intend to book lodging outside of Disney World. It features ads for rental houses, time-shares, and condominiums, as wrll as a directory of attractions, restaurants, and other useful info. To receive a copy, call ☎ 800-327-9159, or view it online at **floridakiss.com.**

7. GUIDEBOOK FOR GUESTS WITH DISABILITIES Available at Guest Relations when entering the theme/water parks, at resort front desks, and wheelchair-rental areas (listed in each theme park chapter). PDF versions are available at **disney world.disney.go.com/guests-with-disabilities.**

WALT DISNEY WORLD ON THE WEB

SEARCHING THE INTERNET for Disney information is like navigating an immense maze for a very small piece of cheese: there's a lot of information out there, but you may have to wade through list after list until you find what you need.

Many individuals maintain elaborate Disney-related sites and chat groups, but the information they provide isn't always accurate.

Recommended Web Sites

UNOFFICIAL GUIDE research director Len Testa combs the Web looking for the best Disney-related sites. His picks follow below.

BEST OFFICIAL THEME PARK SITE The official **Walt Disney World website** (**disneyworld.com** or **disneyworld.disney.go .com**) is slightly more useful than the official sites for Universal Studios (**universalorlando.com**) and SeaWorld (**seaworld .com**). All three websites contain information on ticket options, park hours, height requirements for attractions, disabled-guest access, and the like. Disney's site also allows you to make dining reservations online. On the minus side, the site uses so many high-tech gimmicks that it sometimes just doesn't work.

BEST OFFICIAL MOM'S SITE Who knew? Walt Disney World has a Mom's Panel composed of more than a dozen moms and a few dads. The panelists have a website, **disneyworld moms.com,** where they offer tips, discuss how to plan a Disney World vacation, and answer questions about how those guys got into the henhouse.

BEST GENERAL UNOFFICIAL WALT DISNEY WORLD SITE Besides touringplans.com, Deb Wills's comprehensive **allears.net** is the first site we recommend to friends who are interested in making a trip to Disney World. Want to know what a room at a Disney resort looks like before you book one? This site has photos—sometimes for each floor of a resort. The site is updated several times per week and includes menus from Disney restaurants, ticketing information, maps, and more.

BEST MONEY-SAVING SITE Mary Waring's **MouseSavers** (**mousesavers.com**) is the kind of site for which the Web was invented. It keeps an updated list of discounts and reservation codes for use at Disney resorts, along with discount codes for rental cars and non-Disney hotels in the area.

BEST WALT DISNEY WORLD PREVIEW SITE If you want to see what a particular attraction is like, visit **YouTube** (**youtube .com**). Enter the name of the desired attraction in the search bar at the top of the page, and several videos should come up. Good for previewing potentially scary rides with kids.

OTHER SITES Facebook and **Twitter** are popular places for Disney fans to gather online and share comments, tips, and photos. Following fellow Disneyphiles as they share their in-park experiences can make you feel like you're there, even as you're stuck in a cubicle at work.

BEST DISNEY DISCUSSION BOARDS The best online discussions of all things Disney can be found at **disboards.com.** With tens of thousands of members and millions of posts, these discussion boards are the most active and popular on the Web.

BEST INTERNET RADIO STATION We thought our couple-hundred-hour collection of theme park digital audio was complete until we found **mouseworldradio.com.** Several different radio stations are available (some free, others for a small fee), playing everything from attraction ride scores and hotel background music to old sound clips from Disney resort TV ads. The tracks match what the Disney parks are playing at the time of day you're listening.

BEST MOBILE APPLICATION FOR WDW As far as all-purpose apps go, **E-Ticket** (iPhone; $6) has the most going for it, using the vast resources of **wdwinfo.com** to assist you in organizing the myriad details necessary for a successful trip. It contains satellite maps; locator buttons; information and reviews of all resorts, parks, attractions, and dining; and features for itinerary planning.

BEST DISNEY PLANNING PODCAST *Unofficial Guide* coauthor Len Testa cohosts a thrice-weekly podcast (on Monday, Wednesday, and Friday) on all things related to Disney World. Free subscriptions are available through iTunes. Visit **wdw today.com** for more details.

BEST DISNEY BLOG John Frost's unofficial **thedisneyblog.com** is witty, concise, and updated continually. Topics cover everything in the Disney universe, from theme parks and movies to the latest rumors.

BEST SITE FOR BREAKING NEWS AND RUMORS We try to check **wdwmagic.com** every few days for the latest news and gossip on Disney World. The site also features pages dedicated to major rides, parades, and shows in each park, including audio and video. A caveat: some readers report that maintenance and accuracy have taken a slight hit recently.

BEST THEME-PARK-INSIDER SITE Well researched and supplied with limitless insider information, **jimhillmedia.com** guides you through the internal squabbles, shareholder revolts, and outside competition that have made (and that still make) Walt Disney World what it is.

BEST TRIVIA SITES Lou Mongello's excellent *Walt Disney World Trivia Book* has an equally good online companion; check it out on iTunes and at **wdwradio.com.** You'll find message boards, Disney-theme-park news, and more. Lou hosts live Net chats at his site, usually on Wednesdays. Lou also hosts the WDW Radio Show podcast.

Fans of Steve Barrett's *Hidden Mickeys* book now have an online destination where they can keep updated on the latest tri-circle sightings at **hiddenmickeysguide.com.**

BEST ONLINE TOUR Disney has teamed up with Google to present a 3-D virtual walk-through of the Orlando theme parks and resorts via Google Earth. Visit **disneyworld .com/3dparks.**

BEST ORLANDO WEATHER INFORMATION Printable 15-day Orlando-area forecasts are available from **accuweather.com.**

BEST SAFETY SITE Check **flhsmv.gov/fhp/cps** to learn about state child-restraint requirements.

BEST WEB SITE FOR ORLANDO TRAFFIC, ROADWORK, AND CON- STRUCTION INFORMATION Visit **expresswayauthority.com** for the latest information on roadwork in the Orlando and Orange County areas. The site also contains maps, direc- tions, and toll-rate information.

BEST DRIVING DIRECTIONS The printable directions available at **mapquest.com** are accurate and efficient. We especially like the feature that allows you to get driving directions for the return drive with the click of a button.

WHEN *to* GO *to* WALT DISNEY WORLD

SELECTING THE TIME OF YEAR FOR YOUR VISIT

WALT DISNEY WORLD IS BUSIEST Christmas Day through New Year's Day. Also extremely busy are Thanksgiving weekend, the week of Presidents Day, the first full week of November, spring break for colleges, and late March through the third week of April. On just a single day in these peak times, as many as 92,000 people have toured the Magic Kingdom! This level of attendance isn't typical—only those who simply cannot go at any other time should tackle the parks at their peak.

The least busy time is from Labor Day in September through the beginning of October. Next slowest are the sec- ond full week of November through the weekend preced- ing Thanksgiving, the week after Thanksgiving until the week before Christmas, January 4 through the first week

IMPORTANT WALT DISNEY WORLD ADDRESSES

Compliments, Complaints, and Suggestions
Walt Disney World Guest Communications
P. O. Box 10040
Lake Buena Vista, FL 32830-1000

Convention and Banquet Information
Walt Disney World Resort South
P.O. Box 10000
Lake Buena Vista, FL 32830-1000

**Merchandise Mail Order
(Guest Service Mail Order)**
P.O. Box 10070
Lake Buena Vista, FL 32830-0070

**Walt Disney World
Central Reservations**
P.O. Box 10100
Lake Buena Vista, FL 32830-0100

Walt Disney World Educational Programs
P.O. Box 10000
Lake Buena Vista, FL 32830-1000

Walt Disney World Info/Guest Letters/Letters to Mickey Mouse
P.O. Box 10040
Lake Buena Vista, FL 32830-0040

Walt Disney World Ticket Mail Order
P.O. Box 10140
Lake Buena Vista, FL 32830-0140

IMPORTANT WALT DISNEY WORLD PHONE NUMBERS

General Information	☎ 407-824-4321
	or 407-824-2222
Accommodations/Reservations	☎ 407-934-7639
Convention Information	☎ 407-828-3200
Dining Advance Reservations	☎ 407-939-3463
Disabled Guests Special Requests	☎ 407-939-7807
Lost and Found	☎ 407-824-4245
Merchandise Guest Services	☎ 407-363-6200
Resort Dining	☎ 407-939-3463
Telecommunication for the Deaf Reservations	☎ 407-939-7670
Walt Disney Travel Company	☎ 407-828-3232
Weather Information	☎ 407-827-4545

of February (except the Martin Luther King Jr. holiday weekend and the weekend of the Disney World Marathon), and the last week of April through early June. Late February, March, and early April are dicey. Crowds ebb and flow according to spring-break schedules and the timing of Presidents Day weekend. Though crowds have grown in September and October as a result of promotions aimed at locals and the international market, these months continue to be good for weekday touring at the Magic Kingdom, Disney's Hollywood Studios, and Disney's Animal Kingdom, and for weekend visits to Epcot.

The Downside of Off-season Touring

Though we strongly recommend going to Disney World in the fall, winter, or spring, there are a few trade-offs. The parks often open late and close early during the off-season. When they open as late as 9 a.m., everyone arrives at about the same time. A late opening coupled with an early closing drastically reduces touring hours. Even when crowds are small, it's difficult to see big parks such as the Magic Kingdom between 9 a.m. and 6 p.m. Early closing (before 8 p.m.) also usually means no evening parades or fireworks. And because these are slow times, some rides and attractions may be closed. Finally, Central Florida temperatures fluctuate wildly during late fall, winter, and early spring; daytime highs in the 40s and 50s aren't uncommon.

Given the choice, however, smaller crowds, bargain prices, and stress-free touring are worth risking cold weather or closed attractions. Touring in fall and other "off" periods is so much easier that our research team, at the risk of being blasphemous, would advise taking children out of school for a Disney World visit.

EXTRA MAGIC HOURS

EXTRA MAGIC HOURS IS A PERK FOR families staying at a Walt Disney World resort, including the Swan, Dolphin, and Shades of Green, and the Hilton in the Downtown Disney Resort Area. On selected days of the week, Disney resort guests will be able to enter a Disney theme park 1 hour earlier, or stay in a selected theme park up to 3 hours later than the official park operating hours. Theme park visitors not staying at a Disney resort may stay in the park for Extra Magic Hour evenings but cannot experience any rides, attractions, or shows. In other words, they can shop and eat.

CROWD CONDITIONS AND THE BEST AND WORST PARKS TO VISIT FOR EACH DAY OF THE YEAR We receive thousands of e-mails and letters inquiring about crowd conditions on specific dates throughout the year. Readers also want to know which park is best to visit on each day of their stay. To make things easier for you (and us!), we provide at **touringplans.com** a calendar covering the next year (click "Crowd Calendar" on the home page). For each date, we offer a crowd-level index based on a scale of 1 to 10, with 1 being least crowded and 10 being most crowded. Our calendar takes into account all holidays, special events, and more The same calendar lists the best and worst park(s) to visit in terms of crowd conditions on any given day. Collecting data for the Crowd Calendar requires us to have researchers in the parks year-round. Thus, to keep the calendar current on a daily basis, we have to charge a modest subscription fee. The same fee also provides access to additional touring plans and other features. Owners of the current edition of *The Unofficial Guide to Walt Disney World,* as well as owners of the previous year's edition, are eligible for a substantial discount on the subscription.

SUMMER AND HOLIDAYS If you visit on a nonholiday midsummer day, arrive at the turnstile 30–40 minutes before the stated opening on a non-early-entry day. If you visit during a major holiday period, arrive 1 hour before. Hit your favorite rides early using one of our touring plans, then go back to your hotel for lunch, a swim, and perhaps a nap. If you're interested in the special parades and shows, return to the park in late afternoon or early evening. Assume that unless you use Fastpass, early morning will be the only time you can experience the attractions without long waits. Finally, don't wait until the last minute in the evening to leave the park. The exodus at closing is truly mind-boggling.

Epcot is usually the least crowded park during holidays. Expect the others to be mobbed. To save time in the morning, buy your admission in advance. Also, consider bringing your own stroller or wheelchair instead of renting one of Disney's. If you're touring Epcot or the Magic Kingdom and plan to spend the day, try exiting the park for lunch at a nearby resort hotel. Above all, bring your sense of humor, and pay attention to your group's morale.

PART TWO

MAKING *the* MOST *of* YOUR TIME *and* MONEY

ALLOCATING MONEY

HOW MUCH YOU SPEND DEPENDS ON HOW long you stay at Disney World. But even if you visit only for an afternoon, be prepared to drop a bundle. In Part Three, we'll show you how to save money on lodging, and in Part Eight, you'll find lots of tips for economizing on meals. This section will give you some sense of what you can expect to pay for admission, as well as which admission option will best meet your needs.

WALT DISNEY WORLD ADMISSION OPTIONS

IN AN EFFORT TO ACCOMMODATE various vacation needs, Disney offers a number of different admission options. These range from the humble One-day Base Ticket, good for a single entry into one Disney theme park, to the top-of-the-line Premium Annual Pass, good for 365 days of admission into every Disney theme or water park, plus DisneyQuest.

The sheer number of ticket options available makes it difficult and, yes, daunting to sort out which option represents the least expensive way to see and do everything you want. Finding the optimum admission, or combination of admissions, however, could save the average family a nice little bundle.

HELP IS ON THE WAY!

TO SIMPLIFY THINGS, we tried to define guidelines to help you choose the best ticket options for your vacation. After a day or so, we realized that a handful of general guidelines was an impossible task, so we wrote a computer program to figure it out. You can use the program to determine the best ticket options for you by visiting our website, **touringplans.com** (choose the ticket calculator from the "Walt Disney World" pull-down menu at the top of the page). It aggregates ticket prices from a number of online ticket vendors, including Disney itself. Just answer a few simple questions relating to the size of your party and the theme parks you intend to visit, and the calculator then identifies your four least expensive ticket options.

MAGIC YOUR WAY

WALT DISNEY WORLD OFFERS AN ARRAY of theme park ticket options, grouped into a program called Magic Your Way. The simplest option, visiting one theme park for one day, is called a One-day Base Ticket. Other features, such as the ability to visit more than one park per day ("park hopping"), or the inclusion of admission to Disney's minor venues (Typhoon Lagoon, Blizzard Beach, DisneyQuest, and the like), are available as individual add-ons to the Base Ticket.

The more days of admission you purchase, the lower the cost per day. For example, if you buy an adult five-day Base Ticket for $267.32 (taxes included), each day will cost $53.46, compared with $90.53 a day for a one-day pass. Base Tickets can be purchased from 1 up to 10 days and admit you to exactly one theme park per day.

Base Tickets also expire 14 days from the first day of use. If, say, you purchase a four-day Base Ticket on June 1 and use it that day for admission to the Magic Kingdom, you'll be able to visit a single Disney theme park on any of your three remaining days between June 2 and June 15. After that, the ticket expires and any unused days will be lost. Through another add-on, however, you can avoid the 14-day expiration and make your ticket valid forever. More on that later.

BASE TICKET ADD-ON OPTIONS

THREE ADD-ON OPTIONS ARE OFFERED with the Base Ticket, each at an additional cost:

PARK HOPPER Adding this feature to your Base Ticket allows you to visit more than one theme park per day. The cost is $58.58 (including tax) on top of the price of any Base Ticket. It's an exorbitant price for one or two days, but it becomes more affordable the longer your stay. As an add-on to a seven-day Base Ticket, the flat fee would work out to $8.37 per day for park-hopping privileges. If you want to visit the Magic Kingdom in the morning and dine at Epcot in the evening, this is the feature to request.

NO EXPIRATION Adding this option to your ticket means that unused admissions to the major theme parks and the swimming parks, as well as other minor venues, never expire. If you added this option to a 10-day Base Ticket and used only 4 days this year, the remaining 6 days could be used for admission at any date in the future. The No Expiration option ranges from $26.63 with tax for a 2-day ticket to $239.63 for a 10-day Base Ticket. This option is not available on single-day tickets.

> **unofficial TIP** With the No Expiration option, any admissions you don't use are good forever, including visits to the water parks and the ESPN sports complex).

WATER PARK FUN AND MORE (WPFAM) This option gives you a single admission to one of Disney's water parks (Blizzard Beach and Typhoon Lagoon), DisneyQuest, Oak Trail Golf Course, or the ESPN Wide World of Sports Complex. The cost is a flat $58.58 (including tax). Except for the single-day WPFAM ticket, which gives you two admissions, the number of admissions equals the number of days on your Base Ticket. If you buy an 8-day Base Ticket, for example, and add the WPFAM option, you get eight WPFAM admissions. What you can't do is, say, buy a 10-day Base Ticket with only three admissions or a 3-day Base Ticket with four admissions. You can, however, skip WPFAM entirely and buy an individual admission to any of these minor parks. This last option is almost always the best deal if you want to visit only one of the venues above.

Annual Passes

An Annual Pass provides unlimited use of the major theme parks for one year; a Premium Annual Pass also provides unlimited use of the minor parks. Annual Pass holders also get perks, including free parking and seasonal offers such as room-rate discounts at Disney resorts. The Annual Pass is not valid for special events, such as admission to Mickey's Very Merry Christmas Party. Tax included, Annual Passes run $552.74 for adults and $509.07 for children ages 3–9. A Premium Annual Pass, at $691.19 for adults and $636.87 for children ages 3–9, provides unlimited admission to Blizzard Beach, Typhoon Lagoon, DisneyQuest, and Oak Trail Golf Course, in addition to the four major theme parks. In addition to Annual Passes, Florida residents are eligible for discounts

> **unofficial TIP** The longer your Disney vacation, the more you save with the Annual Pass.

MAGIC YOUR WAY ADMISSION CHART

TICKET TYPE						
7-day	6-day	5-day	4-day	3-day	2-day	1-day
BASE TICKET ADULTS						
$284	$276	$267	$259	$247	$179	$91
$41/day	$46/day	$53/day	$65/day	$82/day	$89/day	–
BASE TICKET CHILDREN (ages 3–9)						
$264	$256	$247	$239	$228	$165	$84
$38/day	$43/day	$49/day	$60/day	$76/day	$83/day	–
PARK HOPPER ADD-ON						
$59	$59	$59	$59	$59	$59	$59
$8/day	$10/day	$12/day	$15/day	$20/day	$29/day	–
WATER PARK FUN AND MORE ADD-ON						
$59 for 7 visits	$59 for 6 visits	$59 for 5 visits	$59 for 4 visits	$59 for 3 visits	$59 for 2 visits	$59 for 2 visits
$8/visit	$10/visit	$12/visit	$15/visit	$20/visit	$30/visit	$30/visit
NO EXPIRATION ADD-ON						
$170	$138	$122	$80	$37	$27	–

All prices include tax and are rounded to the nearest dollar.

on one-day theme park Base Tickets (about 10%) as well as on various add-on options.

HOW TO GET THE MOST FROM MAGIC YOUR WAY

FIRST, HAVE A REALISTIC IDEA OF WHAT you want out of your vacation. As with anything, it doesn't make sense to pay for options you'll never use. A seven-day theme park ticket with five pluses might seem like a wonderful idea, but actually trying to visit all those parks in a week in July might end up feeling more like Navy SEAL training. If you're going to make only one visit to a water park, DisneyQuest, or ESPN Wide World of Sports Complex, you're almost always better off purchasing that admission separately rather than in the WPFAM option.

Next, think carefully about paying for the No Expiration option. An inside source reports that fewer than 1 in 10 admission tickets with rollover days are ever reused at a Disney theme park. The rest are misplaced, discarded, or forgotten. Unless you're absolutely certain you'll be returning to Walt Disney World within the next year or two and have identified a safe place to keep those unused tickets, we don't think the additional cost is worth the risk.

WHERE TO PURCHASE
MAGIC YOUR WAY TICKETS

YOU CAN BUY YOUR ADMISSION PASSES on arrival at Walt Disney World or purchase them in advance. Admission passes are available at Walt Disney World resorts and theme parks. Passes are also available at some non-Disney hotels and certain Walt Disney World–area grocery stores, and from independent ticket brokers. Offers of free or heavily discounted tickets abound, but they generally require you to attend a timeshare sales presentation.

Magic Your Way tickets are available at Disney Stores and at **disneyworld.com** for the same prices listed in the chart on the facing page.

If you're trying to keep costs to an absolute minimum, consider using an online ticket wholesaler, such as **maple leaftickets.com, theofficialticketcenter.com,** or **undercover tourist.com,** especially for trips with five or more days in the theme parks. All tickets sold are brand-new, and savings can range from $2 to more than $41, depending on the ticket and options chosen.

The Official Ticket Center, Maple Leaf Tickets, and Undercover Tourist offer discounts on tickets for almost all Central Florida attractions, including Disney World, Universal Orlando, SeaWorld, and Cirque du Soleil. Discounts for the major theme parks are about 6–8.5%. Tickets for other attractions are more deeply discounted.

Finally, if all this is too confusing, our website will help you navigate all of the choices and find you the least-expensive ticket options for your vacation. Visit **touringplans .com** for more details.

For Additional Information on Passes

If you have a question or concern regarding admissions that can be addressed by talking to a living, breathing human being, call **Disney Ticket Inquiries** at ☎ 407-566-4985, or e-mail **ticket.inquiries@disneyworld.com.** If you need current prices or routine information, you're better off calling ☎ 407-824-4321 for recorded admission information, or visiting **disney world.com.**

Special Passes

Walt Disney World offers a number of special and situational passes that are not known to the general public and are not sold at any Disney World ticket booth. The best information we've found on these passes is available on the Internet at **mousesavers.com.**

ALLOCATING TIME

WHICH PARK TO SEE FIRST?

THIS QUESTION IS LESS ACADEMIC THAN it appears, especially if there are children or teenagers in your party. Children who see the Magic Kingdom first expect more of the same type of entertainment at the other parks. At Epcot, they're often disappointed by the educational orientation and more serious tone (many adults react the same way). Disney's Hollywood Studios offers some pretty wild action, but the general presentation is educational and more adult. Though most children enjoy zoos, animals can't be programmed to entertain. Thus, children may not find Disney's Animal Kingdom as exciting as the Magic Kingdom or Disney's Hollywood Studios.

First-time visitors should see Epcot first; you will be able to enjoy it fully without having been preconditioned to think of Disney entertainment as solely fantasy or adventure. See Disney's Animal Kingdom second. Like Epcot, it's educational, but its live animals provide a change of pace. Next, see Disney's Hollywood Studios, which helps all ages make a fluid transition from the educational Epcot and Animal Kingdom to the fanciful Magic Kingdom. Also, because Disney's Hollywood Studios is smaller, you won't walk as much or stay as long. Save the Magic Kingdom for last.

OPERATING HOURS

DISNEY RUNS A DOZEN OR MORE SCHEDULES each year. Call ☎ 407-824-4321 for the exact hours before you arrive. Off-season, parks may be open as few as 8 hours (9 a.m.– 5 p.m.). At busy times (particularly holidays), they may operate from 8 a.m. until 2 a.m. We also maintain more easily readable park hours and entertainment and Extra Magic Hour schedules at **touringplans.com** and through our mobile application, **Lines** (**touringplans.com/lines**).

Official Opening vs. Real Opening

Operating hours you're quoted when you call are "official hours." Sometimes, the parks actually open earlier. If the official hours are 9 a.m.–9 p.m., for example, Main Street in the Magic Kingdom might open at 8:30 a.m. and the remainder of the park will open at 9 a.m.

Disney surveys local hotel reservations, estimates how many visitors to expect on a given day, and opens the theme parks early to avoid bottlenecks at parking facilities and ticket windows and to absorb crowds as they arrive.

Rides and attractions shut down at approximately the official closing time. Main Street in the Magic Kingdom remains open 30 minutes to an hour after the rest of the park has closed.

THE CARDINAL RULES FOR SUCCESSFUL TOURING

EVEN THE MOST TIME-EFFECTIVE TOURING plan won't allow you to cover two or more major theme parks in one day. Plan to allocate at least an entire day to each park (an exception to this rule is when the parks close at different times, allowing you to tour one park until closing and then proceed to another park).

unofficial **TIP**
If your schedule allows only one day of touring, concentrate on one park and save the others for another visit.

One-day Touring

A comprehensive one-day tour of the Magic Kingdom, Disney's Animal Kingdom, Epcot, or Disney's Hollywood Studios is possible but requires knowledge of the park, good planning, and plenty of energy and endurance. One-day touring doesn't leave much time for sit-down meals, prolonged browsing in shops, or lengthy breaks. One-day touring can be fun and rewarding, but allocating two days per park, especially for the Magic Kingdom and Epcot, is always preferable.

Successful touring of the Magic Kingdom, Animal Kingdom, Epcot, or Disney's Hollywood Studios hinges on *three rules:*

1. Determine in Advance What You Really Want to See

To help you set your touring priorities, we describe the theme parks and every attraction in detail in this book. In each description, we include the author's evaluation of the attraction and the opinions of Walt Disney World guests expressed as star ratings. Five stars is the best possible rating.

Finally, because attractions range from midway-type rides and horse-drawn trolleys to colossal, high-tech extravaganzas, we've developed a hierarchy of categories to pinpoint an attraction's magnitude:

SUPER-HEADLINERS The best attractions that the theme park has to offer. Mind-boggling in size, scope, and imagination, they represent the cutting edge of modern attraction technology and design.

HEADLINERS Full-blown multimillion-dollar themed adventures and theater presentations. They are modern in technology and design and employ a full range of special effects.

unofficial **TIP**
Meeting characters, posing for photos, and collecting autographs can burn hours of touring time.

MAJOR ATTRACTIONS Themed adventures on a more modest scale but which incorporate state-of-the-art technologies, or larger-scale attractions of older design.

MINOR ATTRACTIONS Midway-type rides, small "dark" rides (cars on a track, zig-zagging through the dark), small theater presentations, transportation rides, and walk-through attractions.

DIVERSIONS Exhibits, both passive and interactive, such as playgrounds, video arcades, and street theater.

2. Arrive Early! Arrive Early! Arrive Early!

Have breakfast before you arrive so you won't waste prime touring time sitting in a restaurant. The earlier a park opens, the greater your potential advantage. This is because most vacationers won't make the sacrifice to rise early and get to a theme park before it opens. Fewer people are willing to be on hand for an 8 a.m. opening than for a 9 a.m. opening. On those rare occasions when a park opens at 10 a.m., almost everyone arrives at the same time, so it's almost impossible to get a jump on the crowd. If you are visiting during midsummer, arrive at the turnstile 30–40 minutes before official opening time. During holiday periods, get to the parks 45–60 minutes before official opening.

3. Avoid Bottlenecks

We provide touring plans for the Magic Kingdom, Disney's Animal Kingdom, Epcot, and Disney's Hollywood Studios to help you avoid bottlenecks. In addition, we provide detailed information on all rides and performances, enabling you to estimate how long you may have to wait in line and allowing you to compare rides for their capacity to accommodate large crowds. Touring plans for the Magic Kingdom begin on page 162; Epcot, on page 200; Disney's Animal Kingdom, on page 230; and Disney's Hollywood Studios, on page 255.

TOURING PLANS EXPLAINED

OUR TOURING PLANS ARE STEP-BY-STEP guides for seeing as much as possible with a minimum of standing in line. They're designed to help you avoid crowds and bottlenecks on days of moderate–heavy attendance. On days of lighter attendance (see "Selecting the Time of Year for Your Visit," page 12), the plans will still save time but won't be as critical to successful touring.

What You Can Expect from the Touring Plans

Though we present one-day touring plans for each of the theme parks, you should understand that the Magic Kingdom and Epcot have far more attractions than you can reasonably see in one day, even if you never wait in line. If you must cram your visit into a single day, the one-day touring plans will enable you to see as much as is humanly possible. Under certain circumstances, you may not complete the plan, and you definitely won't be able to see everything. For the Magic Kingdom and Epcot, the most comprehensive, efficient, and relaxing touring plans are the two-day plans. Although Disney's Hollywood Studios has grown considerably since its 1989 debut, you should have no problem seeing everything in one day. Likewise, Disney's Animal Kingdom is a one-day outing.

Variables that Affect the Success of Touring Plans

How quickly you move from one ride to another; when and how many refreshment and restroom breaks you take; when, where, and how you eat meals; and your ability to find your way around will all have an impact on the success of the plans. Smaller groups almost always move faster than larger groups, and parties of adults generally can cover more ground than families with young children. Switching off (see page 75), among other things, inhibits families with little ones from moving expeditiously among attractions. Plus, some children simply cannot conform to the "early to rise" conditions of the touring plans.

If you have young children in your party, be prepared for character encounters. The appearance of a Disney character usually stops a touring plan in its tracks. While some characters stroll the parks, it's equally common that they assemble in a specific venue (such as Exposition Hall on Main Street, U.S.A.) where families queue up for photos and autographs. Meeting characters, posing for photos, and collecting autographs can burn hours of touring time. If your kids collect character autographs, you need to anticipate these interruptions and negotiate some understanding with your children about when you'll follow the plan and when you'll collect autographs.

While we realize that following the touring plans is not always easy, we still recommend continuous, expeditious touring until around noon. After noon, breaks and diversions won't affect the plans significantly. If unforeseen events interrupt a plan, skip one step on the plan for every 20 minutes you're delayed. If you lose your billfold, for example, and spend an hour finding it, skip three steps and pick up from there.

Flexibility

The attractions included in the touring plans are the most popular ones as determined by more than 39,000 reader surveys. Even so, your favorite attractions might be different. Fortunately, the touring plans are flexible. If a plan calls for an attraction you don't wish to experience, simply skip it and move on to the next one. You can also substitute similar attractions in the same area of the park. If a plan calls for, say, riding Dumbo and you're not interested but you'd enjoy the Mad Tea Party (which is not on the plan), then go ahead and substitute it for Dumbo. As long as the substitution is a similar attraction—substituting a show for a ride won't work—and is pretty close to the attraction called for in the touring plan, you won't compromise the plan's overall effectiveness.

A Clamor for Additional Touring Plans

We're inundated by letters urging us to create additional plans. These include a plan for ninth- and tenth-graders, a plan for rainy days, a seniors' plan, a plan for folks who sleep late, a plan omitting rides that "bump, jerk, and clonk," a plan for gardening enthusiasts, a plan for kids who are afraid of skeletons, and a plan for single women.

The plans in this book are flexible. Adapt them to your preferences. If you don't like rides that bump and jerk, skip those when they come up in a plan. If you want to sleep in and go to the park at noon, use the afternoon part of a plan. If you're a ninth-grader and want to ride Space Mountain three times in a row, do it. Will it decrease the plans' effectiveness? Sure, but they were created only to help you have fun. It's your day.

For those using the plans in this guide or the specialized plans at our website, **touringplans.com,** the latter provide updated information on park operating hours, parade times and showtimes, and attractions closed for maintenance.

FASTPASS

YOUR HANDOUT PARK MAP, AS WELL AS signage at respective attractions, will tell you which attractions are included in the Fastpass program. Attractions operating Fastpass will have a regular line and a Fastpass line. A sign at the entrance will tell you how long the wait is in the regular line. If the wait is acceptable to you, hop in line. If the wait seems too long, you can insert your park-admission pass into a special Fastpass machine and receive an appointment time (for sometime later in the day) to come back and ride. When you return at the appointed time, you will enter the Fastpass line and proceed directly to the attraction's preshow or boarding area with no further wait. There is no extra charge to use Fastpass.

Fastpass doesn't eliminate the need to arrive at the theme park early. Because each park offers a limited number of Fastpass attractions, you still need to get an early start if you want to see as much as possible in a single day. Plus, as we'll discuss later, there is a limited supply of Fastpasses available for each attraction on a given day. If you don't arrive until the middle of the afternoon, you might find that all the Fastpasses have been distributed to other guests. Fastpass does make it possible to see more with less waiting than ever before, and it's a great benefit to those who like to sleep late or who enjoy an afternoon or evening at the theme parks on their arrival day at Walt Disney World. It also allows you to postpone wet rides, such as Kali River Rapids at Disney's Animal Kingdom and Splash Mountain at the Magic Kingdom, until the warmer part of the day.

UNDERSTANDING THE FASTPASS SYSTEM When you insert your admission pass into a Fastpass time clock, the machine spits out a small slip of paper about two-thirds the size of a credit card—small enough to fit in your wallet but also small enough to lose easily. Printed on the paper is the name of the attraction and a specific 1-hour time window, for example 1:15–2:15 p.m., during which you can return to enjoy the ride.

When you report back to the attraction during your 1-hour window, you'll enter a line marked FASTPASS RETURN that will route you more or less directly to the boarding or preshow area. Each person in your party must have his or her own Fastpass and be ready to show it to the Disney cast member at the entrance of the Fastpass Return line. Before you enter the boarding area or theater, another cast member will collect your Fastpass.

You can obtain a Fastpass anytime after a park opens, but the Fastpass Return lines do not begin operating until 35–90 minutes after opening. Thus, if the Magic Kingdom opens at 9 a.m., the Fastpass time clock machines will also be available at 9 a.m., and the Fastpass Return line will begin operating at about 9:35 a.m.

WHEN TO USE FASTPASS Except as discussed on the next page, there's no reason to use Fastpass during the first 30–40 minutes a park is open. Lines for most attractions are quite manageable during this period, and this is the only time of day when Fastpass attractions exclusively serve those in the regular line. Regardless of time of day, however, if the wait in the regular line at a Fastpass attraction is 25–30 minutes or less, we recommend joining the regular line.

FASTPASS RULES Disney allows you to obtain a second Fastpass at a time printed on the bottom of your most recent pass, usually 2 hours or less from the time the first was issued. Rules aside, the real lesson here is to check out the posted return time before obtaining a Fastpass. If the return time is hours away, forgo the Fastpass. Especially in the Magic Kingdom, there will be a number of other Fastpass attractions where the return time is only an hour or so away. Disney rarely enforces the expiration time on the return window, meaning that Fastpasses are good from the beginning of the window until park closing.

Fastpass Guidelines

- Don't mess with Fastpass unless it can save you 30 minutes or more.

- If you arrive after a park opens, obtain a Fastpass for your preferred Fastpass attraction first thing.

- Do not obtain a Fastpass for a theater attraction until you have experienced all the Fastpass rides on your itinerary (using Fastpass at theater attractions usually requires more time than using the standby line).

- Always check the Fastpass return period before obtaining your Fastpass.

- Obtain Fastpasses for Peter Pan's Flight, Space Mountain, Splash Mountain, and Winnie the Pooh at the Magic Kingdom; Mission: SPACE, Soarin', and Test Track at Epcot; Expedition Everest at Disney's Animal Kingdom; and Rock 'n' Roller Coaster and Toy Story Mania! at Disney's Hollywood Studios as early in the day as possible.

- Try to obtain Fastpasses for rides not mentioned in the preceding tip by 1 p.m.

- Don't depend on Fastpasses being available for rides after 2 p.m. during busier times of year.

- Make sure everyone in your party has his or her own Fastpass.

- You can obtain a second Fastpass at the time printed at the bottom of your first Fastpass.

TRICKS OF THE TRADE It's possible to acquire a second Fastpass before using the first one (and sooner than 2 hours after getting it). Let's say you obtain a Fastpass to Kilimanjaro Safaris at Disney's Animal Kingdom with a return time of 10:15–11:15 a.m. Any time after your Fastpass window begins, you can get another Fastpass, say for Kali River Rapids. This is possible because the Fastpass computer monitors only the distribution of passes, ignoring whether or when a Fastpass is used.

unofficial **TIP**
Obtain Fastpasses for all members of your party, including those who are too short, too young, or simply not interested in riding. This is a convenient way for parents and kids alike to work in extra rides on attractions they really enjoy.

When obtaining Fastpasses, it's faster and more considerate of other guests if one person obtains passes for your entire party. This means entrusting one individual with both your park-admission passes and your Fastpasses, so choose wisely.

Our mobile wait-times app, **Lines,** will show you which Fastpass attractions still have passes available and when we estimate they'll run out. See Lines in action before you go at **touringplans.com/lines.**

PART THREE

ACCOMMODATIONS

◼ THE BASIC CONSIDERATIONS

BENEFITS OF STAYING IN THE WORLD

WALT DISNEY WORLD RESORT hotel and campground guests have privileges and amenities unavailable to those staying outside the World. Though some of these perks are only advertising gimmicks, others are real and potentially valuable:

1. CONVENIENCE If you don't have a car, the commute to the theme parks is short via the Disney Transportation System. This is especially advantageous if you stay in one of the hotels connected by the monorail or boat service. If you have a car, however, there are dozens of hotels outside Disney World that are within 5–10 minutes of theme-park parking lots.

2. EXTRA MAGIC HOURS AT THE THEME PARKS Disney World lodging guests (excluding guests at the independent hotels of Downtown Disney Resort Area, except for the Hilton) are invited to enter a designated park 1 hour earlier than the general public each day or to enjoy a designated theme park for up to 3 hours after it closes to the general public in the evening. Disney guests are also offered specials on admission, including discount tickets to the water parks. These benefits are subject to change without notice.

3. BABYSITTING AND CHILD-CARE OPTIONS Disney hotel and campground guests have several options for babysitting, child care, and children's programs. The Polynesian and Grand Floridian resorts, connected by the monorail, as well as several other Disney hotels, offer themed child-care centers where potty-trained children ages 3–12 can stay while the adults go out.

5. PRIORITY THEME PARK ADMISSIONS On days of unusually heavy attendance, Disney may restrict admission into the theme parks for all customers. When deciding whom to admit into the parks, priority is given to guests staying at Disney resorts. In practice, no guest is turned away until a park's parking lot is full. When this happens, that park will be packed to gridlock. Under such conditions, you would exhibit the common sense of an amoeba to exercise your priority-admission privilege.

5. CHILDREN SHARING A ROOM WITH THEIR PARENTS There is no extra charge per night for children younger than age 18 sharing a room with their parents. Many hotels outside Disney World also observe this practice.

6. FREE PARKING Disney resort guests with cars don't have to pay for parking in the theme park lots. This privilege saves $14 per day.

7. RECREATIONAL PRIVILEGES Disney resort guests get preferential treatment for tee times at the golf courses.

STAYING IN OR OUT OF THE WORLD: WEIGHING THE PROS AND CONS

1. COST If cost is a primary consideration, you'll lodge much less expensively outside Disney World. Our ratings of hotel quality and cost (see pages 61–66) compare specific hotels both in and out of the World.

2. EASE OF ACCESS Even if you stay in Disney World, you're dependent on some mode of transportation. It may be less stressful to use the Disney transportation system, but with the single exception of commuting to the Magic Kingdom, the fastest, most efficient, and most flexible way to get around is usually a car. Walt Disney World is so large that some destinations within the World can be reached more quickly from off-property hotels than from Disney hotels. For example, guests at hotels and motels on US 192 (near the so-called Walt Disney World main entrance) are closer to Disney's Hollywood Studios, Disney's Animal Kingdom, and Blizzard Beach water park than guests at many hotels inside Disney World.

3. YOUNG CHILDREN Although the hassle of commuting to most non-World hotels is only slightly (if at all) greater than that of commuting to Disney hotels, a definite peace of mind results from staying in Walt Disney World. The salient point, regardless of where you stay, is to make sure you get your young children back to the hotel for a nap each day.

4. SPLITTING UP If you're in a party that probably will split up to tour (as frequently happens in families with children of

varying ages), staying in the World offers more transportation options and, thus, more independence. Mom and Dad
can take the car and return to the hotel for a relaxed dinner
and early bedtime while the teens remain in the park for evening parades and fireworks.

5. FEEDING THE ARMY OF THE POTOMAC If you have a large
crew that chows down like cattle on a finishing lot, you may
do better staying outside the World, where food is far less
expensive.

6. VISITING OTHER ORLANDO-AREA ATTRACTIONS If you will
visit SeaWorld, Kennedy Space Center Visitor Complex,
Universal Orlando, or other area attractions, it may be more
convenient to stay outside the World.

HOW TO GET DISCOUNTS ON LODGING AT WALT DISNEY WORLD

THERE ARE SO MANY GUEST ROOMS in and around Walt
Disney World that competition is brisk, and everyone,
including Disney, wheels and deals to keep them filled. This
has led to a more flexible discount policy for Disney World
hotels. Here are tips for getting price breaks:

1. SEASONAL SAVINGS You can save from $15 to $50 per night
on a Walt Disney World hotel room by scheduling your visit
during the slower times of the year. However, Disney uses so
many adjectives (*regular, holiday, peak, value*, etc.) to describe
its seasonal calendar that it's hard to keep up without a score-
card. To confuse matters more, the dates for each "season"
vary from resort to resort. If you're set on staying at a Disney
resort, obtain a copy of the Walt Disney Travel Company's
Walt Disney World Florida Vacations video and brochure,
described on page 8.

2. ASK ABOUT SPECIALS When you talk to Disney reservationists, inquire specifically about special deals. Ask, for example,
"What special rates or discounts are available at Disney hotels
during the time of our visit?"

3. "TRADE-UP" OR "UPSELL" RATES If you request a room at
a Disney Value resort and none are available, you may be
offered a room in the next category up (Moderate resorts,
in this example) at a discounted price. Similarly, if you ask
for a room in a moderate resort and none are available,
Disney will usually offer a good deal for Disney Deluxe
Villa rooms or a Deluxe resort. You can angle for a trade-up
rate by asking for a resort category that is more likely to be
sold out.

4. KNOW THE CODE The folks at **MouseSavers** (**mousesavers
.com**) keep an updated list of discounts and reservation
codes for use at Disney resorts. The codes are separated into
categories such as "For anyone," "For residents of certain
states," "For Annual Pass holders," and so
on. For example, the site listed code
"CVZ," published in an ad in some Span-
ish-language newspapers and magazines,
offering a rate of $65 per night for Disney's
All-Star Resorts from April 22 through
August 8. Anyone calling the Disney Reservation Center at ☎ 407-W-DISNEY can use
a current code and get the discounted rate

unofficial **TIP**
Dozens of discounts
are usually listed
at the MouseSavers
site, covering
almost all Disney
resort hotels.

Our blog, **blog.touringplans.com,** often provides advance
notice on discount details. Two other sites, **allearsnet.com**
and **wdwinfo.com,** also have discount codes.

5. INTERNET SELLERS Online travel sellers **Expedia** (**expedia
.com**), **Travelocity** (**travelocity.com**), and **One Travel** (**one
travel.com**) discount Disney hotels. Most breaks are in the
7–25% range, but they can go as deep as 40%. Disney also
places its hotel rooms on **Priceline** (**priceline.com**). While still
abstaining from the "Name Your Own Price" aspect of the
site, Disney's hotel rooms are now in Priceline's inventory and
available through its conventional booking engine at a discounted rate.

6. WALT DISNEY WORLD WEBSITE Particularly in the post-
recession economy, Disney has become more aggressive about
offering deals when it sees lower-than-usual future demand.
Go to **disneyworld.com** and look for "Special Offers" just
below the picture of Cinderella Castle. In the same place, also
look for seasonal discounts, usually listed as "Summertime
Savings" or "Fall Savings" or something similar. You can also
go to "Tickets and Packages" at the top right of the home
page, where you'll find a link to Special Offers. You must click
on the specific special to get the discounts: if you fill out the
information on "Price Your Dream Vacation," you'll be
charged the full rack rate. Reservations booked online are
subject to a $200 penalty if canceled less than 45 days before
arrival. Before booking rooms on Disney's or any website,
click on "Terms and Conditions" and read the fine print.

7. ANNUAL PASS–HOLDER DISCOUNTS Annual Pass holders
are eligible for discounts on dining, shopping, parking, and
lodging. Before the last recession, pass holder discounts on
lodging were, on average, so much better than deals to the
general public that it often made sense to get an annual pass,

even if you had no plans to return to Walt Disney World. These days passholder discounts are usually around $5–5% deeper than those found elsewhere. Five percent isn't anything to sneeze at, but it's not usually enough by itself to justify the cost of an Annual Pass.

The number of discounted rooms available to pass holders is limited, and the rooms often are offered only on short notice. Discounts are generally not available from the third week of December through New Year's Day, and occasionally not during other peak seasons.

8. RENTING DISNEY VACATION CLUB POINTS The Disney Vacation Club (DVC) is Disney's time-share-condominium program. DVC resorts (aka Disney Deluxe Villa resorts) at Walt Disney World are **Bay Lake Tower** at the Contemporary Resort, **Disney's Old Key West Resort, Disney's Saratoga Springs Resort & Spa, Treehouse Villas at Saratoga Springs,** the **Beach Club Villas,** the **Villas at Wilderness Lodge, Animal Kingdom Villas,** and the **BoardWalk Villas.**

DVC members receive a number of "points" annually that they use to pay for their Disney accommodations. Sometimes members elect to "rent" (sell) their points instead of using them in a given year. Though Disney is not involved in the transaction, it allows DVC members to make these points available to the general public. You can potentially save a considerable amount of money by renting points rather than booking through the Disney Reservation Center.

When you rent points, you deal with the selling DVC member and pay him or her directly. Arrangements vary widely, but some trust is required from both parties. You should always insist on receiving the confirmation before making more than a one-night deposit.

Disboards (**disboards.com**), the popular Disney discussion site, has a specific message board that deals with DVC rentals, and the unofficial discount website, **MouseSavers,** has a page with tips on renting DVC points: see **mousesavers.com/dvc .html#rentpoints.**

9. TRAVEL AGENTS Once ineligible for commissions on Disney bookings, travel agents now are active players and particularly good sources of information on time-limited special programs and discounts. In our opinion, a good travel agent is the best friend a traveler can have.

10. ORGANIZATIONS AND AUTO CLUBS Disney has developed time-limited programs with some auto clubs and organizations. AAA, for example, can often offer discounts on hotels and packages comparable to those Disney offers its Annual

COSTS PER NIGHT OF DISNEY RESORT HOTEL ROOMS

All-Star Resorts (Movies, Music, Sports)	$82–$179
All-Star Music Resort Family Suites	$194–$365
Animal Kingdom Lodge	$250–$615
Animal Kingdom Villas (Jambo House, Kidani Village)	$280–$2,330
Art of Animation Resort (opens summer 2012)	$82–$179
Bay Lake Tower	$395–$2,550
Beach Club Resort	$335–$815
Beach Club Villas	$345–$1,250
BoardWalk Inn	$345–$885
BoardWalk Villas	$345–$2,330
Caribbean Beach Resort	$154–$309
Contemporary Resort	$300–$905
Coronado Springs Resort	$159–$284
Disney's Old Key West Resort	$305–$1,780
Disney's Saratoga Springs Resort & Spa	$305–$1,780
Dolphin (Sheraton)	$235–$540
Fort Wilderness Resort & Campground (cabins)	$275–$450
Grand Floridian Resort & Spa	$440–$1,145
Polynesian Resort	$385–$1,020
Pop Century Resort	$82–$179
Port Orleans Resort (French Quarter, Riverside)	$154–$269
Swan (Westin)	$270–$425
Treehouse Villas	$545–$950
Wilderness Lodge	$250–$840
Wilderness Lodge Villas	$340–$1,245
Yacht Club Resort	$335–$990

WHAT IT COSTS TO STAY IN THE DOWNTOWN DISNEY RESORT AREA

Best Western Lake Buena Vista Resort Hotel	$104–$250
Buena Vista Palace Hotel & Spa	$179–$1,009
Doubletree Guest Suites	$82–$505
Hilton in the WDW Resort	$95–$329
Holiday Inn in the WDW Resort	$94–$159
Royal Plaza	$109–$249
Wyndham Lake Buena Vista Resort	$77–$399

Pass holders. Such deals come and go, but the market suggests there will be more. If you're a member of AARP, AAA, or any travel or auto club, ask whether the group has a program before shopping elsewhere.

11. ROOM UPGRADES Sometimes, a room upgrade is as good as a discount. If you're visiting Disney World during a slower time, book the least expensive room your discounts will allow. Checking in, ask very politely about being upgraded to a water-view or pool-view room. A fair percentage of the time, you'll get one at no additional charge.

12. MILITARY DISCOUNTS The **Shades of Green Armed Forces Recreation Center,** near the Grand Floridian Resort & Spa, offers luxury accommodations at rates based on a service-man's rank as well as attraction tickets to the theme parks. Call ☎ 888-593-2242 or see **shadesofgreen.org**.

13. YEAR-ROUND DISCOUNTS AT THE SWAN AND DOLPHIN RESORTS Government workers, teachers, nurses, military, and Entertainment Club members can save on their rooms at the Dolphin or Swan (when space is available). Call ☎ 800-227-1500.

CHOOSING A WALT DISNEY WORLD HOTEL

IF YOU WANT TO STAY IN WALT DISNEY WORLD but don't know which hotel to choose, consider:

1. COST Consider your budget. Hotel rooms start at about $82 a night at the All-Star and Pop Century resorts during Value Season and top out near $1,145 at the Grand Floridian Resort & Spa during Holiday Season. Suites, of course, are more expensive than standard rooms.

Animal Kingdom Villas, Bay Lake Tower, Beach Club Villas, BoardWalk Villas, Disney's Old Key West Resort, Disney's Saratoga Springs Resort & Spa, and Wilderness Lodge Villas offer condo-type accommodations with one-, two-, and (at Saratoga Springs, BoardWalk Villas, Disney's Old Key West, Animal Kingdom Villas, and Bay Lake Tower) three-bedroom units with kitchens, living rooms, DVD play-ers, and washers and dryers. Prices range from $269 per night for a studio suite at Animal Kingdom Villas to more than $2,000 per night for a three-bedroom villa at BoardWalk Villas. Fully equipped cabins at Fort Wilderness Resort & Campground cost $265–$410 per night.

Also at Disney World are the seven hotels of the Down-town Disney Resort Area (DDRA). Accommodations range from fairly luxurious to Holiday Inn quality. Though not typically good candidates for bargains, these hotels have surprised us with some great deals over the years. While the DDRA is technically part of Disney World, staying there is like visiting a colony rather than the motherland. Free park-ing at theme parks isn't offered—nor is early entry, with one exception, the Hilton—and hotels operate their own buses rather than use Disney transportation. See our profiles of the Hilton in the Walt Disney World Resort and the Buena Vista Palace in the section beginning on page 51.

2. LOCATION If you intend to use your own car, the location of your Disney hotel isn't especially important unless you plan to spend most of your time at the Magic Kingdom. (Disney transportation is always more efficient than your car in this case because it bypasses the Transportation and Ticket Center and deposits you at the theme park entrance.)

Most convenient to the Magic Kingdom are the three resorts linked by the monorail: the Grand Floridian, Contemporary–Bay Lake Tower, and Polynesian. Commuting to and from the Magic Kingdom by monorail is quick and simple.

The Contemporary Resort–Bay Lake Tower, in addition to being on the monorail, is only a 10- to 15-minute walk to the Magic Kingdom. Guests reach Epcot by monorail but must transfer at the Transportation and Ticket Center. Buses connect the resort complex to Disney's Hollywood Studios and Disney's Animal Kingdom. No transfer is required, but the bus makes several stops before reaching either destination.

The Polynesian Resort is served by the Magic Kingdom monorail and is an easy walk from the transportation center. At the center, you can catch an express monorail to Epcot. This makes the Polynesian the only Disney resort with direct monorail access to both Epcot and the Magic Kingdom. To minimize your walk to the transportation center, request a room in the Rapa Nui, Tahiti, or Tokelau guest buildings.

Most convenient to Epcot and Disney's Hollywood Studios are the BoardWalk Inn, BoardWalk Villas, Yacht and Beach Club Resorts, Beach Club Villas, the Swan, and the Dolphin. Though all are within easy walking distance of Epcot's International Gateway, boat service is also available. Vessels also connect Epcot hotels to DHS. Epcot hotels are best for guests planning to spend most of their time at Epcot or DHS.

Though they're not centrally located, the All-Star, Coronado Springs, and Animal Kingdom Lodge and Villas resorts have very good bus service to all Disney World destinations and are closest to Disney's Animal Kingdom. Wilderness Lodge and Villas and Fort Wilderness Resort & Campground have the most convoluted transportation service.

If you plan to play golf, book Disney's Old Key West Resort or Disney's Saratoga Springs Resort & Spa, both built around golf courses. The military-only Shades of Green resort is adjacent to two courses. Near but not on a golf course are the Grand Floridian, Polynesian, and Port Orleans resorts. For boating and water sports, try the Polynesian, Contemporary, or Grand Floridian resorts, Fort Wilderness Resort & Campground, or the Wilderness Lodge & Villas. The lodge and campground are also great for hikers, bikers, and joggers.

3. ROOM QUALITY Few Disney guests spend much time in their hotel rooms, though these rooms are among the best designed, most well appointed, and most meticulously maintained anywhere. At the top of the line are the luxurious rooms of the Contemporary, Grand Floridian, and Polynesian resorts; bringing up the rear are the small rooms of the Pop Century Resort. But even these economy rooms are sparkling clean and quite livable. Check our hotel table on pages 61–66 for ratings of all Disney and non-Disney hotels.

4. THE SIZE OF YOUR GROUP Larger families and groups may be interested in how many persons can be accommodated in a Disney resort room, but only Lilliputians would be comfortable in a room filled to capacity. Groups requiring two or more guest rooms should consider condo/villa accommodations, either in or out of Walt Disney World. The most cost-efficient lodging in Walt Disney World for groups of five or six persons are the cabins at Fort Wilderness Campground. Both sleep six adults plus a child or toddler in a crib. For detailed room schematics that show the maximum number of persons per room as well as the rooms' relative size and configuration, consult *The Unofficial Guide to Walt Disney World*.

unofficial **TIP**
If there are more than six in your party, you will need either two hotel rooms, a suite, or a condo.

5. THEME All Disney hotels are themed. Each is designed to make you feel you're in a special place or period of history.

Some resorts carry off their themes better than others, and some themes are more exciting. The Wilderness Lodge and Villas, for example, is extraordinary. The lobby opens eight stories to a timbered ceiling supported by giant columns of bundled logs. One look eases you into the Northwest-wilderness theme. Romantic and isolated, the lodge is a great choice for couples and seniors and is heaven for children.

Animal Kingdom Lodge and Villas replicates the grand safari lodges of Kenya and Tanzania and overlooks its own private African game preserve. By far the most exotic of the Disney resorts, it's made to order for couples on a romantic getaway as well as for families with children. The Polynesian, likewise dramatic, conveys the feeling of the Pacific Islands.

It's great for romantics and families. Many waterfront rooms offer a perfect view of Cinderella Castle and the Magic Kingdom fireworks across Seven Seas Lagoon.

Grandeur, nostalgia, and privilege are central to the Grand Floridian and Yacht & Beach Club resorts, and the BoardWalk Inn & Villas. Although modeled after Eastern-seaboard hotels of different eras, the resorts are amazingly similar. Thematic distinctions are subtle.

The Port Orleans French Quarter Resort lacks the mystery and sultriness of the New Orleans French Quarter, but it's hard to replicate the Big Easy in a sanitized Disney version. Old Key West Resort, however, hits the mark with its Florida Keys theme. The Caribbean Beach Resort's theme is much more effective at night, thanks to creative lighting. By day, the resort looks like a Miami condo development.

Coronado Springs Resort offers several styles of Mexican and southwestern American architecture. Though the lake setting is lovely and the resort is attractive and inviting, the theme (with the exception of the main swimming area) isn't especially stimulating—more like a Scottsdale, Arizona, country club than a Disney resort.

The All-Star Resorts comprise 30 three-story, *T*-shaped hotels with almost 6,000 guest rooms. There are 15 themed areas: 5 celebrate sports (surfing, basketball, tennis, football, and baseball), 5 recall Hollywood movies, and 5 have musical motifs. The resort's design, with entrances shaped like giant Dalmatians, Coke cups, footballs, and the like, is pretty adolescent, sacrificing grace and beauty for energy and novelty. Guest rooms are small, with decor reminiscent of a teenage boy's bedroom. Despite the theme, there are no sports, music, or movies at All-Star Resorts. The Pop Century Resort is pretty much a clone of All-Star Resorts, only this time the giant icons symbolize decades of the 20th century (Big Wheels, 45-rpm records, silhouettes of people doing period dances, and such), and period memorabilia decorate the rooms. Across the lake from Pop Century Resort is Disney's Art of Animation Resort (opens summer 2012), with icons and decor based on four animated features: *Cars, Finding Nemo, The Lion King,* and *The Little Mermaid.*

Pretense aside, the Contemporary, Swan, and Dolphin are essentially themeless though architecturally interesting. The original Contemporary Resort is a 15-story A-frame building with monorails running through the middle. Views from guest rooms here and in the brand-new Bay Lake Tower are among the best at Disney World. Swan and Dolphin are massive yet whimsical. Designed by Michael Graves, they're excellent examples of "entertainment architecture." The two resorts' guest rooms, originally avant-garde bordering on garish, have been totally redesigned. Although still visually interesting, they're now more restful and easier on the eye.

6. DINING The best resorts for dining quality and selection are the Epcot resorts: the Beach Club Villas, BoardWalk Inn & Villas, Dolphin, Swan, and Yacht & Beach Club Resorts. Each has good restaurants and is within easy walking distance of the others and of the 14 restaurants in Epcot's World Showcase section. If you stay at an Epcot resort, you have a total of 31 restaurants within a 5- to 12-minute walk.

The only other place in Disney World where restaurants and hotels are similarly concentrated is in the Downtown Disney Resort Area. In addition to restaurants in the hotels themselves, the Hilton, Holiday Inn, Wyndham Lake Buena Vista Resort, and Buena Vista Palace, as well as Disney's Saratoga Springs Resort & Spa, are within walking distance of restaurants in Downtown Disney.

Guests at the Contemporary, Polynesian, and Grand Floridian can eat in their hotels, or they can commute to restaurants in the Magic Kingdom (not recommended) or in other monorail-linked hotels. Riding the monorail to another hotel or to the Magic Kingdom takes about 10 minutes each way, plus waiting for the train.

All the other Disney resorts are somewhat isolated. This means you're stuck dining at your hotel unless (1) you have a car and can go anywhere or (2) you're content to eat at the theme parks or Downtown Disney.

7. AMENITIES AND RECREATION Disney resorts offer staggering variety here: swimming pools, themed shops, restaurants or food courts, bars or lounges, and access to five Disney golf courses. The more you pay for your lodging, the more amenities and opportunities are at your disposal. Animal Kingdom Lodge & Villas, BoardWalk Inn, Wilderness Lodge, and the Contemporary, Grand Floridian, Polynesian, and Yacht & Beach Club resorts, for example, all offer concierge floors.

For swimming and sunning, the Contemporary–Bay Lake Tower, Polynesian, Wilderness Lodge & Villas, and Grand Floridian offer both pools and white-sand nonswimming beaches on Bay Lake or Seven Seas Lagoon. Caribbean Beach Resort, the Dolphin, and the Yacht & Beach Club also provide both pools and nonswimming beaches. Though lacking a lakefront beach, Disney's Saratoga Springs Resort & Spa, Animal Kingdom Lodge & Villas, Port Orleans and

Coronado Springs resorts, and the BoardWalk Inn & Villas have exceptionally creative pools.

Bay Lake and the Seven Seas Lagoon are the best venues for boating. Resorts fronting these lakes are the Contemporary–Bay Lake Tower, Polynesian, Wilderness Lodge & Villas, Grand Floridian, and Fort Wilderness Resort & Campground. Though on smaller bodies of water, BoardWalk Inn & Villas, Caribbean Beach, Coronado Springs, the Dolphin, Old Key West, Port Orleans, Saratoga Springs, and the Yacht & Beach Club also rent watercraft.

Most convenient for golf are Saratoga Springs, Shades of Green, Old Key West, Contemporary, Polynesian, Grand Floridian, and Port Orleans resorts.

While there are many places to bike or jog at Disney World (including golf-cart paths), the best biking and jogging are at Fort Wilderness Resort & Campground and the adjacent Wilderness Lodge & Villas. Caribbean Beach Resort offers a lovely hiking, biking, and jogging trail around the lake. Also good for biking and jogging is the area along Bonnet Creek extending through Port Orleans and Old Key West toward Downtown Disney. Epcot resorts offer a lakefront promenade and bike path, as well as a roadside walkway suitable for jogging.

On-site child-care programs are offered at Animal Kingdom Lodge & Villas, BoardWalk Inn & Villas, Dolphin, Grand Floridian Resort & Spa, Hilton in the Walt Disney World Resort, Polynesian, Swan, Wilderness Lodge & Villas, and Yacht & Beach Club Resorts. All other resorts offer in-room babysitting (see page 87 for details).

8. NIGHTLIFE The boardwalk at BoardWalk Inn & Villas has an upscale dance club (albeit one that has never lived up to its potential), a club with dueling pianos and sing-alongs, a brew pub, and a sports bar. BoardWalk clubs are within easy walking distance of all Epcot resorts. Most non-Disney hotels in the Downtown Disney Resort Area, as well as Disney's Saratoga Springs Resort & Spa, are within walking distance of Downtown Disney nightspots. Nightlife at other Disney resorts is limited to lounges that stay open late.

At the California Grill Lounge, you can relax over dinner and watch the fireworks at the nearby Magic Kingdom.

CAMPING AT WALT DISNEY WORLD

FORT WILDERNESS RESORT & CAMPGROUND is a spacious area for tent and RV camping. Fully equipped, air-conditioned prefabricated log cabins are also available for rent.

Tent/Pop-Up campsites provide water, electricity, and cable TV and run from $46 to $93 depending on season. **Full Hook-Up** sites have all of the above, accommodate large RVs, and run from $61 to $108 per night. **Preferred Hook-Up** sites for tents and RVs add sewer connections and run from $66 to $115 per night. **Premium** sites add an extra-large concrete parking pad and run from $76 to $125 a night. All sites provide picnic tables, waste containers, grills, and high-speed Internet (additional fee). Sites are arranged on 28 loops accessible from one of three main roads. Loops 100–2000 are for tent and RV campers, and Loops 2100–2800 offer cabins at $275–$450 per night. RV sites are roomy by eastern-U.S. standards, but tent campers will probably feel a bit cramped.

Fort Wilderness arguably offers the most recreational facilities and activities of any Disney resort. Among them are nightly campfire programs; a dinner theater; two swimming pools; walking paths; bike, boat, and water-ski rentals; and tennis, basketball, and volleyball courts.

Access to the Magic Kingdom is by boat from Fort Wilderness Landing and to Epcot by bus, with a transfer at the Transportation and Ticket Center (TTC) to the Epcot monorail. Boat service may be suspended during thunderstorms, in which case Disney provides buses. An alternate route to the Magic Kingdom is by internal bus to the TTC, then by monorail or ferry to the park. Transportation to all other Disney destinations is by bus. Motor traffic within the campground is permitted only when entering or exiting. Get around within the campground by bus, golf cart, or bike, the latter two available for rent.

HOTELS *outside* WALT DISNEY WORLD

SELECTING AND BOOKING A HOTEL OUTSIDE WALT DISNEY WORLD

LODGING COSTS OUTSIDE DISNEY WORLD vary incredibly. If you shop around, you can find a clean motel with a pool within 5–20 minutes of the World for as low as $40 a night.

There are four primary out-of-World areas to consider:

1. INTERNATIONAL DRIVE AREA This area, about 15–25 minutes northeast of the World, parallels Interstate 4 on its eastern side and offers a wide selection of hotels and restaurants. Prices range from $56 to $400 per night. The chief

Hotel Concentrations around Walt Disney World

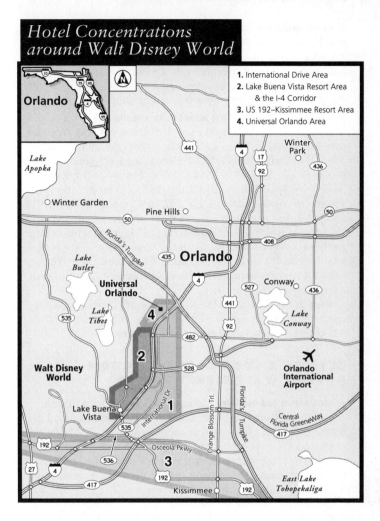

1. International Drive Area
2. Lake Buena Vista Resort Area & the I-4 Corridor
3. US 192–Kissimmee Resort Area
4. Universal Orlando Area

drawbacks of the International Drive area are its terribly congested roads, countless traffic signals, and inadequate access to westbound I-4. While the biggest bottleneck is the intersection with Sand Lake Road, the mile of International Drive between Kirkman Road and Sand Lake Road stays in near-continuous gridlock.

I-Drive hotels are listed in the *Official Vacation Guide,* published by the Orlando–Orange County Convention and Visitors Bureau. For a copy, call ☎ 800-972-3304 or 407-363-5872, or see **orlandoinfo.com.**

2. LAKE BUENA VISTA AND THE I-4 CORRIDOR A number of hotels are along FL 535 and west of I-4 between Disney World and I-4's intersection with Florida's Turnpike. They're easily reached from the interstate and are near many restaurants, including those on International Drive. The *Official Vacation Guide* (see previous page) lists most of them.

3. US 192 (IRLO BRONSON MEMORIAL HIGHWAY) This is the highway to Kissimmee to the south of Disney World. In addition to large, full-service hotels, there are many small, privately owned motels that are often a good value. Several dozen properties on US 192 are nearer Disney parks than are more expensive hotels inside the World. The number and variety of restaurants on US 192 has increased markedly, compensating for the area's primary shortcoming. Locally, US 192 is called Irlo Bronson Memorial Highway. The section to the west of I-4 and the Disney "Maingate" is designated Irlo Bronson Memorial Highway West, while the section from I-4 running southeast toward Kissimmee is Irlo Bronson Memorial Highway East.

Hotels on US 192 and in Kissimmee are listed in the *Kissimmee Visitor's Guide*. Order a copy by calling ☎ 800-327-9159, or view it online at **floridakiss.com.**

GETTING A GOOD DEAL ON A ROOM OUTSIDE WALT DISNEY WORLD

1. ORLANDO MAGICARD Orlando Magicard is a discount program sponsored by Visit Orlando. Cardholders are eligible for discounts of 12–50% at about 50 hotels. The Magicard is also good for discounts at some area attractions, three dinner theaters, museums, performing-arts venues, restaurants, shops, and more. Valid for up to six persons, the card isn't available for larger groups or conventions.

To obtain a free Magicard and a list of participating hotels and attractions, call ☎ 800-643-9492 or 407-363-5872. On the Web, go to **orlandoinfo.com/magicard;** the Magicard and accompanying brochure can be printed from a personal computer. If you miss getting one before you leave home, obtain one at the Convention and Visitors Bureau Information Center at 8723 International Dr. When you call for your Magicard, also request the *Official Vacation Guide.*

2. FLORIDA ROOMSAVER GUIDE This book of coupons for discounts at hotels statewide is free in many restaurants and motels on main highways leading to Florida. Because most travelers make reservations before leaving home, picking up the book en route doesn't help much. To view it online or sign up for a free monthly guide sent by e-mail, visit **roomsaver.com.** For a hard copy ($3 for handling, $5 if shipped to Canada), write to 13709 Progress Blvd., Box 14, Alachua, FL 32615, or call ☎ 800-222-3948 Monday–Friday, 8 a.m.–5 p.m. Eastern time.

3. HOTEL SHOPPING ON THE INTERNET Hotels use the Internet to fill rooms during slow periods and to advertise limited-time specials. Hotels also use more-traditional communication avenues, such as promoting specials through travel agents. If you enjoy cybershopping, have at it, but hotel shopping on the Internet isn't as quick or convenient as handing the task to your travel agent. When we bump into a great deal on the Web, we call our agent. Often she can beat the deal or improve on it (perhaps with an upgrade). A good agent working with a savvy, helpful client can work wonders.

The secret to shopping on the Internet is, well, shopping. The chart below lists the websites we've found most dependable for discounts on Disney-area hotels. When we're really looking for a deal, we check all the sites listed in the chart. Flexibility on dates and location is helpful, and we always give our travel agent the opportunity to beat any deal we find.

mousesavers.com	Best site for hotels in Disney World.
dreamsunlimitedtravel.com	Excellent for both Disney and non-Disney hotels.
2000orlando-florida.com	Comprehensive hotel site.
valuetrips.com	Specializes in budget accommodations.
travelocity.com	Multidestination travel superstore.
roomsaver.com	Provides discount coupons for hotels.
floridakiss.com	Primarily US 192–Kissimmee area hotels.
orlandoinfo.com	Good for hotel info; not user-friendly for booking.
orlandovacation.com	Great rates for a small number of properties, including condos and home rentals.
expedia.com	Largest of the multidestination travel sites.
hotels.com	Largest Internet hotel-booking service; manyother sites link to this site and its subsidiary, **hoteldiscounts.com.**

We recommend choosing a hotel based on location, room quality, price, and commuting times to the parks, plus any features important to you. Next, check each of the applicable sites that follow. You'll be able to ferret out the best Internet deal in about 30 minutes. Then call the hotel to see if you can save more by booking directly. Start by asking the hotel for specials. If their response doesn't beat the Internet deal, tell them what you've found and ask if they can do better.

4. IF YOU MAKE YOUR OWN RESERVATION Always call the hotel in question, not the chain's national toll-free number. Often, reservationists at the toll-free number are unaware of local specials. Always ask about specials before you inquire about corporate rates. Don't hesitate to bargain, but do it before you check in. If you're buying a hotel's weekend package and want to extend your stay, for example, you can often obtain at least the corporate rate for the extra days.

5. CONDOMINIUM AND VACATION-HOME DEALS The best deals in lodging in the Walt Disney World area are vacation homes and single-owner condos. Prices range from about $65 a night for two-bedroom condos and town homes to $200–$500 a night for three- to seven-bedroom vacation homes. Look for bargains, especially during off-peak periods. Reservations and information can be obtained from the following online resources:

All Star Vacation Homes	**allstarvacationhomes.com**
Orlando's Finest Vacation Homes	**orlandosfinest.com**
Last Minute Villas	**lastminutevillas.net**
Vacation Rental by Owner	**vrbo.com**
Vacation Rentals 411	**vacationrentals411.com**
Visit Orlando	**visitorlando.com**

Because condos tend to be part of large developments (frequently time-shares), amenities such as swimming pools, playgrounds, game arcades, and fitness centers often rival those found in the best hotels. Generally speaking, condo developments don't have restaurants, lounges, or spas. In a condo, if something goes wrong, there will be someone on hand to fix the problem. Vacation homes rented from a property-management company likewise will have someone to come to the rescue, though responsiveness tends to vary vastly from company to company.

THE BEST HOTELS FOR FAMILIES OUTSIDE WALT DISNEY WORLD

International Drive & Universal Areas

CoCo Key Hotel and Water Resort–Orlando
7400 International Dr., Orlando; ☎407-351-2626 or
877-875-4681; cocokeywaterresort.com

Rate per night $99–$149. **Pools** ★★★★. **Fridge in room** Not yet. **Shuttle to parks** Yes (Aquatica, SeaWorld, Universal, Wet 'n Wild). **Maximum number of occupants per room** 4. **Special comments** A daily $19/room fee is charged for use of the water park; day guests may use the water park for a fee of $19.95/person ($14.95/person for Florida residents).

DESCRIPTION AND COMMENTS On International Drive, not far from the Universal Orlando theme parks, CoCo Key combines a tropical-themed hotel with a canopied water park featuring 3 pools and 14 waterslides, as well as poolside food and arcade entertainment. A full-service restaurant serves breakfast and dinner; a food court offers family favorites such as burgers, chicken fingers, and pizza. The spacious guest rooms include 37-inch flat-screen TVs, Wi-Fi, granite showers and counter-tops, and plenty of accessible outlets for guests' electronics.

Hard Rock Hotel
5800 Universal Blvd., Orlando; ☎ 407-503-2000;
hardrockhotelorlando.com

Rate per night $234–$724. **Pool** ★★★★. **Fridge in room** $15/day. **Shuttle to parks** Yes (Universal, SeaWorld, Discovery Cove, Aquatica, and Wet 'n Wild). **Maximum number of occupants per room** 5 (double-queen) or 3 (king). **Special comments** Microwaves available for $15/day.

DESCRIPTION AND COMMENTS On Universal property, the 650-room Hard Rock Hotel is nirvana for kids older than 8, especially those interested in music. Architecture is California Mission–style, and rock memorabilia is displayed throughout. Guests receive theme park privileges such as all-day access to the Universal Express line-breaking program, as well as delivery of packages to their rooms and priority seating at select Universal restaurants. The music-filled pool area has a white-sand beach, a 260-foot waterslide, a 12,000-square-foot pool, an underwater audio system, and an ultrahip pool bar. You'll also find four restaurants and lounges, including the Palm Restaurant, a chic lounge, fitness center, and Hard Rock merchandise store.

Guest rooms are ultrahip, too, with cutting-edge contemporary decor, a CD sound system, TV with pay-per-view movies and video games, coffeemaker, iron and board, minibar, robes, hair dryer, and two phones. A supervised activity center, Camp Lil' Rock, serves kids ages 4–14. Pet-friendly rooms available.

Doubletree Resort Orlando–International Drive
10100 International Dr., Orlando; ☎ 407-352-1100 or 800-327-0363; doubletreeorlandoidrive.com

Rate per night $89–$499. **Pools** ★★★½. **Fridge in room** Standard in some rooms; available in others for $10/day. **Shuttle to parks** Yes. **Maximum number of occupants per room** 4. **Special comments** A good option if you're visiting SeaWorld or Aquatica.

DESCRIPTION AND COMMENTS Formerly the International Plaza Resort & Spa, this hotel has undergone a comprehensive $35 million renovation. Situated on 28 lush, tropical acres with a Balinese feel, the Doubletree is adjacent to SeaWorld and Aquatica water park. All 1,094 rooms and suites—classified as "resort" or "tower"—have been completely refurbished and are equally suitable for business travelers or families. We recommend the tower rooms for good views and the resort rooms for maximum convenience. The Bamboo Grille serves steak and seafood along with breakfast; you can also get a quick bite at Bangli Lounge, the deli, or the pool bar. Relax and cool off at one of the three pools (there are three more just for kids), or indulge in a special spa treatment. A fitness center, minigolf course, children's day camp, and game area afford even more diversions. The resort is about a 15-minute drive to Walt Disney World, a 12-minute drive to Universal, or a short walk to SeaWorld.

Holiday Inn Resort–The Castle
8629 International Dr., Orlando; ☎ 407-345-1511 or 800-952-2785; thecastleorlando.com

Rate per night $100–$230. **Pool** ★★★. **Fridge in room** Yes ($15/day). **Shuttle to parks** Yes (Disney and Universal; additional fee). **Maximum number of occupants per room** 4. **Special comments** For an additional fee ($13.95 adults, $7.95 kids), up to 4 people receive a full breakfast; 2 signature chocolate-chip cookies come with every room. Pets up to 75 pounds welcome for an additional $75.

DESCRIPTION AND COMMENTS You can't miss this one; it's the only castle on I-Drive. Inside you'll find royal colors (purple predominates), opulent fixtures, European art, Renaissance music, and a mystic Castle Creature at the door. The 216 guest rooms also receive the royal treatment in decor, though some guests may find them gaudy. All, however, are fairly large and well equipped with TV plus PlayStation, minibar (fridge is available at an extra charge), three phones, coffeemaker, iron and board, hair dryer, and safe. The Castle Café off the lobby serves full or Continental breakfast. For lunch or dinner, you might walk next door to Vito's Chop House (dinner only) or Café Tu Tu Tango (an *Unofficial* favorite). The heated circular pool is 5 feet deep and features a fountain in the center, a poolside bar, and a whirlpool. There's no separate kiddie pool. Other amenities include a fitness center, gift shop, lounge, valet laundry service and facilities, and a guest-services desk with park passes for sale and babysitting recommendations. Security feature: elevators require an electronic key card.

Loews Portofino Bay Hotel
5601 Universal Blvd., Orlando; ☎ 407-503-1000 or 888-273-1311; tinyurl.com/portofinobay

---

Rate per night $269–$714. **Pools ★★★★. Fridge in room** Minibar; fridge available for $15/day. **Shuttle to parks** Yes (Universal, SeaWorld, Discovery Cove, and Wet 'n Wild). **Maximum number of occupants per room** 4. **Special comments** Character dinner on Friday.

DESCRIPTION AND COMMENTS In Universal Orlando, the 750-room Portofino Bay Hotel is themed like an Italian Riviera village. Guests receive theme park privileges such as all-day access to the Universal Express line-breaking program, as well as delivery of packages to their room and priority seating at select Universal restaurants. The rooms are ultraluxurious, with Italian furnishings, opulent baths, and soothing neutral hues. Standard guest-room amenities include minibar, coffeemaker, iron and board, hair dryer, safe, and TV with pay-per-view movies. Microwaves are available ($15 per day). Campo Portofino offers supervised activities (movies, video games, crafts, and such) for children ages 4–14. The cost is $15 per hour plus $15 per meal, per child; hours vary. Trattoria del Porto restaurant offers a character dinner from 6:30 until 9:30 p.m. on Friday, with characters such as Scooby Doo and Woody Woodpecker in attendance. Portofino has four other Italian restaurants (each with a children's menu), an Italian bakery (also serves gelato), and two bars. Three elaborate pools, gardens, jogging trails, pet-friendly rooms, and a spa and fitness center round out major amenities. If you can afford it and plan to spend time at Universal, you can't go wrong here.

Nickelodeon Suites Resort Orlando
**14500 Continental Gateway, Orlando; ☎ 407-387-5437
or 877-NICK-111; nickhotel.com**

Rate per night $159–$529. **Pools** ★★★★. **Fridge in room** Yes.
Shuttle to parks Yes. **Maximum number of occupants per room**
8. **Special comments** Daily character breakfast; resort fee of $25/night.

DESCRIPTION AND COMMENTS   This resort is as kid-friendly as they come
and is sure to please any fan of TV shows the likes of *SpongeBob
SquarePants, Dora the Explorer, Avatar: The Last Airbender,* and *iCarly.*
Nickelodeon characters hang out in the resort's lobby and mall
area, greeting kids while parents check in. Guests can choose from
among 777 suites—one-bedroom Family Suites and two- and
three-bedroom KidSuites—executed in a number of different
themes—all very brightly and creatively decorated. All suites include kitchenettes or full kitchens; also standard are a microwave,
fridge, coffeemaker, TV, iron and board, hair dryer, and a safe.
KidSuites feature a semiprivate kids' bedroom with bunk or twin
beds, pull-out sleeper bed, 32-inch TV, CD player, and activity
table. Additional amenities include a high-tech video arcade, Studio Nick—a game-show studio that hosts several game shows a
night for the entertainment of a live studio audience, a buffet (kids
3 and younger eat free with a paying adult), a food court offering
Subway and other choices, the full-service Nicktoons Cafe (offers
character breakfasts), a convenience store, a lounge, a gift shop, a
fitness center, a washer and dryer in each courtyard, and a guest-
activities desk (buy Disney tickets and get recommendations on
babysitting). Not to be missed—don't worry, your kids won't let
you—are the resort's two pools, Oasis and Lagoon. Oasis features
a water park complete with water cannons, rope ladders, geysers,
and dump buckets, as well as a hot tub for adults (with a view of
the rest of the pool to keep an eye on little ones) and a smaller play
area for younger kids. Kids will love the huge, zero-depth-entry
Lagoon Pool, replete with 400-gallon dump bucket, plus nearby
basketball court and nine-hole minigolf course.

Rosen Shingle Creek
**9939 Universal Blvd., Orlando; ☎ 407-996-9939 or
866-996-9939; rosenshinglecreek.com**

Rate per night $99–$285. **Pools** ★★★★. **Fridge in room** Yes.
Shuttle to parks Yes (Universal, Wet 'n Wild, Discovery Cove,
Aquatica, and SeaWorld only). **Maximum number of occupants
per room** 4.

DESCRIPTION AND COMMENTS   Beautiful rooms (east-facing ones
have great views) and excellent restaurants distinguish this

mostly meeting- and convention-oriented resort. The pools are large and lovely and include a lap pool, a family pool, and a kiddie wading pool. There's an 18-hole golf course on-site as well as a superior spa and an adequate fitness center. Child care is provided as well. Though a state-of-the-art video arcade will gobble up your kids' pocket change, the real kicker, especially for the 8-years-and-up crowd, is a natural area encompassing lily ponds, grassy wetlands, Shingle Creek, and an adjacent cypress swamp. Running through the area is a nature trail complete with signs to help you identify wildlife. Great blue herons, wood storks, coots, egrets, mallard ducks, anhingas, and ospreys are common, as are sliders (turtles), chameleons, and skinks (lizards). Oh yeah, there are alligators and snakes, too—real ones, but that's part of the fun. Hotel shuttle service is limited, departing and picking up at rather inconvenient times and stopping at three other hotels before delivering you to your destination.

Lake Buena Vista and I-4 Corridor

Buena Vista Palace Hotel & Spa
1900 E. Buena Vista Dr., Lake Buena Vista; ☎ 407-827-2727 or 866-397-6516; buenavistapalace.com

---

Rate per night $99–$380. **Pools** ★★★½. **Fridge in room** Yes. **Shuttle to parks** Yes (Disney only). **Maximum number of occupants per room** 4. **Special comments** Sunday character brunch available.

DESCRIPTION AND COMMENTS   In the Downtown Disney Resort Area, the Buena Vista Palace is upscale and convenient. Surrounded by an artificial lake and plenty of palms, the spacious pool area contains three heated pools, the largest of which is partially covered (nice for when you need a little shade); a whirlpool and sauna; a basketball court; and a sand volleyball court. Plus, a pool concierge will fetch your favorite magazine or fruity drink. On Sunday, the Watercress Café hosts a character brunch ($22 for adults and $10 for children). The 897 guest rooms are posh and spacious; each comes with a desk, coffeemaker, hair dryer, satellite TV with pay-per-view movies, iron and board, and minifridge. There are also 117 suites. In-room babysitting is available through All About Kids. One lighted tennis court, a European-style spa offering 60 services, a fitness center, an arcade, a playground, and a beauty salon round out amenities. Two restaurants and a mini-market are on-site. And if you aren't wiped out after time in the parks, consider dropping by the Lobby Lounge or the full-menu sports bar for a nightcap. *Note:* All these amenities and services come at a price—a $17-per-night resort fee will be added to your bill.

Hilton in the Walt Disney World Resort
1751 Hotel Plaza Blvd., Lake Buena Vista;
☎ **407-827-4000 or 800-782-4414; hilton-wdwv.com**

Rate per night $99–$309. **Pools** ★★★½. **Fridge in room** Minibar; minifridge available free on request. **Shuttle to parks** Yes (Disney theme and water parks only). **Maximum number of occupants per room** 4. **Special comments** Sunday character breakfast and Disney Extra Magic Hours program.

DESCRIPTION AND COMMENTS The Hilton occupies 23 acres in the Downtown Disney Resort Area. The Hilton's 814 guest rooms and suites are spacious, luxurious, and tasteful. Decorated in earth tones, all standard rooms have a granite bath, iron and board, hair dryer, two phones, desk, minibar, coffeemaker, and cable TV with pay-per-view movies and video games. A character-breakfast buffet is served from 8:30 to 11 a.m. on Sunday (reservations recommended). Five characters attend (only two are present at a time). Other important family amenities include babysitting services; an arcade and pool table; and two beautifully landscaped heated swimming pools, as well as a kiddie pool. Adults and older children can relax in the fitness center after a long day touring. Seven restaurants, including Benihana, add to the hotel's convenience.

Holiday Inn Resort Lake Buena Vista
13351 FL 535, Lake Buena Vista; ☎ **407-239-4500 or**
866-808-8833; hisunspreelbv.com

Rate per night $80–$75. **Pool** ★★★. **Fridge in room** Yes. **Shuttle to parks** Yes (Disney only). **Maximum number of occupants per room** 4–6. **Special comments** The first hotel in the world to offer KidSuites; resort fee of $9.53/night entitles guests to numerous perks, including use of fitness center and daily fountain drinks for kids.

DESCRIPTION AND COMMENTS The big lure here is KidSuites—405-square-foot rooms, each with a separate children's area. Themes include a tree house, jail, space capsule, and fort, among others. The kids' area sleeps two to four children in one or two sets of bunk beds. The separate adult area has its own TV, safe, hair dryer, and mini-kitchenette with fridge, microwave, sink, and coffeemaker. Other kid-friendly amenities include the tiny Castle Movie Theater, which shows movies all day, every day; a playground; an arcade with video games and air hockey, among its many games; and a basketball court. Other amenities include a fitness center for the grown-ups and a large free-form pool complete with kiddie

pool and two whirlpools. Applebee's serves breakfast and dinner and offers an à la carte menu for dinner. There's also a
minimart. More perks: kids age 12 and younger eat free from
a special menu when dining with one paying adult (maximum
four kids per adult), and "Dive-Inn" poolside movies are
shown Saturday nights. Finally, pets weighing 30 pounds or
less are welcome for an additional $40 nonrefundable fee.

Hyatt Regency Grand Cypress
**1 Grand Cypress Blvd., Orlando; ☎ 407-239-1234;
grandcypress.hyatt.com**

Rate per night $215–$355. **Pool** ★★★★★. **Fridge in room** Yes,
plus minibar. **Shuttle to parks** Yes (Disney, Universal, SeaWorld).
Maximum number of occupants per room 4. **Special comments**
Wow, what a pool!

DESCRIPTION AND COMMENTS There are myriad reasons to stay at
this 1,500-acre resort, but the pool ranks as number one. The
800,000-gallon tropical paradise has two 45-foot waterslides,
waterfalls, caves and grottoes, and a suspension bridge. The
Hyatt also is a golfer's paradise. With 45 holes of Jack Nicklaus–
designed championship golf, a 9-hole pitch-and-putt course,
and a golf academy, there's something for golfers of all abilities.
Other recreational perks include a racquet facility with hard
and clay courts, a private lake with beach, a fitness center, and
miles of trails for biking, walking, and jogging. (*Note:* A daily
$23 resort fee applies.) The 683 standard guest rooms are 360
square feet and have a Florida ambience, with green and red-
dish hues, touches of rattan, and private balconies. Amenities
include minibar, iron and board, safe, hair dryer, ceiling fan, and
cable/satellite TV with pay-per-view movies and video games.
Camp Hyatt provides supervised programs for kids ages 3–12;
in-room babysitting is available. Six restaurants offer dining
options. Four lounges provide nighttime entertainment.

Marriott Village at Lake Buena Vista
**8623 Vineland Ave., Lake Buena Vista; ☎ 407-938-9001 or
877-682-8552; marriottvillage.com**

Rate per night $119–$219. **Pools** ★★★. **Fridge in room** Yes.
Shuttle to parks Disney only, $7. **Maximum number of occupants
per room** 4 (Courtyard and Fairfield) or 5 (SpringHill). **Special
comments** Free Continental breakfast at Fairfield and SpringHill.

DESCRIPTION AND COMMENTS This gated hotel community includes
a 388-room Fairfield Inn, a 400-suite SpringHill Suites, and a

312-room Courtyard. Amenities at all three properties include fridge, cable TV, iron and board, hair dryer, and microwave. Cribs and roll-away beds are available at no extra charge at all locations. Swimming pools at all three hotels are attractive and medium-sized, featuring children's interactive splash zones and whirlpools; in addition, each property has its own fitness center. The incredibly convenient Village Marketplace food court includes Pizza Hut, Village Grill, Village Coffee House, along with a 24-hour convenience store. Bahama Breeze and Golden Corral full-service restaurants are within walking distance. Other services and amenities include a Disney planning station and ticket sales, an arcade, and a Hertz car-rental desk. Shoppers will find the Orlando Premium Outlets adjacent.

Sheraton Safari Hotel & Suites Lake Buena Vista
12205 S. Apopka–Vineland Rd., Lake Buena Vista;
☎ **407-239-0444 or 800-423-3297; sheratonsafari.com**

Rate per night $89–$174. **Pool** ★★★. **Fridge in room** Standard in suites, $10/day in standard rooms. **Shuttle to parks** Yes (Disney free; other parks for a fee). **Maximum number of occupants per room** 4–6. **Special comments** Cool python waterslide. Dogs allowed.

DESCRIPTION AND COMMENTS The safari theme is nicely executed throughout the property—from the lobby dotted with African artifacts and native decor to the 79-foot python waterslide dominating the pool. The 393 guest rooms and 90 safari suites sport African-inspired art and tasteful animal-print soft goods in brown, beige, and jewel tones. Amenities include cable TV, coffeemaker, iron and board, hair dryer, and safe. The first thing your kids will probably want to do is take a turn on the python waterslide. Other on-site amenities include a restaurant (children's menu available), lounge, arcade, and fitness center.

Sheraton Vistana Resort
8800 Vistana Centre Dr., Lake Buena Vista;
☎ **866-208-0003; sheraton.com**

Rate per night $139–$279. **Pools** ★★★½. **Fridge in room** Yes. **Shuttle to parks** Yes (Disney free; other parks for a fee). **Maximum number of occupants per room** 4–8. **Special comments** Though time-shares, the villas are rented nightly as well.

DESCRIPTION AND COMMENTS The Vistana is one of Orlando's best off-Disney properties. If you want a serene retreat from your days in the theme parks, this is an excellent base. The spacious villas come in one-bedroom, two-bedroom, and two-bedroom-with-lock-off models (which can be reconfigured as one studio room and a one-bedroom suite). All are decorated in beachy pastels, but the emphasis is on the profusion of amenities. Each villa has a full kitchen (including fridge/freezer, microwave, oven/range, dishwasher, toaster, and coffeemaker, with an option to prestock with groceries and laundry products), clothes washer and dryer, TVs in the living room and each bed-room (one with DVD player), stereo with CD player in some villas, separate dining area, and private patio or balcony in most. Grounds offer seven swimming pools (three with bars), four playgrounds, two restaurants, game rooms, fitness cen-ters, a minigolf course, sports equipment rental (including bikes), and courts for basketball, volleyball, tennis, and shuffle-board. A mind-boggling array of activities for kids (and adults) ranges from crafts to games and sports tournaments. Of special note: Vistana is highly secure, with locked gates bordering all guest areas, so children can have the run of the place without parents worrying about them wandering off.

Waldorf Astoria Orlando
14200 Bonnet Creek Resort Lane, Lake Buena Vista;
☎ **407-597-5500; waldorfastoriaorlando.com**

Rate per night $199–$379. **Pool** ★★★★. **Fridge in room** Yes. **Shuttle to parks** Yes. **Maximum number of occupants per room** 4, plus child in crib. **Special comments** A good alternative to Disney's Deluxe properties.

DESCRIPTION AND COMMENTS Opened in 2009, the Waldorf Astoria is between I-4 and Disney's Pop Century Resort, near the Hilton Orlando at the back of the Bonnet Creek Resort prop-erty. Getting here requires a GPS or good directions, so be prepared with those before you travel. Once you arrive, how-ever, you'll know the trip was worth it. Beautifully decorated and well manicured, the Waldorf is more elegant than any Disney resort. Service is excellent, and the staff-to-guest ratio is far lower than at Disney properties.

At just under 450 square feet, standard rooms feature either two queen beds or one king. A full-size desk allows you to get work done if it's absolutely necessary, and rooms also have flat-screen televisions, high-speed Internet, and Wi-Fi. The bathrooms are spacious and gorgeous, with cool marble floors, glass-walled showers, separate tubs, and enough coun-ter space for a Broadway makeup artist. This space is so nice that when we stayed here in 2009, we debated whether we'd rather stay at Pop Century with three others or sleep in a Waldorf bathroom by ourselves.

Amenities include a fitness center, a spa, a golf course, six restaurants, and two pools (including one zero-entry for kids). Pool-size cabanas are available for rent. The resort offers shuttle service to the Disney parks about every half hour, but check with the front desk for the exact schedule when you arrive. Runners will enjoy the relative solitude—it's about a 1-mile round-trip to the nearest busy road, and the route is flat as a pancake.

Wyndham Bonnet Creek Resort
9560 Via Encinas, Lake Buena Vista; ☎ 407-238-3500; wyndhambonnetcreek.com

Rate per night $179–$359. **Pool** ★★★★. **Fridge in room** Yes. **Shuttle to parks** Disney only. **Maximum number of occupants per room** 4–12 depending on room/suite. **Special comments** A non-Disney suite hotel within Walt Disney World.

DESCRIPTION AND COMMENTS   This condo hotel lies on the south side of Buena Vista Drive, about a quarter mile east of Disney's Caribbean Beach Resort. The property has an interesting history: When Walt Disney began secretly buying up real estate in the 1960s under the names of numerous front companies, the land on which this resort stands was the last holdout and was never sold to Disney, though the company tried repeatedly to acquire it through the years. (The owners reportedly took issue with the way Disney went about acquiring land and preferred to see the site languish undeveloped.) The 482-acre site was ultimately bought by Marriott, which put up a Fairfield Inn time-share development in 2004. The Wyndham is part of a luxury-hotel complex on the same site that includes a 500-room Waldorf Astoria (see previous page) and a 1,000-room Hilton. The development is surrounded on three sides by Disney property and on one side by I-4.

The Bonnet Creek Resort offers upscale, family-friendly accommodations: one- and two-bedroom condos with fully equipped kitchens, washer-dryers, jetted tubs, and balconies. Activities and amenities on-site include two outdoor swimming pools, a "lazy river" float stream, a children's activities program, a game room, a playground, and miniature golf. Free scheduled transportation serves all the Disney parks. One-bedroom units are equipped with a king bed in the bedroom and a sleeper sofa in the living area; two-bedroom condos have two double beds in the second bedroom, a sleeper sofa in the living area, and an additional bath.

US 192

Comfort Suites Maingate

7888 W. Irlo Bronson Memorial Hwy., Kissimmee; ☎ 407-390-9888 or 888-390-9888; comfortsuiteskissimmee.com

---

Rate per night $70–$170. **Pool** ★★★. **Fridge in room** Yes. **Shuttle to parks** Yes (Disney, Universal, and SeaWorld). **Maximum number of occupants per room** 6 for most suites. **Special comments** Complimentary Continental breakfast daily.

DESCRIPTION AND COMMENTS This property has 150 spacious one-room suites, each with double sofa bed, microwave, fridge, coffeemaker, TV, hair dryer, and safe. The suites are clean and contemporary, with muted deep-purple and beige tones. The large, heated pool has plenty of lounge chairs and moderate landscaping. A kiddie pool, whirlpool, and poolside bar complete the courtyard. Other amenities include an arcade and a gift shop. But Maingate's big plus is its location next door to a shopping center with about everything a family could need. There, you'll find 10 dining options, including Outback Steakhouse, Red Lobster, Subway, T.G.I. Friday's, and Chinese, Italian, and Japanese eateries; a Winn-Dixie Marketplace; a liquor store; a bank; a dry cleaner; and a tourist-information center with park passes for sale, among other services.

Gaylord Palms Hotel and Convention Center

6000 W. Osceola Pkwy., Kissimmee; ☎ 407-586-0000; gaylordpalms.com

---

Rate per night $129–$279. **Pool** ★★★★. **Fridge in room** Yes. **Shuttle to parks** Disney only. **Maximum number of occupants per room** 4. **Special comments** Probably the closest you'll get off-World to Disney-level extravagance. Resort fee of $15/day.

DESCRIPTION AND COMMENTS This decidedly upscale resort has a colossal convention facility and caters strongly to business clientele, but it's still a nice (if pricey) family resort. Hotel wings are defined by the three themed, glass-roofed atriums they overlook. Key West's design is reminiscent of island life in the Florida Keys; Everglades is an overgrown spectacle of shabby swamp chic, complete with piped-in cricket noise and a robotic alligator; and the immense, central St. Augustine harks back to Spanish Colonial Florida. Lagoons, streams, and waterfalls cut through and connect all three, and walkways and bridges abound. Rooms reflect the colors of their respective areas, though there's no particular connection in decor (St. Augustine atrium-view rooms are the most opulent, but they're not

Spanish). A fourth wing, Emerald Bay Tower, overlooks the Emerald Plaza shopping and dining area of the St. Augustine atrium. These rooms are the nicest and the most expensive, and they're mostly used by convention-goers. Though rooms have fridges and alarm clocks with CD players (as well as other perks such as high-speed Internet access), the rooms themselves really work better as retreats for adults than for kids. However, children will enjoy wandering the themed areas, playing in the family pool (with water-squirting octopus); in-room child care is provided by Kid's Nite Out.

Orange Lake Resort
8505 W. Irlo Bronson Memorial Hwy., Kissimmee;
☎ **407-239-0000 or 800-877-6522; orangelake.com**

Rate per night $126–$270 (2-bedroom summer rate). **Pools** ★★★★. **Fridge in room** Yes. **Shuttle to parks** Yes (fee varies depending on destination). **Maximum number of occupants per room** Varies. **Special comments** This is a time-share property, but if you rent directly through the resort (as opposed to the sales office), you can avoid time-share sales pitches.

DESCRIPTION AND COMMENTS You could spend your entire vacation never leaving this property, about 6–10 minutes from the Disney theme parks. From its 10 pools and two mini–water parks to its golfing opportunities (36 holes of championship greens plus two 9-hole executive courses), Orange Lake offers an extensive menu of amenities and recreational opportunities. If you tire of lazing by the pool, try waterskiing, wakeboarding, tubing, fishing, or other activities on the 80-acre lake. There's also a live alligator show, exercise programs, organized competitive sports and games, arts-and-crafts sessions, and miniature golf. Activities don't end when the sun goes down. Karaoke, live music, a Hawaiian luau, and movies at the resort cinema are some of the evening options.

The 2,412 units are tastefully decorated and comfortably furnished, ranging from suites and studios to three-bedroom villas, all containing fully equipped kitchens. If you'd rather not cook on vacation, try one of the seven restaurants scattered across the resort: two cafes, three grills, one pizzeria, and a fast-food eatery. If you need help with (or a break from) the kids, babysitters are available.

Radisson Resort Orlando-Celebration
2900 Parkway Blvd., Kissimmee; ☎ **407-396-7000 or 800-634-4774; radissonorlandoresort.com**

Rate per night $107–$168. **Pool** ★★★★½. **Fridge in room** Yes. **Shuttle to parks** Yes (Disney, Universal, and SeaWorld). **Maximum number of occupants per room** 5. **Special comments** $12.50/ day resort fee; kids age 10 and younger eat free with a paying adult at Mandolin's restaurant.

DESCRIPTION AND COMMENTS The free-form swimming pool alone is worth a stay here, but the Radisson Resort gets high marks in all areas. The pool is huge, with a waterfall and waterslide surrounded by palms and flowering plants, plus a smaller heated pool, two whirlpools, and a kiddie pool. Other outdoor amenities include two lighted tennis courts, sand volleyball, a playground, and jogging areas. Kids can also blow off steam at the arcade, while adults might visit the fitness center. Rooms are elegant, featuring Italian furnishings and marble baths. They're of ample size and include a minibar (some rooms), coffeemaker, TV, iron and board, hair dryer, and safe. Dining options include Mandolin's for breakfast (buffet) and dinner, and a 1950s-style diner serving burgers, sandwiches, shakes, and Pizza Hut pizza, among other fare. A sports lounge with an 11 × 6-foot TV offers nighttime entertainment. Guest services can help with tours, park passes, car rental, and babysitting. While there are no children's programs per se, there are still plenty of activities for little ones to enoy, such as face painting by a clown, juggling classes, bingo, and arts and crafts at the pool.

HOTELS *and* MOTELS: *Rated and Ranked*

IN THIS SECTION, WE COMPARE HOTELS in four main areas outside Walt Disney World (see next page) with those inside the World.

ROOM RATINGS

TO EVALUATE PROPERTIES FOR THEIR QUALITY, tastefulness, state of repair, cleanliness, and size of their standard rooms, we have grouped the hotels and motels into classifications denoted by stars—the overall star rating. Star ratings in this guide apply only to Orlando-area properties and don't necessarily correspond to ratings awarded by *Frommer's*, Mobil, AAA, or other travel critics. Because stars have little relevance when awarded in the absence of recognized standards of comparison, we have tied our ratings to

WHAT THE RATINGS MEAN		
★★★★★	Superior rooms	Tasteful and luxurious by any standard
★★★★	Extremely nice rooms	What you would expect at a Hyatt Regency or Marriott
★★★	Nice rooms	Holiday Inn or comparable quality
★★	Adequate rooms	Clean, comfortable, and functional without frills—like a Motel 6
★	Super-budget	These exist but are not included in our coverage

expected levels of quality established by specific American hotel corporations.

Overall star ratings apply only to room quality and describe the property's standard accommodations. For most hotels, a standard accommodation is a room with one king bed or two queen beds. In an all-suite property, the standard accommodation is either a studio or one-bedroom suite. Star ratings for rooms are assigned without regard to whether a property has restaurant(s), recreational facilities, entertainment, or other extras.

In addition to stars (which delineate broad categories), we use a numerical rating system—the room-quality rating. Our scale is 0–100, with 100 being the best possible rating and zero (0) the worst. Numerical ratings show the difference we perceive between one property and another. For instance, rooms at both the Courtyard Orlando Lake Buena Vista and the Courtyard Orlando I-Drive are rated 3½ stars (★★★½). In the supplemental numerical ratings, the former is an 82 and the latter a 76. This means that within the 3½-star category, the Courtyard LBV has slightly nicer rooms than the Courtyard I-Drive.

The location column identifies the area around Walt Disney World where you'll find a particular property. The designation **WDW** means the property is inside Walt Disney

LODGING AREAS
WDW Walt Disney World
1 International Drive
2 I-4 Corridor
3 US 192 (Irlo Bronson Memorial Highway)
4 Universal Orlando Area

World. A **1** means it's on or near International Drive. Properties on or near US 192 (aka Irlo Bronson Memorial Highway, Vine Street, and Space Coast Parkway) are indicated by a **3,** those in the vicinity of Universal Orlando as **4.** All others are marked with **2** and for the most part are along FL 535 and the I-4 corridor, though some are in nearby locations that don't meet any other criteria.

How the Hotels Compare

HOTEL	LOCATION	OVERALL QUALITY RATING	ROOM QUALITY RATING	COST ($ = $50)
Omni Orlando Resort at ChampionsGate	2	★★★★★	96	$$$$–
Bay Lake Tower at Contemporary Resort	WDW	★★★★½	95	$ × 9+
Disney's Animal Kingdom Villas (Kidani Village)	WDW	★★★★½	95	$ × 8
Hilton Grand Vacations Club at SeaWorld International	1	★★★★½	95	$$$
Sheraton Vistana Resort Villas	2	★★★★½	95	$$$+
The Ritz-Carlton Orlando, Grande Lakes	1	★★★★½	94	$ × 6–
Contemporary Resort	WDW	★★★★½	93	$ × 7
Grand Floridian Resort & Spa	WDW	★★★★½	93	$ × 10
Hard Rock Hotel	4	★★★★½	93	$ × 6+
JW Marriott Orlando Grande Lakes	1	★★★★½	93	$ × 6–
Orange Lake Resort	3	★★★★½	93	$$$$$–
Waldorf Astoria Orlando	2	★★★★½	93	$ × 9–
Westgate Vacation Villas (town center)	2	★★★★½	93	$$+
Bohemian Hotel Celebration	2	★★★★½	92	$$$$–
Doubletree Resort Orlando–I-Drive (resort)	1	★★★★½	92	$$$$–
Doubletree Resort Orlando–I-Drive (tower)	1	★★★★½	92	$$$+
Loews Portofino Bay Hotel	4	★★★★½	92	$ × 7–
Marriott's Grande Vista	1	★★★★½	92	$$$+
Polynesian Resort	WDW	★★★★½	92	$ × 9+
Westgate Lakes Resort & Spa	2	★★★★½	92	$$$
Disney's Animal Kingdom Villas (Jambo House)	WDW	★★★★½	91	$ × 7–
Rosen Centre Hotel	1	★★★★½	91	$ × 8+
Shades of Green	WDW	★★★★½	91	$$
Vacation Village at Parkway	3	★★★★½	91	$$
Beach Club Resort	WDW	★★★★½	90	$ × 8
Beach Club Villas	WDW	★★★★½	90	$ × 8
BoardWalk Villas	WDW	★★★★½	90	$ × 7–
CoCo Key Water Resort–Orlando	1	★★★★½	90	$$$
Disney's Old Key West Resort	WDW	★★★★½	90	$ × 7–
Disney's Saratoga Springs Resort & Spa	WDW	★★★★½	90	$ × 7–
Dolphin	WDW	★★★★½	90	$$$$–
Four Points by Sheraton Orlando Studio City	1	★★★★½	90	$$$–
Gaylord Palms Hotel & Convention Center	3	★★★★½	90	$$$$$–
Holiday Inn in the Walt Disney World Resort	WDW	★★★★½	90	$$$–
Holiday Inn Main Gate East	3	★★★★½	90	$$–

How the Hotels Compare (continued)

HOTEL	LOCATION	OVERALL QUALITY RATING	ROOM QUALITY RATING	COST ($ = $50)
Hyatt Regency Grand Cypress	2	★★★★½	90	$$$$–
Liki Tiki Village	3	★★★★½	90	$$–
Loews Royal Pacific Resort at Universal Orlando	4	★★★★½	90	$ × 6–
Marriott's Harbour Lake	2	★★★★½	90	$$$+
Peabody Orlando	1	★★★★½	90	$ × 7
Rosen Plaza Hotel	1	★★★★½	90	$ × 7–
Swan	WDW	★★★★½	90	$$$$
Treehouse Villas at Disney's Saratoga Springs Resort & Spa	WDW	★★★★½	90	$ × 14–
Westgate Vacation Villas (villas)	2	★★★★½	90	$$+
Wilderness Lodge Villas	WDW	★★★★½	90	$ × 8–
BoardWalk Inn	WDW	★★★★	89	$ × 8+
Courtyard Orlando Lake Buena Vista at Vista Centre	2	★★★★	89	$$–
Disney's Animal Kingdom Lodge	WDW	★★★★	89	$ × 6+
Doubletree Universal	4	★★★★	89	$$$–
Hilton Orlando Bonnet Creek	1	★★★★	89	$$$+
Orlando World Center Marriott Resort	2	★★★★	89	$$$$+
Renaissance Orlando SeaWorld	1	★★★★	89	$$$$$
Yacht Club Resort	WDW	★★★★	89	$ × 8
Caribe Royale All-Suite Hotel & Convention Center	1	★★★★	88	$$$
Floridays Resort Orlando	1	★★★★	88	$$$$–
Hilton Grand Vacations Club on I-Drive	1	★★★★	88	$$$+
Rosen Shingle Creek	1	★★★★	88	$ × 6–
Wyndham Bonnet Creek Resort	2	★★★★	88	$$$$$–
Hawthorn Suites Lake Buena Vista	2	★★★★	87	$$+
Hilton in the Walt Disney World Resort	WDW	★★★★	87	$$$$+
Mystic Dunes Resort & Golf Club	3	★★★★	87	$$–
Royal Plaza (tower)	WDW	★★★★	87	$$+
Westin Imagine Orlando	1	★★★★	87	$$$$$–
Wyndham Cypress Palms	3	★★★★	87	$$
Doubletree Guest Suites	WDW	★★★★	86	$$$
Fort Wilderness Resort (cabins)	WDW	★★★★	86	$ × 7
Marriott Cypress Harbour Villas	1	★★★★	86	$ × 6+
Marriott Imperial Palm Villas	1	★★★★	86	$ × 8
Radisson Resort Orlando-Celebration	3	★★★★	86	$$–
Wilderness Lodge	WDW	★★★★	86	$ × 6+
Monumental Hotel	1	★★★★	85	$+

HOTEL	LOCATION	OVERALL QUALITY RATING	ROOM QUALITY RATING	COST ($ = $50)
Best Western Lake Buena Vista Resort Hotel	WDW	★★★★	85	$$
Celebrity Resorts Lake Buena Vista	2	★★★★	85	$+
Marriott Residence Inn Orlando SeaWorld/ International Center	2	★★★★	85	$$$
Extended Stay Deluxe Orlando Convention Center	1	★★★★	84	$$−
Hyatt Place Orlando/Universal	4	★★★★	84	$$+
Port Orleans Resort (French Quarter)	WDW	★★★★	84	$$$$−
Star Island Resort & Club	3	★★★★	84	$$$+
Buena Vista Suites	1	★★★★	83	$$+
Coronado Springs Resort	WDW	★★★★	83	$ × 8
Extended Stay Deluxe Orlando Lake Buena Vista	2	★★★★	83	$$−
Orlando Vista Hotel	2	★★★★	83	$$−
Polynesian Isles Resort (Phase 1)	3	★★★★	83	$$+
Port Orleans Resort (Riverside)	WDW	★★★★	83	$$$$−
Sheraton Safari Hotel & Suites Lake Buena Vista	2	★★★★	83	$$
Wyndham Orlando Resort	1	★★★★	83	$$+
Country Inn & Suites Orlando Maingate at Calypso	3	★★★½	82	$$
Courtyard Orlando LBV in Marriott Village	2	★★★½	82	$$
Hawthorn Suites Universal	1	★★★½	82	$$−
Hilton Garden Inn Orlando at SeaWorld	1	★★★½	82	$$$
Hilton Garden Inn Orlando I-Drive North	1	★★★½	82	$$+
Holiday Inn Resort Orlando–The Castle	1	★★★½	82	$$+
Nickelodeon Suites Resort	1	★★★½	82	$$$$+
Parkway International Resort	3	★★★½	82	$$
Radisson Hotel Orlando Lake Buena Vista	2	★★★½	82	$$$−
Embassy Suites Orlando–Lake Buena Vista	2	★★★½	81	$$$
Holiday Inn SunSpree Resort Lake Buena Vista	2	★★★½	81	$$
Homewood Suites by Hilton I-Drive	1	★★★½	81	$$$$−
Westgate Vacation Villas (towers)	2	★★★½	81	$$$−
Buena Vista Palace Hotel & Spa	WDW	★★★½	80	$$$−
Caribbean Beach Resort	WDW	★★★½	80	$$$$−
Celebrity Resorts Orlando	3	★★★½	80	$$+
Embassy Suites Orlando I-Drive/ Jamaican Court	1	★★★½	80	$$$$
Fairfield Inn & Suites Near Universal Orlando Resort	4	★★★½	80	$$+
Hawthorn Suites Orlando Convention Center	1	★★★½	80	$$−

How the Hotels Compare (continued)

HOTEL	LOCATION	OVERALL QUALITY RATING	ROOM QUALITY RATING	COST ($ = $50)
Holiday Inn Express Lake Buena Vista	2	★★★½	80	$$+
Residence Inn Orlando Convention Center	1	★★★½	80	$$$+
SpringHill Suites Orlando Convention Center	1	★★★½	80	$$$−
Country Inn & Suites Orlando Lake Buena Vista (rooms)	2	★★★½	78	$+
Country Inn & Suites Orlando Lake Buena Vista (suites)	2	★★★½	78	$$−
International Palms Resort & Conference Center	1	★★★½	77	$+
Radisson Resort Worldgate	3	★★★½	77	$$+
Comfort Suites Maingate	3	★★★½	76	$$
Courtyard Orlando I-Drive	1	★★★½	76	$$$−
Grand Lake Resort	3	★★★½	76	$$
Hampton Inn Orlando/Lake Buena Vista	2	★★★½	76	$$+
Palms Hotel & Villas	3	★★★½	76	$$+
Embassy Suites Orlando I-Drive	1	★★★½	75	$$$+
Extended Stay America Universal	4	★★★½	75	$$−
Extended Stay Deluxe Orlando Universal	4	★★★½	75	$+
Fairfield Inn & Suites Orlando LBV in Marriott Village	2	★★★½	75	$$
Holiday Inn Main Gate to Universal Orlando	4	★★★½	75	$$
Quality Suites Royal Parc Suites	3	★★★½	75	$$+
Residence Inn Orlando I-Drive	1	★★★½	75	$$+
Residence Inn Orlando Lake Buena Vista	2	★★★½	75	$$$−
Rosen Inn at Pointe Orlando	1	★★★½	75	$$+
Staybridge Suites Orlando	1	★★★½	75	$$$−
Wyndham Lake Buena Vista Resort	WDW	★★★½	75	$$$−
Galleria Palms Kissimmee Hotel	3	★★★	74	$+
Hampton Inn I-Drive/Convention Center	1	★★★	74	$$$
Holiday Inn Hotel & Suites Orlando Convention Center	1	★★★	74	$$
Quality Suites Orlando	2	★★★	74	$+
Quality Suites Orlando Lake Buena Vista	2	★★★	74	$$−
All-Star Resorts	WDW	★★★	73	$$$−
La Quinta Inn Orlando I-Drive	1	★★★	73	$$−
Extended Stay America Orlando Convention Center	1	★★★	72	$$−
Ramada Inn Orlando I-Drive Lakefront	1	★★★	72	$$−
Staybridge Suites Lake Buena Vista	2	★★★	72	$$$−
Pop Century Resort	WDW	★★★	71	$$$−
Ramada Gateway Kissimmee (tower)	3	★★★	71	$$−

HOTEL	LOCATION	OVERALL QUALITY RATING	ROOM QUALITY RATING	COST ($ = $50)
Royal Plaza (garden)	WDW	★★★	71	$$+
Seralago Hotel & Suites Main Gate East	3	★★★	71	$+
SpringHill Suites Orlando LBV in Marriott Village	2	★★★	71	$$+
Best Western Orlando Gateway Hotel	1	★★★	70	$$
Holiday Inn Express at Summer Bay Resort	3	★★★	70	$$−
Super 8 Kissimmee/Orlando Area	3	★★★	70	$
Monumental MovieLand Hotel	1	★★★	68	$+
Westgate Palace	1	★★★	68	$$$+
Enclave Suites	1	★★★	67	$+
Maingate Lakeside Resort	3	★★★	67	$+
Hampton Inn Universal	4	★★★	67	$$−
Champions World Resort	3	★★★	66	$
Comfort Inn Universal Studios Area	1	★★★	66	$
Comfort Suites Universal	4	★★★	66	$$−
Destiny Palms Maingate West	3	★★★	65	$−
Ramada Inn Convention Center I-Drive	1	★★★	65	$$−
Ramada Maingate West Kissimmee	3	★★★	65	$+
Best Western Universal Inn	1	★★½	64	$$−
Clarion Inn & Suites at I-Drive	1	★★½	64	$$−
Clarion Inn Lake Buena Vista	2	★★½	64	$$−
Inn Nova Kissimmee	3	★★½	64	$−
Ramada Gateway Kissimmee (garden)	3	★★½	64	$+
Silver Lake Resort	3	★★½	64	$$$$−
Baymont Inn & Suites	1	★★½	63	$
Country Inn & Suites Orlando Universal	1	★★½	63	$$
The Inn at Summer Bay	3	★★½	63	$$$−
La Quinta Inn Orlando–Universal Studios	4	★★½	63	$$−
Orlando Metropolitan Express	1	★★½	63	$+
Days Inn Clermont South	3	★★½	62	$+
Econo Lodge Inn & Suites I-Drive	1	★★½	62	$+
Celebration Suites	3	★★½	61	$$−
Days Inn Orlando/I-Drive	1	★★½	61	$−
Imperial Swan Hotel & Suites	1	★★½	61	$
Motel 6 Orlando–I-Drive	1	★★½	61	$
Clarion Hotel Maingate	3	★★½	60	$+
Comfort Inn I-Drive	1	★★½	60	$+
Continental Plaza Hotel Kissimmee	3	★★½	60	$−

How the Hotels Compare *(continued)*

HOTEL	LOCATION	OVERALL QUALITY RATING	ROOM QUALITY RATING	COST ($ = $50)
Days Inn Orlando/Convention Center	1	★★½	60	$+
Days Inn Orlando/Universal Maingate	4	★★½	60	$+
Lexington Suites Orlando	1	★★½	60	$$−
Royal Celebration Inn	3	★★½	60	$
Super 8 Main Gate	3	★★½	60	$
Howard Johnson Enchanted Land Hotel	3	★★½	59	$−
Howard Johnson Inn Maingate East	3	★★½	59	$−
Howard Johnson Inn Orlando I-Drive	1	★★½	59	$
Rodeway Inn Maingate	3	★★½	59	$−
Blue Palm Hotel	1	★★½	58	$+
Extended Stay Deluxe Pointe Orlando	1	★★½	58	$$−
Red Roof Inn Orlando Convention Center	1	★★½	58	$+
HomeSuiteHome Eastgate	3	★★½	57	$−
Quality Inn International Hotel	1	★★½	57	$$−
Quality Inn & Suites	3	★★½	56	$
Knights Inn Maingate Kissimmee	3	★★	55	$−
Masters Inn Kissimmee	3	★★	55	$−
Quality Inn & Suites Eastgate	3	★★	55	$+
Travelodge Suites East Gate Orange	3	★★	55	$+
Best Western I-Drive	1	★★	54	$$−
Golden Link Resort Motel	3	★★	54	$
Baymont Inn & Suites Celebration	3	★★	53	$+
Motel 6 Main Gate West	3	★★	52	$−
Rosen Inn	1	★★	52	$+
Central Motel	3	★★	51	$−
Key Motel	3	★★	51	$−
America's Best Inn Main Gate East	3	★★	50	$−
Howard Johnson Express Inn & Suites	3	★★	50	$
La Quinta Inn Orlando I-Drive North	1	★★	50	$+
Magic Castle Inn & Suites	3	★★	50	$−
HomeSuiteHome Kissimmee Maingate	3	★★	48	$−
Monte Carlo Motel	3	★★	48	$−
Motel 6 Main Gate East	3	★★	47	$−
Orlando Continental Plaza Hotel	1	★★	47	$
Red Roof Inn Kissimmee	3	★★	47	$−
Vacation Lodge Maingate	3	★½	46	$−

Names of properties along US 192 also designate location (for example, Holiday Inn Maingate West). The consensus in Orlando seems to be that the main entrance to Disney World is the broad interstate-type road that runs off US 192. This is called the **Maingate.** Properties along US 192 call themselves Maingate East or West to differentiate their positions along the highway. So, driving southeast from Clermont or Florida's Turnpike, the properties before you reach the Maingate turnoff are called Maingate West, while the properties after you pass the Maingate turnoff are called Maingate East.

Cost estimates are based on the hotel's published rack rates for standard rooms. Each **$** represents $50. Thus a cost symbol of **$$$** means that a room (or suite) at that hotel will be about $150 a night.

We've focused on room quality and excluded consideration of location, services, recreation, or amenities. In some instances, a one- or two-room suite is available for the same price or less than that of a single standard hotel room.

If you've used an earlier edition of this guide, you'll notice that new properties have been added and many ratings and rankings have changed, some because of room renovation or improved maintenance or housekeeping. Failure to maintain rooms or lax housekeeping can bring down ratings.

The key to avoiding disappointment in a room is to snoop in advance. When you or your travel agent calls, ask how old the property is and when the guest room you're being assigned was last renovated. Note that some chains use the same guest-room photo in promotional literature for all their hotels and that the room in a specific property may not resemble the photo. If you're assigned a room inferior to expectations, demand to be moved.

THE 30 BEST HOTEL VALUES

LET'S LOOK AT THE BEST COMBINATIONS of quality and value in a room. Listed on page 69 are our top 30 buys for the money regardless of location or star rating, based on average rack rates. These rankings were made without consideration for the availability of restaurant(s), recreational facilities, entertainment, and/or amenities.

A reader recently wrote to complain that he had booked one of our top-ranked rooms in terms of value and had been very disappointed in the room. We noticed that the room the reader occupied had a quality rating of ★★½. Remember that the list of top deals is intended to give you some sense of value received for dollars spent. A ★★½ room at $40 may have the same value as a ★★★★ room at $115, but that doesn't mean the rooms will be of comparable quality. Regardless of whether it's a good deal, a ★★½ room is still a ★★½ room.

For example, the Magic Castle Inn and Suites is a clean, reasonably comfortable motel with an exceptionally friendly staff, within 15 minutes of every Disney theme park. During one Christmas season they had available basic rooms for around $54 per night when every other hotel within 20 miles of Walt Disney World was charging $150. The catch? They're right next door to a place that gives helicopter tours of Orlando . . . all day long. You won't notice a thing if you don't plan on midday breaks, but our midafternoon naps were filled with visions of *M*A*S*H* and *Apocalypse Now*. We'd still stay there again, but our wives have different opinions.

The Top 30 Best Deals

RANK	HOTEL	LOCATION	RATING	QUALITY	($ = $50)
1.	Monumental Hotel	1	★★★★	85	$+
2.	Rodeway Inn Maingate	3	★★½	59	$−
3.	Liki Tiki Village	3	★★★★½	90	$$−
4.	Vacation Village at Parkway	3	★★★★½	91	$$
5.	Destiny Palms Maingate West	3	★★★	65	$−
6.	Celebrity Resorts Lake Buena Vista	2	★★★★	85	$+
7.	Holiday Inn Main Gate East	3	★★★★½	90	$$−
8.	HomeSuiteHome Eastgate	3	★★½	57	$−
9.	Shades of Green	WDW	★★★★½	91	$$
10.	Continental Plaza Hotel Kissimmee	3	★★½	60	$−
11.	Extended Stay Deluxe Orlando Convention Center	1	★★★★	84	$$−
12.	Extended Stay Deluxe Orlando Lake Buena Vista	2	★★★★	83	$$−
13.	Orlando Vista Hotel	2	★★★★	83	$$−
14.	Radisson Resort Orlando-Celebration	3	★★★★	86	$$−
15.	Champions World Resort	3	★★★	66	$
16.	Inn Nova Kissimmee	3	★★½	64	$−
17.	Courtyard Orlando Lake Buena Vista at Vista Centre	2	★★★★	89	$$−
18.	Country Inn & Suites Orlando Lake Buena Vista (rooms)	2	★★★½	78	$+
19.	Days Inn Orlando/I-Drive	1	★★½	61	$−
20.	Mystic Dunes Resort & Golf Club	3	★★★★	87	$$−
21.	Super 8 Kissimmee/Orlando Area	3	★★★	70	$
22.	Knights Inn Maingate Kissimmee	3	★★	55	$−
23.	Central Motel	3	★★	51	$−
24.	Extended Stay Deluxe Orlando Universal	4	★★★½	75	$+
25.	Quality Inn & Suites	3	★★½	56	$
26.	Seralago Hotel & Suites Main Gate East	3	★★★	71	$+
27.	Howard Johnson Enchanted Land Hotel	3	★★½	59	$−
28.	Howard Johnson Inn Maingate East	3	★★½	59	$−
29.	Comfort Inn Universal Studios Area	1	★★★	66	$
30.	Best Western Lake Buena Vista Resort Hotel	WDW	★★★★	85	$$

PART FOUR

WALT DISNEY WORLD *with* KIDS

RECOMMENDATIONS *for* MAKING *the* DREAM COME TRUE

WHEN PLANNING A DISNEY WORLD vacation with young children, consider the following:

AGE Although the color and festivity of Disney World excite all children, and specific attractions delight toddlers and preschoolers, Disney entertainment is generally oriented to older children and adults. Children should be a fairly mature 7 years old to *appreciate* the Magic Kingdom and Disney's Animal Kingdom, and a year or two older to get much out of Epcot or Disney's Hollywood Studios.

TIME OF YEAR TO VISIT Avoid the hot, crowded summer months, especially if you have preschoolers. Go in October, November (except Thanksgiving), early December, January, February, or May. If you have children of varied ages and they're good students, take the older ones out of school and visit during the cooler, less congested off-season. Arrange special assignments relating to the educational aspects of Disney World. If your children can't afford to miss school, take your vacation as soon as the school year ends in late May or early June. Alternatively, try late August before school starts.

BUILD NAPS AND REST INTO YOUR ITINERARY The theme parks are huge; don't try to see everything in one day. Tour in early morning and return to your hotel around 11:30 a.m. for lunch, a swim, and a nap. Even during off-season when the crowds are smaller and the temperatures more pleasant, the size of the major theme parks will exhaust most children under age 8 by lunchtime. Return to the park in late afternoon or early evening and continue touring. If you plan to return to your hotel in midday and would like your room made up, let housekeeping know.

unofficial **TIP**
Naps and relief from the frenetic pace of the theme parks, even during the off-season, are indispensable.

WHERE TO STAY The time and hassle involved in commuting to and from the theme parks will be lessened if you stay in a hotel close to the theme parks. We should point out that this doesn't necessarily mean you have to lodge at a hotel in Walt Disney World. Because Walt Disney World is so geographically dispersed, many off-property hotels are actually closer to the theme parks than some Disney resorts. Regardless of whether you stay in or out of the World, it's imperative that you take young children out of the parks each day for a few hours of rest. Neglecting to relax is the best way we know to get the whole family in a snit and ruin the day (or the vacation).

If you have young children, you must plan ahead. Make sure your hotel is within 20 minutes of the theme parks. It's true you can revive somewhat by retreating to a Disney hotel for lunch or by finding a quiet restaurant in the theme parks, but there's no substitute for returning to the familiarity and comfort of your own hotel. Regardless of what you have heard, children too large to sleep in a stroller won't relax unless you take them back to your hotel. If it takes renting a car to make returning to your hotel practicable, rent the car.

If you are traveling with children ages 12 and younger and want to stay in the World, we recommend the Polynesian, Grand Floridian, or Wilderness Lodge and Villas Resorts (in that order) if they fit your budget. For less expensive rooms, try the Port Orleans Resort. Bargain accommodations are available at the All-Star and Pop Century resorts. Fully equipped log cabins at Fort Wilderness Campground are also good economy lodging. Outside Walt Disney World, check out our top hotels for families (see page 47).

BE IN TOUCH WITH YOUR FEELINGS When you or your children get tired and irritable, call time out and regroup. Trust your instincts. What would feel best? Another ride, an ice cream break, or going back to the room for a nap? *The way to protect your considerable investment in your Disney vacation is to stay happy and have a good time.* You don't have to meet a quota for experiencing attractions. Do what you want.

LEAST COMMON DENOMINATORS Somebody is going to run out of steam first, and when he or she does, the whole family will be affected. Sometimes a snack break will revive the flagging member. Sometimes, however, it's better to just return to your hotel. Pushing the tired or discontented beyond their capacity will spoil the day for them—and you. Accept that energy levels vary and be prepared to respond to members of your group who poop out.

BUILDING ENDURANCE Though most children are active, their normal play usually doesn't condition them for the exertion required to tour a Disney theme park. We recommend starting a program of family walks four to six weeks before your trip to get in shape.

SETTING LIMITS AND MAKING PLANS Avoid arguments and disappointment by establishing guidelines for each day, and get everybody committed.

BE FLEXIBLE Any day at Walt Disney World includes some surprises; be prepared to adjust your plan. Listen to your intuition.

OVERHEATING, SUNBURN, AND DEHYDRATION These are the most common problems of younger children at Disney World. Carry and use sunscreen. Be sure to put some on children in strollers, even if the stroller has a canopy. To avoid overheating, rest regularly in the shade or in an air-conditioned restaurant or show. Plastic squeeze bottles with caps are sold in all major parks for about $3.

unofficial **TIP**
We recommend renting a stroller for children age 6 and younger and carrying plastic bottles of water.

BLISTERS AND SORE FEET Guests of all ages should wear comfortable, well-broken-in shoes and two pairs of thin socks (better than one pair of thick socks). If you or your children are susceptible to blisters, bring precut moleskin bandages, available at most drugstores. When you feel a hot spot, stop, air out your foot, and place a moleskin bandage over the area before a blister forms. Young children may not tell their parents about a developing blister until it's too late, so inspect the feet of preschoolers two or more times a day.

FIRST AID Each major theme park has a first-aid center. In the Magic Kingdom, it's at the end of Main Street to your left, between Casey's Corner and The Crystal Palace. At Epcot, it's on the World Showcase side of Odyssey Center. At Disney's Hollywood Studios, it's in the Guest Relations Building inside the main entrance. At Disney's Animal

Kingdom, it's in Discovery Island, on your left just before you cross the bridge to Africa. If you or your children have a medical problem, go to a first-aid center. They're friendlier than most doctor's offices and are accustomed to treating everything from paper cuts to allergic reactions.

CHILDREN ON MEDICATION Some parents of hyperactive children on medication discontinue or decrease the child's dosage at the end of the school year. If you have such a child, be aware that Disney World might overstimulate him or her. Consult your physician before altering your child's medication regimen.

WALKIE-TALKIES An increasing number of readers stay in touch while on vacation by using walkie-talkies. If you go the walkie-talkie route, get a set that operates on multiple channels, or opt for cellular phones.

SUNGLASSES If you want your younger children to wear sunglasses, put a strap or string on the frames so that the glasses will stay on during rides and can hang from the child's neck while indoors.

THINGS YOU FORGOT OR THINGS YOU RAN OUT OF Rain gear, diapers, diaper pins, formula, film, painkillers, topical sunburn treatments, and other sundries are sold at all major theme parks and at Typhoon Lagoon, Blizzard Beach, and Downtown Disney. Rain gear is a bargain, but most other items are high. Ask for goods you don't see displayed.

INFANTS AND TODDLERS AT THE THEME PARKS The major parks have centralized facilities for infant and toddler care. Everything necessary for changing diapers, preparing formulas, and warming bottles and food is available. Supplies are for sale, and rockers and special chairs for nursing mothers are provided. At the Magic Kingdom, the Baby Care Center is next to The Crystal Palace at the end of Main Street. At Epcot, the Baby Care Center is in the Odyssey Center, between Test Track in Future World and Mexico in World Showcase. At Disney's Hollywood Studios, the Baby Care Center is in the Guest Relations Building left of the main entrance. At Disney's Animal Kingdom, the Baby Care Center is behind Creature Comforts. Dads are welcome at the centers and can use most services. In addition, many men's restrooms in the major parks have changing tables.

Infants and toddlers are allowed to experience any attraction that doesn't have minimum height or age restrictions. If you think you might try nursing during a theater attraction, be advised that most shows run about 17–20 minutes. Exceptions are *The Hall of Presidents* at the Magic Kingdom and

The American Adventure at Epcot, which run 23 and 29 minutes, respectively.

STROLLERS The good news is that strollers are available for a modest rental fee at all four theme parks. If you rent a stroller at the Magic Kingdom and decide to go to Epcot, Disney's Animal Kingdom, or Disney's Hollywood Studios, turn in your Magic Kingdom stroller and present your receipt at the next park. You'll be issued another stroller without additional charge.

Obtain strollers at the Magic Kingdom entrance, to the left of Epcot's Entrance Plaza and at Epcot's International Gateway, and at Oscar's Super Service just inside the entrance of Disney's Hollywood Studios. At Disney's Animal Kingdom, they're at Garden Gate Gifts, to the right just inside the entrance. Rental at all parks is fast and efficient, and returning the stroller is a breeze. You can ditch your rental stroller anywhere in the park when you're ready to leave.

When you enter a show or board a ride, you must park your stroller, usually in an open, unprotected area. If it rains before you return, you'll need a cloth, towel, or diaper to dry it. Strollers are a must for infants and toddlers, but we have observed many sharp parents renting strollers for somewhat older children (up to 5 or so years old). The stroller prevents parents from having to carry children when they sag and provides a convenient place to carry water and snacks.

If you go to your hotel for a break and intend to return to the park, leave your rental stroller by an attraction near the park entrance, marking it with something personal like a bandanna. When you return, you'll know in an instant which one is yours.

unofficial **TIP**
Orlando Stroller Rentals (☎ 800-281-0884; **orlando strollerrentals .com**) offers folding strollers of higher quality than Disney's all-plastic models. OSR will drop your stroller off at your hotel before you arrive and pick it up there when you're done.

Be aware that rental strollers are too large for all infants and many toddlers.

It's permissible to bring your own stroller. Remember, however, that only collapsible strollers are allowed on monorails, parking-lot trams, and buses.

DISNEY, KIDS, AND SCARY STUFF

MONSTERS AND SPECIAL EFFECTS AT Disney's Hollywood Studios are more real and sinister than those in the other parks. If your child has difficulty coping with the ghouls of The Haunted Mansion, think twice about exposing him to machine-gun battles, earthquakes, and the creature from *Alien* at the Studios.

Preschoolers should start with Dumbo and work up to the Jungle Cruise in late morning, after being revved up and before getting hungry, thirsty, or tired. Pirates of the Caribbean is out for preschoolers. You get the idea.

SWITCHING OFF (AKA THE BABY SWAP)

SEVERAL ATTRACTIONS HAVE MINIMUM HEIGHT and/ or age requirements. Some couples with children too small or too young forgo these attractions, while others take turns to ride. Missing some of Disney's best rides is an unnecessary sacrifice, and waiting in line twice for the same ride is a tremendous waste of time.

Instead, take advantage of the "switching off" option, also called "The Baby Swap." To switch off, there must be at least two adults. Everybody waits in line together, adults and children. When you reach an attendant (called a "greeter"), say you want to switch off. The greeter will allow everyone, including the young children, to enter the attraction. When you reach the loading area, one adult rides while the other stays with the kids. Then the riding adult disembarks and takes charge of the children while the other adult rides. A third adult in the party can ride twice, once with each of the switching off adults, so that the switching-off adults don't have to experience the attraction alone.

ATTRACTIONS WHERE SWITCHING OFF IS COMMON

Magic Kingdom

Big Thunder Mountain Railroad

Seven Dwarfs Mine Train

Space Mountain

Splash Mountain

Stitch's Great Escape!

Epcot

Mission: SPACE

Test Track

Disney's Hollywood Studios

Rock 'n' Roller Coaster	Star Tours—The Adventures Continue
The Twilight Zone Tower of Terror	

Disney's Animal Kingdom

DINOSAUR	Expedition Everest
Kali River Rapids	Primeval Whirl

Small-child Fright-potential Chart

This is a quick reference to identify attractions to be wary of, and why. The chart represents a generalization, and all kids are different. It relates specifically to kids ages 3–7. On average, children at the younger end of the range are more likely to be frightened than children in their sixth or seventh year.

The Magic Kingdom

MAIN STREET, U.S.A.

Main Street Vehicles Not frightening in any respect.
Walt Disney World Railroad Not frightening in any respect.

ADVENTURELAND

The Enchanted Tiki Room A thunderstorm, loud volume level, and simulated explosions frighten some preschoolers.
Jungle Cruise Moderately intense, some macabre sights. A good test attraction for little ones.
Pirates of the Caribbean Slightly intimidating queuing area; intense boat ride with gruesome (though humorously presented) sights and a short, unexpected slide down a flume.
The Magic Carpets of Aladdin Much like Dumbo. A favorite of young children.
Swiss Family Treehouse May be unsuitable for kids who are afraid of heights.

FRONTIERLAND

Big Thunder Mountain Railroad Visually intimidating from outside, with moderately intense visual effects. The roller coaster is wild enough to frighten many adults, particularly seniors. Switching-off option provided (see page 75).
Country Bear Jamboree Not frightening in any respect.
Frontierland Shootin' Arcade Not frightening in any respect.
Splash Mountain Visually intimidating from outside, with moderately intense visual effects. The ride, culminating in a 52-foot plunge down a steep chute, is somewhat hair-raising for all ages. Switching-off option provided (see page 75).
Tom Sawyer Island Some very young children are intimidated by dark walk-through tunnels that can be easily avoided.

LIBERTY SQUARE

The Hall of Presidents Not frightening, but boring for young ones.
The Haunted Mansion Name raises anxiety, as do the spooky sounds and sights of the waiting area. The ride itself is gentle, though.
Liberty Belle **Riverboat** Not frightening in any respect.

FANTASYLAND

Cinderella's Golden Carousel Not frightening in any respect.

Dumbo the Flying Elephant A tame midway ride; a great favorite of most young children.

The Great Goofini *(children's roller coaster)* May frighten some preschoolers.

It's a Small World Not frightening in any respect.

Mad Tea Party Midway-type ride can induce motion sickness in all ages.

The Many Adventures of Winnie the Pooh Frightens a small percentage of preschoolers.

Peter Pan's Flight Not frightening in any respect.

Prince Charming Regal Carrousel Not frightening in any respect.

Seven Dwarfs Mine Train Not open at press time.

Under the Sea: Journey of the Little Mermaid Not open at press time.

TOMORROWLAND

Astro Orbiter Visually intimidating from the waiting area, but the ride is relatively tame.

Buzz Lightyear's Space Ranger Spin Dark ride with cartoonlike aliens may frighten some preschoolers.

Monsters, Inc. Laugh Floor May frighten a small percentage of preschoolers.

Space Mountain Very intense roller coaster in the dark—the Magic Kingdom's wildest ride, and a scary roller coaster by any standard. Switching-off option provided (see page 75).

Stitch's Great Escape! Very intense. May not the best attraction for children age 9 and younger. Switching-off option provided (see page 75).

Tomorrowland Speedway Noise of waiting area slightly intimidates preschoolers; otherwise, not frightening.

Tomorrowland Transit Authority PeopleMover Not frightening in any respect.

Walt Disney's Carousel of Progress Not frightening in any respect.

Epcot

FUTURE WORLD

Honey, I Shrunk the Audience/Captain EO Extremely intense visual effects and loud noises frighten many young children.

Innoventions East and West Not frightening in any respect.

Small-child Fright-potential Chart (cont'd)

Epcot (continued)

FUTURE WORLD (CONTINUED)

Journey into Imagination with Figment Loud noises and unexpected flashing lights can startle younger children.

The Land—*Circle of Life* **Theater** Not frightening in any respect.

The Land—*Living with the Land* Not frightening in any respect.

The Land—*Soarin'* May frighten children age 7 and younger.

Mission: SPACE Extremely intense space-simulation ride that has been known to frighten guests of all ages. Switching-off option provided (see page 75).

The Seas—Main Tank and Exhibits Not frightening in any respect.

The Seas—*The Seas with Nemo & Friends* Very sweet but may frighten some toddlers.

The Seas—*Turtle Talk with Crush* Not frightening in any respect.

Spaceship Earth Intimidates a few preschoolers.

Test Track Intense thrill ride may frighten any age. Switching-off option provided (see page 75).

Universe of Energy: *Ellen's Energy Adventure* Dinosaur segment frightens some preschoolers; some intimidating effects.

WORLD SHOWCASE

The American Adventure Not frightening in any respect.

Canada—*O Canada!* Not frightening in any respect.

China—*Reflections of China* Not frightening in any respect.

France—*Impressions de France* Not frightening in any respect.

Germany Not frightening in any respect.

Italy Not frightening in any respect.

Japan Not frightening in any respect.

Mexico—Gran Fiesta Tour Not frightening in any respect.

Morocco Not frightening in any respect.

Norway—Maelstrom A few preschoolers are frightened.

United Kingdom Not frightening in any respect.

Disney's Animal Kingdom

The Oasis Not frightening in any respect.

Rafiki's Planet Watch Not frightening in any respect.

DISCOVERY ISLAND

It's Tough to Be a Bug! Very intense and loud with special effects that startle viewers of all ages and potentially terrify young children.

CAMP MINNIE-MICKEY

Festival of the Lion King A bit loud, but otherwise not frightening.

AFRICA

Kilimanjaro Safaris Makes a few young children anxious.
Pangani Forest Exploration Trail Not frightening in any respect.
Wildlife Express Train Not frightening in any respect.

ASIA

Expedition Everest Frightening to guests of all ages.
Flights of Wonder Swooping birds alarm a few small children.
Kali River Rapids Potentially frightening and certainly wet for guests of all ages. Switching-off option provided (see page 75).
Maharajah Jungle Trek Some children may balk at the bat exhibit.

DINOLAND U.S.A.

The Boneyard Not frightening in any respect.
DINOSAUR High-tech thrill ride rattles riders of all ages. Switching-off option provided (see page 75).
Finding Nemo: The Musical Not frightening in any respect, but loud.
Primeval Whirl Most children age 7 and older will take it in stride.
TriceraTop Spin Frightens only a small percentage of younger kids.

Disney's Hollywood Studios

HOLLYWOOD BOULEVARD

The Great Movie Ride Intense in parts, with very realistic special effects. Frightens many preschoolers.

SUNSET BOULEVARD

Beauty and the Beast—Live on Stage Not frightening in any respect.
Fantasmic! Terrifies some preschoolers.
Rock 'n' Roller Coaster May frighten guests of any age. Switching-off option provided (see page 75).
The Twilight Zone Tower of Terror The plummeting elevator at the ride's end frightens many adults as well as kids. Switching-off option provided (see page 75).

ECHO LAKE

The American Idol Experience At times, the singing may frighten anyone.
Indiana Jones Epic Stunt Spectacular! An intense show with powerful special effects, but young children generally handle it well.
Sounds Dangerous with Drew Carey Noises in the dark frighten children as old as 8.

Small-child Fright-potential Chart (continued)

Disney's Hollywood Studios (continued)

ECHO LAKE (CONTINUED)

Star Tours—The Adventures Continue Extremely intense visually for all ages. Switching-off option provided (see page 75).

STREETS OF AMERICA

Honey, I Shrunk the Kids Movie Set Adventure Not scary.

Jim Henson's Muppet-Vision 3-D Boisterous but not frightening.

Lights, Motors, Action! Extreme Stunt Show Intense but not threatening.

Studio Backlot Tour Nonintimidating except for Catastrophe Canyon, where an earthquake and a flash flood are simulated.

PIXAR PLACE

Toy Story Mania! Dark ride may frighten some preschoolers.

MICKEY AVENUE

Walt Disney: One Man's Dream Not frightening in any respect.

ANIMATION COURTYARD

Disney Junior—Live on Stage! Not frightening in any respect.

The Magic of Disney Animation Not frightening in any respect.

Voyage of the Little Mermaid Not frightening in any respect.

On most Fastpass attractions, when you tell the cast member that you want to switch off, you get a "rider exchange" Fastpass good for three people. One parent and the nonriding child/children will then be asked to leave the line. When those riding reunite with the waiting adult, the waiting adult and two other persons from the party can ride using the pass.

MEETING *the* DISNEY CHARACTERS

YOU CAN SEE DISNEY CHARACTERS in live shows at all the theme parks and in parades at the Magic Kingdom and Disney's Hollywood Studios. Consult your daily entertainment schedule for times. If you want to *meet* the characters, get autographs, and take photos, consult the park map or the handout *Times Guide* sometimes provided to supplement the park map. If there is a particular character you're itching to meet, ask any cast member to call the character hotline for you. The hotline will tell you (via the cast member) if the character is out and about, and if so, where to find it.

AT THE MAGIC KINGDOM Character encounters are more frequent here than anywhere else in Walt Disney World. A character will almost always be next to City Hall on Main Street, and there will usually be one or more in Town Square or near the railroad station. Characters appear in all of the lands but are usually most plentiful around Fantasyland. In Fantasyland, Cinderella regularly greets diners at Cinderella's Royal Table in the castle. Nearby, check out the Fantasyland Character Festival by the lagoon opposite Dumbo.

unofficial **TIP**
If it's rainy at the Magic Kingdom, look for characters on the veranda of Tony's Town Square Restaurant or in the Town Square Theater next to Tony's.

The Town Square Theater on Main Street is being converted to meet-and-greet use for Mickey and the princesses. Also look for characters in the Central Plaza, by Splash Mountain in Frontierland, and by *Walt Disney's Carousel of Progress* in Tomorrowland. Because of the construction in Fantasyland, check the daily entertainment schedule when you enter the park for the appearance times and locations of your favorite characters.

Characters are featured in afternoon and evening parades and also play a major role in Castle Forecourt shows (at the castle entrance on the central-hub side). Find performance times for shows and parades in the daily entertainment schedule (*Times Guide*). Characters sometimes stay to mingle after shows.

AT EPCOT Characters are plentiful at Epcot and usually appear in their normal garb. In Future World, one or more characters, including Mickey, Minnie, Pluto, Goofy, and Chip 'n' Dale can be found from opening until early evening at the Epcot Character Spot in Innoventions West (waits of an hour or more are not uncommon). In the World Showcase, most pavilions host a character or two. Donald struts his stuff in Mexico, while Mulan and Mushu greet guests in China. Princess Aurora, Belle, and the Beast hang out in France, and Snow White and Dopey are regulars in Germany, as are Jasmine, Aladdin, and the Genie in Morocco. Pooh and friends, Alice in Wonderland, and Mary Poppins appear in the United Kingdom. In addition, character shows are performed

unofficial **TIP**
Many children particularly enjoy meals with "face characters" such as Snow White, Belle, Jasmine, Cinderella, and Aladdin, who speak and are thus able to engage children in a way not possible for the mute animal characters.

daily at the America Gardens Theatre in World Showcase. Check the daily entertainment schedule (*Times Guide*) for showtimes.

AT DISNEY'S ANIMAL KINGDOM Camp Minnie-Mickey in Animal Kingdom is designed specifically for meeting characters. Meet Mickey, Minnie, Goofy, and Donald on designated character-greeting "trails." Elsewhere in the park, Pooh, Eeyore, Tigger, and Piglet appear at the river landing opposite Flame Tree Barbecue, and you might encounter a character or two at Rafiki's Planet Watch. Also at Camp Minnie-Mickey is a stage show featuring characters from *The Lion King*.

AT DISNEY'S HOLLYWOOD STUDIOS Characters are likely to turn up anywhere at the Studios but are most frequently found inside the Magic of Disney Animation building, along Pixar Place (leading to the soundstages), by Al's Toy Barn, at Star Tours, and on Streets of America. The main meet-and-greet area, however, is at the giant sorcerer's hat at the end of Hollywood Boulevard, where up to four characters hold court from 9 a.m. until about 1 p.m. Characters are also prominent in shows, with *Voyage of the Little Mermaid* running almost continuously and an abbreviated version of *Beauty and the Beast* performed several times daily at the Theater of the Stars. Check the daily entertainment schedule (*Times Guide*) for showtimes.

CHARACTER DINING

FRATERNIZING WITH CHARACTERS HAS become so popular that Disney offers character breakfasts, brunches, and dinners where families can dine in the presence of Mickey, Minnie, Goofy, and other costumed versions of animated celebrities. Besides grabbing customers from Denny's and Hardee's, character meals provide a familiar, controlled setting in which young children can warm gradually to characters. All meals are attended by several characters. Adult prices apply to persons ages 10 or older, children's prices to ages 3–9; little ones under age 3 eat free. For additional information on character dining, call ☎ 407-939-3463 (WDW-DINE).

Because character dining is very popular, we recommend arranging Advance Reservations as far in advance as possible by calling ☎ 407-939-3463 (WDW-DINE). An Advance Reservation is not a eservation per se, only a commitment to seat you ahead of walk-in patrons at the scheduled date and time.

At very popular character meals like the breakfast at Cinderella's Royal Table, you're required to make a for-real reservation and guarantee it with a for-real deposit.

How to Choose a Character Meal

We receive a lot of mail asking for advice about character meals. Some *are* better than others, sometimes much better. Here's what we look for when we evaluate character meals:

1. THE CHARACTERS The various meals offer a diverse assortment of Disney characters. Selecting a meal that features your children's special favorites is a good first step. Check the Character-meal Hit Parade chart following to see which characters are assigned to each meal.

2. ATTENTION FROM THE CHARACTERS In all character meals, the characters circulate among the guests hugging children, posing for pictures, and signing autographs. How much time a character spends with you and your children will depend primarily on the ratio of characters to guests. The more characters and fewer guests the better. Because many character meals never fill to capacity, the character–guest ratios found in our Character-meal Hit Parade chart have been adjusted to reflect an average attendance as opposed to a sell-out crowd. Even so, there's quite a range.

3. THE SETTING Some character meals are in exotic settings. For others, moving the event to an elementary-school cafeteria would be an improvement. Our chart rates each meal's setting with the familiar scale of zero (worst) to five (best) stars. Two restaurants, Cinderella's Royal Table in the Magic Kingdom and The Garden Grill Restaurant in the Land Pavilion at Epcot, deserve special mention. Cinderella's Royal Table is on the first and second floors of Cinderella Castle in Fantasyland, offering guests a look inside the castle. The Garden Grill is a revolving restaurant overlooking several scenes from the Living with the Land boat ride. Also at Epcot, the popular Princess Storybook Meals are held in the castlelike Akershus Royal Banquet Hall. Though Chef Mickey's at the Contemporary Resort is rather sterile in appearance, it affords a great view of the monorail running through the hotel. Themes and settings of the remaining character-meal venues, while apparent to adults, will be lost on most children.

Character-meal Hit Parade

1. CINDERELLA'S ROYAL TABLE	**2. AKERSHUS ROYAL BANQUET HALL**	**3. CHEF MICKEY'S**
LOCATION Magic Kingdom	**LOCATION** Epcot	**LOCATION** Contemporary Resort
MEALS SERVED Breakfast, lunch, dinner	**MEALS SERVED** Breakfast, lunch, dinner	**MEALS SERVED** Breakfast, dinner
CHARACTERS Cinderella, Fairy Godmother, Aurora, Belle, Jasmine, Snow White	**CHARACTERS** 4–6 characters chosen from Alice, Ariel, Belle, Jasmine, Mary Poppins, Mulan, Sleeping Beauty, Snow White	**CHARACTERS** *Breakfast:* Mickey, Minnie, Donald, Goofy, Pluto (sometimes Chip 'n' Dale)
SERVED Daily	**SERVED** Daily	*Dinner:* Mickey, Minnie, Donald, Goofy, Pluto (sometimes Chip 'n' Dale)
SETTING ★★★★★	**SETTING** ★★★★	**SERVED** Daily
SERVICE Fixed menu	**SERVICE** Family-style and menu (all you care to eat)	**SETTING** ★★★
FOOD VARIETY AND QUALITY ★★★	**FOOD VARIETY AND QUALITY** ★★★½	**SERVICE** Buffet
NOISE LEVEL Quiet	**NOISE LEVEL** Quiet	**FOOD VARIETY AND QUALITY** ★★★ (breakfast) ★★★½ (dinner)
CHARACTER–GUEST RATIO 1:26	**CHARACTER–GUEST RATIO** 1:54	**NOISE LEVEL** Loud
		CHARACTER–GUEST RATIO 1:56

7. TUSKER HOUSE RESTAURANT	**8. CAPE MAY CAFE**	**9. 'OHANA**
LOCATION Disney's Animal Kingdom	**LOCATION** Beach Club	**LOCATION** Polynesian Resort
MEALS SERVED Breakfast	**MEALS SERVED** Breakfast	**MEALS SERVED** Breakfast
CHARACTERS Donald, Daisy, Mickey, Goofy	**CHARACTERS** Goofy, Donald, Minnie	**CHARACTERS** Lilo and Stitch, Mickey, Pluto
SERVED Daily	**SERVED** Daily	**SERVED** Daily
SETTING ★★★	**SETTING** ★★★	**SETTING** ★★
SERVICE Buffet	**SERVICE** Buffet	**SERVICE** Family-style
FOOD VARIETY AND QUALITY ★★★	**FOOD VARIETY AND QUALITY** ★★½	**FOOD VARIETY AND QUALITY** ★★½
NOISE LEVEL Very loud	**NOISE LEVEL** Moderate	**NOISE LEVEL** Moderate
CHARACTER–GUEST RATIO 1:112	**CHARACTER–GUEST RATIO** 1:67	**CHARACTER–GUEST RATIO** 1:57

4. THE CRYSTAL PALACE

LOCATION
Magic Kingdom

MEALS SERVED
Breakfast, lunch, dinner

CHARACTERS
Pooh, Eeyore, Piglet, Tigger

SERVED Daily

SETTING ★★★

SERVICE Buffet

FOOD VARIETY AND QUALITY
★★½ (breakfast)
★★★ (dinner)

NOISE LEVEL Very loud

CHARACTER–GUEST RATIO
1:67 (breakfast),
1:89 (dinner)

5. 1900 PARK FARE

LOCATION
Grand Floridian Resort

MEALS SERVED
Breakfast, dinner

CHARACTERS
Breakfast:
Mary Poppins, Alice,
Mad Hatter, Pooh

Dinner:
Cinderella and friends

SERVED Daily

SETTING ★★★

SERVICE Buffet

FOOD VARIETY AND QUALITY
★★★ (breakfast)
★★★½ (dinner)

NOISE LEVEL Moderate

CHARACTER–GUEST RATIO
1:54 (breakfast),
1:44 (dinner)

6. THE GARDEN GRILL RESTAURANT

LOCATION
Epcot

MEALS SERVED
Dinner

CHARACTERS
Mickey, Pluto,
Chip 'n' Dale

SERVED Daily

SETTING ★★★★½

SERVICE Family-style

FOOD VARIETY AND QUALITY
★★★½

NOISE LEVEL Very quiet

CHARACTER–GUEST RATIO
1:46

10. HOLLYWOOD & VINE

LOCATION
Disney's Hollywood Studios

MEALS SERVED
Breakfast, lunch

CHARACTERS
June, Leo, Handy Manny,
Agent Oso

SERVED Daily

SETTING ★★½

SERVICE Buffet

FOOD VARIETY AND QUALITY
★★★

NOISE LEVEL Moderate

CHARACTER–GUEST RATIO
1:71

11. GARDEN GROVE

LOCATION
Swan

MEALS SERVED
Breakfast
(Sat & Sun only), dinner

CHARACTERS
Rafiki, Timon, Goofy, Pluto

SERVED
Saturday and Sunday

SETTING ★★★

SERVICE Buffet

FOOD VARIETY AND QUALITY
★★★½

NOISE LEVEL Moderate

CHARACTER–GUEST RATIO
1:198, but often
much better

4. THE FOOD Although some food served at character meals is quite good, most is average—in other words, palatable but nothing to get excited about. In terms of variety, consistency, and quality, restaurants generally do a better job with breakfast than with lunch or dinner (if served). Some restaurants offer a buffet, while others opt for "one-skillet" family-style service, in which all the hot items on the bill of fare are served from the same pot or skillet. To help you sort it out, we rate the food at each character meal in our chart using the tried-and-true five-star scale.

5. THE PROGRAM Some larger restaurants stage modest performances where the characters dance, head a parade around the room, or lead songs and cheers. For some guests, these activities give the meal a celebratory air; for others, they turn what was already mayhem into absolute chaos. Either way, the antics consume time the characters could spend with families at their table.

6. NOISE If you want to eat in peace, character meals are a bad choice. That said, some are much noisier than others. Once again, our chart gives you some idea of what to expect.

7. WHICH MEAL? Although character breakfasts seem to be the most popular, character lunches and dinners are usually more practical because they do not interfere with your early-morning touring. During hot weather especially, a character lunch at midday can be heavenly.

8. COST Dinners cost more than lunches and lunches more than breakfasts. Prices for meals (except at Cinderella Castle) vary only about $10 from the least expensive to the most expensive restaurant. Breakfasts run $21–$50 for adults and $11–$32 for kids ages 3–9. For character lunches, expect to pay $25–$53 for adults and $14–$33 for kids. Dinners are $30–$62 for adults and $14–$37 for children. Little ones ages 2 years and younger eat free.

9. ADVANCE RESERVATIONS The Disney dining reservations system makes Advance Reservations for character meals up to 180 days prior to the day you wish to dine. Advance Reservations for most character meals are easy to obtain even if you forget to call until a couple of weeks before you leave home. Meals at Cinderella's Royal Table are another story; they are without doubt the hottest ticket at Disney World.

10. CHECKING IT TWICE Disney occasionally shuffles the characters and theme of a character meal. If your little one's heart is set on Pooh and Piglet, getting Hook and Mr. Smee is just a waste of time and money. Reconfirm all character-meal

Advance Reservations three weeks or so before you leave home by calling ☎ 407-WDW-DINE.

11. "FRIENDS" For some venues, Disney has stopped specifying characters scheduled for a particular meal. Instead, they say it's a given character "and friends"—for example, "Pooh and friends," meaning Eeyore, Piglet, and Tigger, or some combination thereof, or "Mickey and friends" with some assortment chosen among Minnie, Goofy, Pluto, Donald, Daisy, Chip, and Dale.

12. THE BUM'S RUSH Most character meals are leisurely affairs, and you can usually stay as long as you want. An exception is Cinderella's Royal Table. Because Cindy's is in such high demand, the restaurant does everything short of pre-chewing your food to move you through.

BABYSITTING

CHILD-CARE CENTERS Child care isn't available inside the theme parks, but three Magic Kingdom resorts connected by monorail or boat (Polynesian, Grand Floridian, and Wilderness Lodge & Villas), four Epcot resorts (the Yacht & Beach Club Resorts, the Swan, and the Dolphin), and Animal Kingdom Lodge have child-care centers for potty-trained children older than age 3 (see chart on the following page). Services vary, but children generally can be left between 4:30 p.m. and midnight. Milk and cookies and blankets and pillows are provided at all centers, and dinner is provided at most. Play is supervised but not organized, and toys, videos, and games are plentiful. Guests at any Disney resort or campground may use the services.

The most elaborate of the child-care centers (variously called "clubs" or "camps") is **Never Land Club** at the Polynesian Resort. The rate for ages 4–12 is $12 per hour, per child (2-hour minimum).

All the clubs accept reservations (some six months in advance!) with a credit card guarantee. Call the club directly, or reserve through Disney at ☎ 407-WDW-DINE. Most clubs require a 24-hour cancellation notice and levy a hefty penalty of 2 hours' time or $22.50 per call for no-shows. A limited number of walk-ins are usually accepted on a first-come, first-served basis.

IN-ROOM BABYSITTING Three companies provide in-room sitting in Walt Disney World and surrounding areas. They're **Kid's Nite Out, All About Kids,** and **Fairy Godmothers** (no

CHILD-CARE CLUBS*

HOTEL/PHONE	NAME OF PROGRAM	AGES
Animal Kingdom Lodge and Villas ☎ 407-938-4785	Simba's Cubhouse	4–12
Dolphin ☎ 407-934-4241	Camp Dolphin	4–12
Grand Floridian Resort & Spa ☎ 407-824-1666	Mouseketeer Club	4–12
Polynesian Resort ☎ 407-824-2000	Neverland Club	4–12
Swan ☎ 407-934-1621	Camp Dolphin	4–12
Yacht and Beach Club Resorts ☎ 407-934-7000	Sandcastle Club	4–12
Wilderness Lodge and Villas ☎ 407-824-1083	Cub's Den	4–12

*Child-care clubs operate afternoons and evenings. Before 4 p.m., call the hotels rather than the numbers listed above. All programs require reservations; call ☎ 407-WDW-DINE (939-3463).

kidding). Kid's Nite Out also serves hotels in the greater Orlando area, including downtown. All three provide sitters older than age 18 who are insured, bonded, screened, reference-checked, police-checked, and trained in CPR. In addition to caring for your kids in your room, the sitters will, if you direct (and pay), take your children to the theme parks or other venues. All three services offer bilingual sitters.

SPECIAL TIPS
for SPECIAL PEOPLE

WALT DISNEY WORLD *for* SINGLES

WALT DISNEY WORLD IS GREAT FOR SINGLES. It is safe, clean, and low-pressure. If you're looking for a place to relax without being hit on, Disney World is perfect. Bars, lounges, and nightclubs are the most laid-back and friendly you're likely to find anywhere. In many, you can hang out and not even be asked to buy a drink (or asked to let someone buy a drink for you). Parking lots are well lit and constantly patrolled. For women alone, safety and comfort are unsurpassed.

unofficial **TIP** Virtually every type of entertainment performed fully clothed is available at an amazingly reasonable price at a Disney nightspot.

There's also no need to while away the evening hours alone in your hotel room. Between the BoardWalk and Downtown Disney, nightlife options abound. If you drink more than you should and are a Disney resort guest, Disney buses will return you safely to your hotel.

WALT DISNEY WORLD *for* COUPLES

WEDDINGS AND HONEYMOONS

DISNEY'S ESCAPE WEDDING (maximum 18 or fewer guests, plus bride and groom) includes a cake and Champagne toast for the couple and four guests, a personalized wedding website, a

Disney wedding certificate, a photographer, an Annual Pass for the bride and groom, and a wedding album. Packages require a four-night stay at a Disney-owned and -operated resort; some ceremony locations have a limit of 10 guests. The cost starts at $4,750; prices also include a musician, cake, bouquet, limousine ride, and wedding coordinator. If you invite more than 18 guests, you must buy one of Disney's customized wedding packages, which start at $12,000 (Monday–Thursday), $15,000 (Friday and Sunday), and $20,000 (Saturday), not including taxes and gratuities.

ROMANTIC GETAWAYS

DISNEY WORLD IS A FAVORITE GETAWAY FOR COUPLES, but not all Disney hotels are equally romantic. Some are too family-oriented; others swarm with convention-goers. For romantic (though expensive) lodging, we recommend Animal Kingdom Lodge & Villas, Bay Lake Tower at the Contemporary Resort, the Polynesian Resort, Wilderness Lodge & Villas, the Grand Floridian, BoardWalk Inn & Villas, and the Yacht & Beach Club Resorts. The Alligator Bayou section at Port Orleans Riverside, a Moderate Disney resort, also has secluded rooms.

QUIET, ROMANTIC PLACES TO EAT

RESTAURANTS WITH GOOD FOOD *and* a couple-friendly ambience are rare in the theme parks. Only a handful of dining locales satisfy both requirements: **Coral Reef Restaurant,** an alfresco table at **Tutto Italia,** the terrace at the **Rose & Crown,** and the upstairs tables at the France Pavilion's **Bistro de Paris,** all in Epcot; and the corner booths at **The Hollywood Brown Derby** in Disney's Hollywood Studios. Waterfront dining (though not necessarily quiet or romantic) is available at **Fulton's Crab House, Paradiso 37,** and **Portobello** at Downtown Disney and **Narcoossee's** at the Grand Floridian.

Victoria & Albert's at the Grand Floridian is the World's showcase gourmet restaurant; expect to pay big bucks. Other good choices for couples include **Artist Point** at Wilderness Lodge, **Cítricos** at the Grand Floridian, **Shula's Steakhouse** at the Dolphin, **Jiko—The Cooking Place** at Animal Kingdom Lodge, and the **Flying Fish Cafe** at the BoardWalk.

Eating later in the evening and choosing a restaurant we've mentioned will improve your chances for intimate dining; nevertheless, children—well behaved or otherwise—are everywhere at Walt Disney World, and there's no way to escape them.

WALT DISNEY WORLD *for* SENIORS

MOST SENIORS WE INTERVIEW ENJOY Disney World much more when they tour with folks their own age. If, however, you're considering going to Disney World with your grandchildren, we recommend an orientation visit without them first. If you know first-hand what to expect, it's much easier to establish limits, maintain control, and set a comfortable pace when you visit with the youngsters.

If you're determined to take the grandkids, read carefully those sections of this book that discuss family touring. Because seniors are a varied and willing lot, there aren't any attractions we would suggest they avoid. For seniors, as with other Disney visitors, personal taste is more important than age. We hate to see mature visitors pass up an exceptional attraction like Splash Mountain because younger visitors call it a "thrill ride." A full-blown adventure, Splash Mountain gets its appeal more from music and visual effects than from the thrill of the ride. Because you must choose among attractions that might interest you, we provide facts to help you make informed decisions.

GETTING AROUND

MANY SENIORS LIKE TO WALK, but a 7-hour visit to one of the theme parks normally includes four to eight miles on foot. If you aren't up for that much hiking, let a more athletic member of your party push you in a rented wheelchair. The theme parks also offer fun-to-drive electric carts (convenience vehicles). You can rent a cart at the Magic Kingdom in the morning, return it, go to Epcot, present your deposit slip, and get another cart at no additional charge.

LODGING

IF YOU CAN AFFORD IT, STAY IN Walt Disney World. If you're concerned about the quality of your accommodations or the availability of transportation, staying inside the Disney complex will ease your mind. The rooms are some of the nicest in the Orlando area and are always clean and well maintained. Plus, transportation is always available to any destination in Disney World at no additional cost.

Disney hotels reserve rooms closer to restaurants and transportation for guests of any age who can't tolerate much walking. They also provide golf carts to pick up from and deliver guests to their rooms. Cart service can vary dramatically depending on the time of day and the number of guests requesting service. At check-in time (around 3 p.m.), for example, the wait for a ride can be as long as 40 minutes.

Seniors intending to spend more time at Epcot and Disney's Hollywood Studios than at the Magic Kingdom or Disney's Animal Kingdom should consider the Yacht & Beach Club Resorts, the Swan, the Dolphin, or BoardWalk Inn & Villas.

The Contemporary Resort and the adjacent Bay Lake Tower are good choices for seniors who want to be on the monorail system. So are the Grand Floridian and Polynesian resorts, though they cover many acres, necessitating a lot of walking. For a restful, rustic feeling, choose the Wilderness Lodge & Villas. If you want a kitchen and the comforts of home, book Old Key West Resort, the Beach Club Villas, Animal Kingdom Villas, or BoardWalk Villas. If you enjoy watching birds and animals, try Animal Kingdom Lodge & Villas. Try Saratoga Springs for golf.

RV-ers will find pleasant surroundings at Disney's Fort Wilderness Resort & Campground. Several independent campgrounds are within 30 minutes of Disney World. None offers the wilderness setting or amenities that Disney does, but they cost less.

SENIOR DINING

EAT BREAKFAST AT YOUR HOTEL RESTAURANT, or save money by having juice and rolls in your room. Although you aren't allowed to bring food into the parks, fruit, fruit juice, and soft drinks are sold throughout Disney World. Follow with an early dinner and be out of the restaurants, rested and ready for evening touring and fireworks, long before the main crowd begins to think about dinner. We recommend fitting dining and rest times into the day. Plan lunch as your break in the day. Sit back, relax, and enjoy. Then return to your hotel for a nap or a swim.

unofficial TIP
Make your dining Advance Reservations for before noon to avoid the lunch crowds.

WALT DISNEY WORLD *for* DISABLED GUESTS

VALUABLE INFORMATION FOR TRIP PLANNING is available at **disneyworld.com.** At Walt Disney World, each of the major theme parks offers a free booklet describing disabled services and facilities at that park. The Disney people are somewhat resistant to mailing you the theme park booklets in advance, but if you are polite and persistent, they can usually be persuaded. PDF versions are available at **disneyworld.disney .go.com/guests-with-disabilities.** Or get a booklet at wheelchair-rental locations in the parks. For specific requests, such as those for special accommodations at hotels or on the Disney transportation system, call ☎ 407-939-7807 (voice) or 407-939-7670 (TTY). When the recorded menu comes up, press 1. Limit your questions and requests to those regarding disabled services and accommodations (address other questions to ☎ 407-824-4321 or 407-827-5141 [TTY]).

VISITORS WITH SPECIAL NEEDS

WHOLLY OR PARTIALLY NONAMBULATORY Guests may easily rent wheelchairs. Most rides, shows, attractions, restrooms, and restaurants in the World accommodate the nonambulatory disabled. If you're in a theme park and need assistance, go to Guest Relations. A limited number of electric carts (motorized convenience vehicles) are available for rent. Easy and fun to drive, they give nonambulatory guests a tremendous degree of freedom and mobility.

Close-in parking is available for disabled visitors at all Disney lots. Request directions when you pay your parking fee. All monorails and most rides, shows, restrooms, and restaurants accommodate wheelchairs.

An information booklet for disabled guests is available at wheelchair-rental locations in each park. PDF versions are available at **disneyworld.disney.go.com/guests-with-disabilities.** Theme park maps issued to each guest on admission are symbol-coded to show nonambulatory guests which attractions accommodate wheelchairs.

Even if an attraction doesn't accommodate wheelchairs, nonambulatory guests still may ride if they can transfer from their wheelchair to the ride's vehicle. Disney staff, however, aren't trained or permitted to assist in transfers. Guests must be able to board the ride unassisted or have a member of their party assist them. Either way, members of the nonambulatory guest's party will be permitted to go along on the ride.

Because waiting areas of most attractions won't accommodate wheelchairs, nonambulatory guests and their party should request boarding instructions from a Disney attendant as soon as they arrive at an attraction. Almost always, the entire group will be allowed to board without a lengthy wait.

DIETARY RESTRICTIONS Visitors with dietary restrictions can find assistance at Guest Relations in the parks. For Disney World sit-down restaurants outside the parks, call three days ahead for assistance.

SIGHT- AND/OR HEARING-IMPAIRED GUESTS Guest Relations at the parks provides free assistive-technology devices to visually and hearing-impaired guests ($25–$100 refundable deposit, depending on the device). Sight-impaired guests can customize the given information (such architectural details, restroom locations, and descriptions of attractions and restaurants) through an interactive audio menu that is guided by a wireless GPS system in the device. Hearing-impaired guests can benefit from amplified audio and closed-captioning for attractions loaded into the same device.

Braille guidebooks are available from Guest Relations at all parks ($25 refundable deposit). Closed captioning is provided on some rides, while many theater attractions provide reflective captioning. A sign-language interpreter performs at some live-theater presentations; for show information, call ☎ 407-824-4321 (voice) or 407-939-8255 (TTY).

NONAPPARENT DISABILITIES We receive many letters from readers whose traveling companion or child requires special assistance, but who, unlike an individual on crutches or in a wheelchair, is not visibly disabled. Some conditions—autism, for example—make it very difficult or even impossible to wait in lines for more than a few minutes, or in queues surrounded by a large number of people.

One of the first things to do is obtain a letter from the disabled party's primary physician that explains the specific condition and any special needs the condition implies. The doctor's letter should be explicit enough to fully convey the nature of the condition to the Disney cast member reading the letter. Bring your doctor's note to the Guest Relations window at any Disney theme park and ask for a Guest Assistance Card. This is a special pass designed to allow the disabled individual and his or her touring companions to wait in a separate, uncrowded area, apart from the regular queues at most attractions. One card is good for all four parks, so you do not need to obtain separate cards at each park. You should also pick up a copy of each park's *Guidebook for Guests with Disabilities* (also available online at **disneyworld.disney.go.com/guests-with-disabilities**).

PART SIX

ARRIVING *and* GETTING AROUND

GETTING THERE

DIRECTIONS

MOTORISTS CAN REACH ANY Walt Disney World destination via World Drive off US 192, via Epcot Drive off Interstate 4, or from FL 429 (see map on following page).

WARNING! I-4 is an east–west highway but takes a north–south slant through the Orlando-Kissimmee area. This directional change complicates getting oriented in and around Disney World. Logic suggests that highways branching off I-4 should run north and south, but most run east and west here.

FROM INTERSTATE 10 Take I-10 east across Florida to I-75 southbound, then take Exit 267A/Tampa onto Florida's Turnpike. Take FL 429 (toll) southbound off the turnpike. Leave FL 429 at Exit 8, the Hartzog Road/Walt Disney World interchange, in the direction of Walt Disney World, and follow the signs to your Disney destination. Also use these directions to reach hotels along US 192, the Irlo Bronson Memorial Highway.

FROM INTERSTATE 75 SOUTHBOUND Exit I-75 southbound onto Florida's Turnpike via Exit 267A/Tampa. Take FL 429 (toll) southbound off the turnpike. Leave FL 429 at Exit 8, the Hartzog Road/Walt Disney World interchange, in the direction of Walt Disney World, and follow the signs to your Disney destination. Also use these directions to reach hotels along US 192, the Irlo Bronson Memorial Highway.

FROM INTERSTATE 95 SOUTHBOUND Follow I-95 south to I-4. Go west on I-4 through Orlando. Take Exit 67/FL 536,

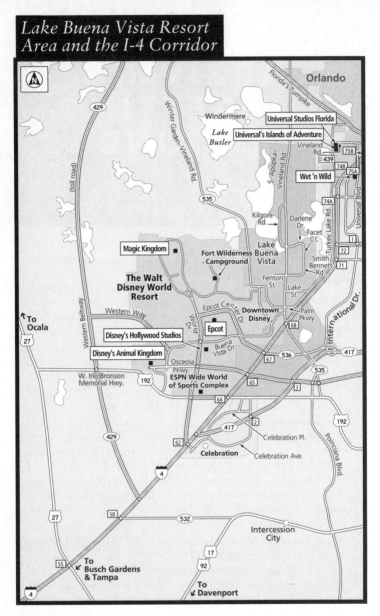

Lake Buena Vista Resort Area and the I-4 Corridor

marked Epcot/Downtown Disney, and follow the signs. During rush hours take FL 417/ Central Florida GreeneWay; take Exit 6 to FL 536 West, and follow the signs.

FROM DAYTONA OR ORLANDO Head west on I-4 through Orlando. Take Exit 67/FL 536, marked Epcot/Downtown Disney, and follow the signs.

FROM THE ORLANDO INTERNATIONAL AIRPORT There are two routes from the airport to Walt Disney World. Both take almost exactly the same time to drive except during rush-hour traffic, when Route One via FL 417 is far less congested than Route Two via the Beachline Expressway. Also, Route One eliminates the need to drive on I-4, which is always horribly congested. Both FL 417 and the Beachline Expressway are toll roads, so make sure you have a dollar's worth of quarters before leaving the airport. *Route One:* Leaving the airport, go southwest on the Central Florida GreeneWay (FL 417), a toll road. Take Exit 6 toward FL 535. FL 536 will cross over I-4 and become Epcot Drive. From here, follow the signs to your destination. *Route Two:* Take FL 528 (Beachline Expressway, a toll road) west for about 12 miles to the intersection with I-4. Go west on I-4 to Exit 67, marked Epcot/Downtown Disney, and follow the signs.

FROM MIAMI, FORT LAUDERDALE, AND SOUTHEASTERN FLORIDA Head north on Florida's Turnpike to I-4 westbound. Take Exit 67/FL 536, marked Epcot/Downtown Disney, and follow the signs.

FROM TAMPA AND SOUTHWESTERN FLORIDA Take I-75 northbound to I-4. Go east on I-4, take Exit 64 onto US 192 westbound, and follow the signs.

Walt Disney World Exits Off I-4

Going east to west (in the direction of Orlando to Tampa), four I-4 exits serve Walt Disney World.

EXIT 68 (marked FL 535/Lake Buena Vista) primarily serves the Downtown Disney Resort Area and Downtown Disney, including Downtown Disney Marketplace and Downtown Disney West Side. It also serves non-Disney hotels with a Lake Buena Vista address. This exit puts you on a road with lots of traffic signals. Avoid it unless you're headed to one of the preceding destinations.

EXIT 67 (marked FL 536/Epcot/Downtown Disney) delivers you to a four-lane expressway into the heart of Disney World. It's the fastest and most convenient way for westbound travelers to access almost all Disney destinations except Disney's Animal Kingdom and ESPN Wide World of Sports Complex.

EXIT 65 (marked Osceola Parkway) is the best exit for west-bound travelers to access Animal Kingdom, Animal Kingdom Lodge, Pop Century Resort, Art of Animation Resort, All Star Resorts, and ESPN Wide World of Sports Complex.

EXIT 64 (US 192/MAGIC KINGDOM) is the best route for eastbound travelers to all Disney World destinations. For westbound travelers, it's the best exit for accessing Disney's Animal Kingdom and ESPN Wide World of Sports.

EXIT 62 (DISNEY WORLD/CELEBRATION) is the first Disney exit you'll encounter if you're headed eastbound. This four-lane, controlled-access highway connects to the so-called Maingate of Walt Disney World.

TRANSPORTATION TO WALT DISNEY WORLD FROM THE AIRPORT

IF YOU ARRIVE IN ORLANDO BY PLANE, there are four basic options for getting to Walt Disney World:

1. TAXI Taxis carry four to eight passengers (depending on vehicle type). Rates vary according to distance. If your hotel is in the World, your fare will be about $60, plus tip. For the US 192 Maingate area, it will be about $55. To International Drive or downtown Orlando, expect to pay about $33–$39.

2. SHUTTLE SERVICE Mears Transportation Group (☎ 407-423-5566; **mearstransportation.com**) provides your transportation if your vacation package includes airport transfers. Nonpackage travelers can also use the service. The shuttles collect passengers until they fill a van (or bus). They're then dispatched. Mears charges *per-person* rates (children under age 3 ride free). One-way and round-trip services are available.

From your hotel to the airport, you're likely to ride in a van (unless you're part of a tour group, for which Mears might send a bus). Because shuttles make several pickups, they ask you to leave much earlier than you'd depart if you were taking a cab or returning a rental car.

FROM THE AIRPORT TO:	ONE-WAY Adult/Child	ROUND-TRIP Adult/Child
International Drive	$19/$15	$30/$24
Downtown Orlando	$18/$15	$29/$23
Walt Disney World–Lake Buena Vista	$21/$17	$34/$27
US 192 Maingate Area	$27/$22	$46/$37

3. TOWN-CAR SERVICE Similar to taxi service, a town-car service will transport you directly from Orlando International Airport to your hotel. Instead of hailing a car outside the airport, however, the town-car driver will usually be waiting for you in the baggage claim area of your airline.

Tiffany Towncar Service (☎ 888-838-2161 or 407-370-2196; **tiffanytowncars.com**) provides a prompt, clean ride. The round-trip fee to a Disney or non-Disney resort is $109 plus tip; one-way is about $60. Tiffany offers a free stop at a Publix supermarket en route to your hotel.

unofficial **TIP**
Check Tiffany's website for a coupon worth $5 off a round-trip.

Quicksilver Tours & Transportation (☎ 888-GO-TO-WDW [468-6939] or 407-299-1434; **quicksilver-tours.com**) offers 8-person limos and 10-person vans in addition to town cars. Round-trip rates in a town car range from $110 to $120 depending on location; round-trip rates in a van range from $125 to $135; round-trip limo rate is $240. Like Tiffany, Quicksilver throws in a stop at the supermarket en route.

4. RENTAL CARS Rental cars are readily available for both short- and long-term rentals. Most rental companies allow you to drop a rental car at certain hotels or one of their subsidiary locations in the Walt Disney World general area if you do not want the car for your entire stay. Likewise, you can pick up a car at any time during your stay at the same hotels and locations without trekking back to the airport. A list of discount codes for rental cars also can be found at **mousesavers .com.** With a little effort, you can often get a great deal.

DISNEY'S MAGICAL EXPRESS

DISNEY'S MAGICAL EXPRESS IS A FREE bus service running between the Orlando International Airport and most Walt Disney World hotels. All guests staying at a Disney-owned and -operated resort are eligible. (Guests staying at the Swan, Dolphin, Shades of Green, and the hotels of the Downtown Disney Resort Area are ineligible.) In addition to transportation, Magical Express provides free luggage-delivery service between your airline and Disney hotel, except for flights arriving after 10 p.m., when you'll need to pick up your suitcases from baggage claim.

You should receive special Magical Express luggage tags about two weeks prior to your departure date. Put a tag on any piece of luggage you plan to check with the airline. When you arrive at the airport, check the bags as you normally would. If you're traveling within the United States, you'll arrive in Orlando and follow the Magical Express signs to your bus; your luggage should be waiting in your hotel room when you check in. (International travelers must retrieve their bags to go through customs. After passing through customs, you'll also head for a bus. Your bags are returned to baggage claim and Disney takes over from there.) Behind the scenes, Disney baggage handlers work with your airline to retrieve suitcases marked with those special tags. All tagged luggage is sent to an airport warehouse, where it's sorted by destination then loaded onto a truck for delivery. At the resort, the luggage is matched to your reservation. If your room is ready, the luggage is brought up; otherwise it's held by the bellhops until you can check in.

In practice the logistical challenge of matching totes and tourists is proving to be a bit more than Disney bargained for, with lost and delayed baggage marring the service's reputation.

RENTING A CAR

READERS PLANNING TO STAY IN THE WORLD frequently ask if they will need a car. If your plans don't include restaurants, attractions, or other destinations outside of Disney World, the answer is a very qualified no. However, consider the following:

unofficial **TIP**
Sign up for your car-rental company's frequent-renter program before your trip. Most programs are free and let you skip long waits in line to receive your car.

Plan to Rent a Car:

1. If your hotel is outside Walt Disney World.

2. If your hotel is in Walt Disney World and you want to dine someplace other than the theme parks and your own hotel.

3. If you plan to return to your hotel for naps or swimming during the day.

4. If you plan to visit other area theme parks or water parks (including Disney's).

GETTING ORIENTED

A GOOD MAP

READERS FREQUENTLY COMPLAIN about signs and maps provided by Disney. While it's easy to find the major theme parks, locating other Disney destinations can be challenging. Many Disney-supplied maps are stylized and hard to read, while others provide incomplete information. The most easily obtained map is in Walt Disney World's "Your Guide to the Magic" guide. Available at any resort or theme park Guest Relations office, the guide provides a reduced version of the Walt Disney World Property Map and information on the Disney transportation system. The guide also covers dining, recreation, and shopping. Unfortunately, Disney isn't very good about updating its property map. New interstate and expressway interchanges take months or even years to show up. For example, the huge new west entrance to Walt Disney World off FL 429, open since 2007, is yet to make an appearance. In fact, FL 429 itself isn't shown! The Disney map is fine for sorting out bus routes, but if you really need to navigate, the maps in this guide are much more current.

A very good map of the Orlando–Kissimmee–Disney World area is free at the **AAA Car Care Center** operated by Goodyear near the Magic Kingdom parking lot.

HOW *to* TRAVEL *around* *the* WORLD

TRANSPORTATION TRADE-OFFS FOR GUESTS: LODGING OUTSIDE WALT DISNEY WORLD

DISNEY DAY GUESTS (THOSE NOT STAYING inside Disney World) can use the monorail system, the bus system, and the boat system. If, for example, you go to Disney's Hollywood Studios in the morning, then decide to go to Epcot for lunch, you can take a bus directly there. The most important advice we can give day guests is to park their cars in the lot of the theme park (or other Disney destination) where they plan to finish their day. This is critical if you stay at a park until closing time.

ALL YOU NEED TO KNOW ABOUT DRIVING TO THE THEME PARKS

1. POSITIONING OF THE PARKING LOTS Disney's Animal Kingdom, Disney's Hollywood Studios, and Epcot parking lots are adjacent to the park entrance. The Magic Kingdom parking lot is adjacent to the Transportation and Ticket Center (TTC). From the TTC you can take a ferry or monorail to the Magic Kingdom entrance.

2. PAYING TO PARK Disney resort guests and Annual Pass

;olders park free. All others pay. If you pay to park, keep your receipt. If you move your car during the day to another theme park you will not have to pay again if you show your receipt.

3. FINDING YOUR CAR WHEN IT'S TIME TO DEPART The theme-park parking lots are huge. Jot down the section and row where you park. If you are driving a rental car, jot down the license number (you wouldn't believe how many white rental cars there are).

4. GETTING FROM YOUR CAR TO THE PARK ENTRANCE Each parking lot provides trams to transport you to the park entrance or, in the case of the Magic Kingdom, to the TTC. If you arrive early in the morning, you may find that it is faster to walk to the entrance (or to the TTC) than to take the tram.

5. GETTING TO DISNEY'S ANIMAL KINGDOM FOR PARK OPENING If you're staying on-property and are planning to be at this theme park when it opens, take a Disney bus from your resort instead of driving. Animal Kingdom's parking lot frequently opens 15 minutes before the park itself—which doesn't leave enough time to park, hop on a tram, and pass through security before park opening.

unofficial **TIP**
If you plan to park-hop, make sure your car is parked in the lot of the theme park where you plan to finish the day.

6. HOW MUCH TIME TO ALLOT FOR PARKING AND GETTING TO THE PARK ENTRANCE For Epcot and Disney's Animal Kingdom, it takes 10–15 minutes to pay, park, and walk or ride to the park entrance. At Disney's Hollywood Studios, allow 8–12 minutes; at the Magic Kingdom, it's 10–15 minutes to get to the TTC and another 20–30 to reach the park entrance via the monorail or the ferry. Allot another 10–20 minutes if you didn't buy your park admission in advance.

7. COMMUTING FROM PARK TO PARK You can commute to the other theme parks via Disney bus, or to and from the Magic Kingdom and Epcot by monorail. You can also, of course, commute via your own car. Using Disney transportation or your own car, allow 45–60 minutes entrance-to-entrance one-way.

8. LEAVING THE PARK AT THE END OF THE DAY If you stay at a park until closing, expect the parking lot trams, the monorails, and the ferries to be mobbed. If the wait for the parking-lot tram is unacceptable, you can either walk to your car, or walk to the first tram stop on the route and wait there until a tram arrives. When some people get off, you can get on and continue to your appropriate stop.

9. DINNER AND A QUICK EXIT One way to beat closing crowds at the Magic Kingdom is to arrange an Advance Reservation for dinner at one of the restaurants at the Contemporary Resort. When you leave the Magic Kingdom to go to dinner, move your car from the TTC lot to the Contemporary Resort. After dinner, either walk (8–10 minutes) or take the monorail back to the Magic Kingdom. When the park closes and everyone else is fighting their way onto the monorail or ferry, you can stroll leisurely back to the Contemporary, pick up your car, and be on your way. You can pull the same trick at Epcot by arranging an Advance Reservation at one of the Epcot resorts. After *IllumiNations* when the park closes, simply exit the park by the International Gateway and walk back to the resort where your car is parked.

10. CAR TROUBLE All the parking lots have security patrols that circulate through the lots. If you have a dead battery or some other automotive problem, the security patrols will help get you going. If you have more serious trouble, the **AAA Car Care Center** (☎ 407-824-0976), operated by Goodyear and located in Walt Disney World near the Magic Kingdom parking lot, will help you. Prices are comparable to what you'd pay at home for most services. The Car Center stays pretty busy, so expect to leave your car for a while unless the fix is simple.

11. SCORING A GREAT PARKING PLACE Anytime you arrive at a park after noon, there will be some empty spots up front vacated by early arriving guests who have already departed.

Taking a Shuttle Bus from Your Out-of-the-World Hotel

Many independent hotels and motels near Walt Disney World provide trams and buses. They're fairly carefree, depositing you near theme park entrances and saving you parking fees. The rub is that they might not get you there as early as you desire (a critical point if you take our touring advice) or be available when you wish to return to your lodging. Also, some shuttles go directly to Disney World, while others stop at additional area lodgings. Each service is a bit different; check the particulars before you make reservations.

If you're depending on shuttles, you'll want to leave the park at least 45 minutes before closing. If you stay until closing and lack the energy to hassle with the shuttle, take a cab. Cab stands are near the Bus Information buildings at Disney's Animal Kingdom, Epcot, Disney's Hollywood Studios, and the TTC. If no cabs are on hand, staff at Bus Information will call one for you.

THE DISNEY TRANSPORTATION SYSTEM

IN THE MOST BASIC TERMS, the Disney Transportation System is a "hub and spoke" system. Hubs include the TTC, Downtown Disney, and all four major theme parks (from 2 hours before official opening time to 2–3 hours after closing). Although there are some exceptions, there is direct service from Disney resorts to the major theme parks and to Downtown Disney, and from park to park. If you want to go from resort to resort or most anywhere else, you will have to transfer at one of the hubs.

If a hotel offers boat or monorail service, its bus service will be limited; you'll have to transfer at a hub for many destinations. If you're staying at a Magic Kingdom resort served by monorail (Polynesian, Contemporary–Bay Lake Tower, Grand Floridian), you'll be able to commute efficiently to the Magic Kingdom. If you want to visit Epcot, you must take the monorail to the TTC and transfer to the Epcot monorail. (Guests at the Polynesian can eliminate the transfer by walking 5–10 minutes to the TTC and catching the direct monorail to Epcot.)

Walt Disney World Bus Service

Disney buses have an illuminated panel above the windshield that flashes the bus's destination. Also, theme parks have designated waiting areas for each Disney destination. To catch the bus to the Caribbean Beach Resort from Disney's Hollywood Studios, for example, go to the bus stop and wait in the area marked TO THE CARIBBEAN BEACH RESORT. At the resorts, go to any bus stop and wait for the bus displaying your destination on the illuminated panel. Directions to Disney destinations are available when you check in or at your hotel's Guest Relations desk. Guest Relations also can answer questions about the transportation system.

Service from resorts to major theme parks is fairly direct. You may have intermediate stops, but you won't have to transfer. Service to the water parks and other Disney World hotels sometimes requires transfers.

Buses begin service to the theme parks at about 7 a.m. on days when the parks' official opening time is 9 a.m. Generally, buses run every 20 minutes. Buses to all four parks deliver you to the park entrance.

To be on-hand for the real opening time (when official opening is 9 a.m.), catch direct buses to Epcot, Disney's Animal Kingdom, and Disney's Hollywood Studios between 7:30 and 8 a.m. Catch direct buses to the Magic Kingdom between

8 and 8:15 a.m. If you must transfer to reach your park, leave 15–20 minutes earlier. On days when official opening is 7 or 8 a.m., move up your departure time accordingly.

For your return bus trip in the evening, leave the park 40 minutes to an hour before closing to avoid the rush. If you're caught in the exodus, you may be inconvenienced, but you won't be stranded. Buses and and boats continue to operate for 2 hours after the parks close.

Walt Disney World Monorail Service

Picture the monorail system as three loops. Loop A is an express route that runs counterclockwise connecting the Magic Kingdom with the TTC. Loop B runs clockwise alongside Loop A, making all stops, with service to (in this order) the TTC, Polynesian Resort, Grand Floridian Resort & Spa, Magic Kingdom, Contemporary Resort–Bay Lake Tower, and back to the TTC. The long Loop C dips southeast, connecting the TTC with Epcot. The hub for all loops is the TTC (where you usually park to visit the Magic Kingdom).

unofficial **TIP**
Monorails run for 1 hour after the Magic Kingdom and Epcot close. If a train is too crowded or you need transportation after the monorails have stopped, catch a bus or boat. *Note:* As a safety measure, Disney no longer lets guests ride in the front of a train.

The monorail serving Magic Kingdom resorts usually starts an hour and a half before official opening. If you're staying at a Magic Kingdom resort and wish to be among the first in the Magic Kingdom when official opening is 9 a.m., board the monorail at these times:

From the Contemporary Resort	7:45–8 a.m.
From the Polynesian Resort	7:50–8:05 a.m.
From the Grand Floridian Resort & Spa	8–8:10 a.m.

If you're a day guest, you'll be allowed on the monorail at the TTC between 8:15 and 8:30 a.m. when official opening is 9 a.m. If you want to board earlier, walk from the TTC to the Polynesian Resort and board there.

The monorail connecting Epcot and the TTC begins operating at 7:30 a.m. when Epcot's official opening is 9 a.m. To be at Epcot when it opens, catch the Epcot monorail at the TTC by 8:05 a.m.

PART SEVEN

BARE NECESSITIES

CREDIT CARDS *and* MONEY

CREDIT CARDS

AMERICAN EXPRESS, DINERS CLUB, DISCOVER, Japan Credit Bureau, MasterCard, and Visa are accepted throughout Walt Disney World.

BANKING SERVICES

BANK SERVICE AT THE THEME PARKS is limited to ATMs, which are marked on the park maps and are plentiful throughout Walt Disney World; most MasterCard and Visa cards are accepted. To use an American Express card, you must sign an agreement with Amex before your trip. If your credit card doesn't work in the ATMs, a teller at any **SunTrust Bank** full-service location will process your transaction (visit **suntrust.com** for Orlando and WDW-area branches).

A LICENSE TO PRINT MONEY

ONE OF DISNEY'S MORE SUBLIME PLOYS for separating you from your money is the printing and issuing of **Disney Dollars.** Available throughout Disney World or by phone (☎ 407-566-4985) in denominations of $1, $5, $10, and $50, each emblazoned with a Disney character, the colorful cash can be used for purchases in Disney World, Disneyland, and Disney Stores nationwide. Disney Dollars can also be exchanged one-for-one with U.S. currency, but only while you're in Disney World. Also, you need your sales receipt to exchange for U.S. dollars. Disney money is sometimes a perk (for which you're charged dollar-for-dollar) in Walt Disney Travel Company packages.

PROBLEMS *and* HOW TO SOLVE THEM

ATTRACTIONS CLOSED FOR REPAIRS

FIND OUT IN ADVANCE WHAT RIDES AND ATTRACTIONS may be closed during your visit (check online at **touringplans .com** for complete refurbishment schedules).

CAR TROUBLE

SECURITY PATROLS WILL HELP if you lock the keys in your parked car or find the battery dead. For more serious problems, the closest repair facility is the **AAA Car Care Center** near the Magic Kingdom parking lot (☎ 407-824-0976).

The nearest off-World repair center is **Maingate Citgo** (US 192 west of Interstate 4; ☎ 407-396-2721). Disney security can help you find it. Farther away but highly recommended by one of our Orlando-area researchers is **Riker's Automotive & Tire** (5700 Central Florida Parkway, near SeaWorld; ☎ 407-238-9800; **rikersauto.com**). Says our source, "They do great work and are the only car place that has never tried to get extra money out of me 'cause I'm a woman and know nothing about cars. I love this place!"

GASOLINE

THERE ARE THREE FILLING STATIONS on Disney property. One station is adjacent to the AAA Car Care Center on the exit road from the Transportation and Ticket Center (Magic Kingdom) parking lot. It's also convenient to the Shades of Green, Grand Floridian, and Polynesian resorts. Most centrally located is the station at the corner of Buena Vista Drive and Epcot Resorts Boulevard, near the BoardWalk Inn. A third station, also on Buena Vista Drive, is across from the former Pleasure Island site in Downtown Disney.

LOST AND FOUND

IF YOU LOSE (OR FIND) SOMETHING in the **Magic Kingdom,** go to **City Hall.** At **Epcot,** go to the **Entrance Plaza.** At **Disney's Hollywood Studios,** go to **Hollywood Boulevard Guest Relations;** at **Disney's Animal Kingdom,** go to **Guest Relations** at the main entrance. If you discover your loss after you've left the park(s), call ☎ 407-824-4245 (all parks). If you're still on-site, call and ask to be transferred to the specific park's Lost and Found. Items not claimed by the end of the day are sent to Lost and Found at the Transportation and Ticket Center.

MEDICAL MATTERS

HEADACHE RELIEF Aspirin and other sundries are sold at the Emporium on Main Street in the Magic Kingdom (they're behind the counter; you must ask), at most retail shops in Epcot's Future World and World Showcase, and in Disney's Hollywood Studios and Disney's Animal Kingdom.

ILLNESSES REQUIRING MEDICAL ATTENTION A **Centra Care** walk-in clinic is at 12500 South Apopka–Vineland Road (☎ 407-934-CARE). It's open 8 a.m.–midnight weekdays and 8 a.m.–8 p.m. weekends. Centra Care also operates a 24-hour physician-house-call service and runs a free shuttle (☎ 407-938-0650). **Buena Vista Urgent Care** (8216 World Center Dr., Suite D; ☎ 407-465-1110) is highly recommended by *Unofficial Guide* readers.

 EastCoast Medical Network (☎ 407-648-5252) has board-certified physicians available 24-7 for house calls to your hotel room. They offer in-room X-rays and IV therapy service as well as same-day dental and specialist appointments. Walk-in clinics are also available.

 DOCS (Doctors on Call Service; ☎ 407-399-DOCS; **doctors oncallservice.com**) offers 24-hour house-call service.

 Physician Room Service (☎ 407-238-2000; **physicianroom service.com;** formerly Florida Hospital Centra Care In-Room Medical Service) provides board-certified doctor house calls to Walt Disney World–area guest rooms for adults and children.

DENTAL EMERGENCIES Call **Celebration Dental Group** (☎ 407-566-2222).

PRESCRIPTION MEDICINE Two nearby pharmacies are **Walgreens Lake Buena Vista** (☎ 407-238-0600) and **Winn-Dixie Pharmacy Lake Buena Vista** (☎ 407-465-8606). **Turner Drugs** (☎ 407-828-8125) charges $5 to deliver a filled prescription to your hotel's front desk. The service is available to Disney and non-Disney hotels in Turner Drugs' area. The delivery fee will be charged to your hotel account.

unofficial **TIP**
Rain gear is one of the few bargains at the parks. It isn't always displayed in shops; you have to ask for it.

RAIN

WEATHER BAD? Go to the parks anyway. The crowds are lighter on rainy days, and most of the attractions and waiting areas are under cover. Showers, especially during the warmer months, usually don't last very long.

Ponchos are about $7; umbrellas, about $13. All ponchos sold at Disney World are made of clear plastic, so picking out somebody in your party on a rainy day can be tricky. Walmart sells an inexpensive green poncho that will make your family emerald beacons in a plastic-covered sea of humanity.

SERVICES

MESSAGES

MESSAGES LEFT AT CITY HALL IN THE Magic Kingdom, Guest Relations at Epcot, Hollywood Boulevard Guest Relations at Disney's Hollywood Studios, or Guest Relations at Disney's Animal Kingdom can be retrieved at any of the four.

LOCKERS AND PACKAGE PICK-UP

LOCKERS ARE AVAILABLE ON THE GROUND FLOOR of the Main Street railroad station in the Magic Kingdom, to the right of Spaceship Earth in Epcot, and on the Transportation and Ticket Center's east and west ends. At Disney's Hollywood Studios, lockers are to the right of the entrance at Oscar's Classical Car Souvenirs. Disney's Animal Kingdom lockers are to the left inside the entrance. Cost is $7 a day for small lockers and $9 a day for large lockers; prices include a $5 refundable deposit. Lockers at Blizzard Beach and Typhoon Lagoon cost $8 (small) and $10 (large), also with a $5 refundable deposit.

Package Pick-Up is available at each major theme park. Ask the salesperson to send your purchases to Package Pick-Up. When you leave the park, they'll be waiting for you. Epcot has two exits, thus two Package Pick-Ups; specify main entrance or International Gateway. If you're staying at a Disney resort, you can also have the packages delivered to your room. If you're leaving within 24 hours, however, take them with you or use the in-park pickup location.

CAMERAS AND FILM

CAMERA CENTERS AT THE PARKS sell disposable cameras for about $12 ($19 with flash). Film is available throughout the World. Developing is available at most Disney hotel gift shops and at Camera Centers. You can also have images from your digital camera's memory card burned to a CD while you're in the parks. The cost is

unofficial **TIP**
Disney no longer offers film developing at the theme parks.

around $13 for 120 images and around $6.50 for an additional 120 images. Prints are around 75¢ each. You'll need to leave your digital media with Disney while they create the CD, typically around 2–5 hours, so make sure you've got extra media on hand.

GROCERY STORES

LOCATED IN THE Crossroads Shopping Center, across FL 535 from the Disney World entrance, **Gooding's Supermarket** is a large designer grocery. While its location makes it undeniably convenient, its gourmet selections (cheese, wine, and such) aren't nearly as extensive as they used to be, and if you're just looking for staples, you'll find the prices higher than the Tower of Terror, and just as frightening. For down-to-earth prices, try **Publix** at either the intersection of International Drive and US 192 or at the intersection of Reames Road and FL-535, or **Winn-Dixie** on Apopka–Vineland Road about a mile north of Crossroads Shopping Center.

If you don't have a car or you don't want to take the time to go to the supermarket, **GardenGrocer** (**gardengrocer.com**) will shop for you and deliver your groceries. The best way to compile your order is on GardenGrocer's website before you leave home. It's simple, and the selection is huge. If there's something you want that's not on their list of available items, they'll try to find it for you. Delivery arrangements are per your instructions. If you're staying at a hotel, you can arrange for your groceries to be left with bell services. For the sake of order-fulfillment accuracy and customer service, GardenGrocer is primarily set up for online ordering. If you can't get online, though, you can order by phone (☎ 866-855-4350). For orders of $200 or more, there's no delivery charge; for orders less than $200, the delivery charge is $12; a minimum order of $40 is required. Prices for individual items are pretty much the same as you'd pay at the supermarket.

You can also order online from **Gooding's** (**goodings.com**); a $50 minimum order is required, and a $25 service charge applies (no holiday delivery, and they don't deliver ice cream).

PART EIGHT

DINING *in* WALT DISNEY WORLD

DISNEY DINING 101

ADVANCE RESERVATIONS

DISNEY CEASELESSLY TINKERS WITH ITS dining-reservations policy. In 2005, Disney abruptly decided to change the name from Priority Seating to the somewhat redundant Advance Reservations. The current system, however, is exactly the same as the old one except in name. When you call, your name and essential information are taken as if you were making an honest-to-goodness reservation. The Disney representative then says you have Advance Reservations for your restaurant of choice on the date and time you've requested and usually explains that this means you will be seated ahead of walk-ins—that is, those without Advance Reservations.

DRESS

unofficial **TIP**
The only restaurant that requires jackets for men and dressy clothes for women is **Victoria & Albert's** at the Grand Floridian Resort.

DRESS IS INFORMAL AT MOST THEME PARK restaurants, but a business-casual dress code applies at Disney's Signature (read: upscale) restaurants: khakis, dress slacks, jeans, or dress shorts with a collared shirt for men and jeans, skirts, or dress shorts with a blouse or sweater (or a dress) for women. A full listing of these restaurants is available at the Walt Disney World website (go to **tinyurl .com/wdwsignaturedining**).

SMOKING

WALT DISNEY WORLD RESTAURANTS adopted a nonsmoking policy several years ago, after Florida voters passed an amendment to the state's constitution that also prohibits smoking in restaurant lounges. (Freestanding bars—those that get less than 10% of their revenues from food sales—are exempt.)

WALT DISNEY WORLD
RESTAURANT CATEGORIES

IN GENERAL, FOOD AND BEVERAGE offerings at Walt Disney World are defined by service, price, and convenience:

FULL-SERVICE RESTAURANTS Full-service restaurants are in all Disney resorts (except the All-Star complex, Port Orleans French Quarter, Pop Century, and Art of Animation) and all major theme parks, Downtown Disney Marketplace, and Downtown Disney West Side. Advance Reservations are recommended for all full-service restaurants except those in the Downtown Disney Resort Area, which are operated independently of the Walt Disney Compmany. The restaurants accept American Express, Carte Blanche, Diners Club, Japan Credit Bureau, MasterCard, and Visa.

BUFFETS AND FAMILY-STYLE RESTAURANTS Many of these have Disney characters in attendance, and most have a separate children's menu featuring dishes such as hot dogs, burgers, chicken nuggets, pizza, macaroni and cheese, and spaghetti and meatballs. In addition to the buffets, several restaurants serve a family-style, all-you-can-eat, fixed-price meal.

unofficial **TIP**
Food at Disney's family-style restaurants tends to be a little better than what you'll find on a buffet line.

Advance Reservations arrangements are required for character buffets and recommended for all other buffets and family-style restaurants. Most major credit cards are accepted.

If you want to eat a lot but don't feel like standing in yet another line, then consider one of the all-you-can-eat family-style restaurants. These feature platters of food brought to your table in courses by a server. You can sample everything on the menu and eat as much as you like. You can even go back to a favorite appetizer after you finish the main course.

Family-style all-you-can-eat service is available at **Cinderella's Royal Table** (breakfast only) and the **Liberty Tree Tavern** (dinner only) in the Magic Kingdom; **The Garden Grill Restaurant** in the Land Pavilion in Epcot; **'Ohana** in the Polynesian

Resort; **Garden Grove** (breakfast and lunch only) in the Swan; and **Whispering Canyon Cafe** in the Wilderness Lodge.

FOOD COURTS Featuring a collection of counter-service eateries under one roof, food courts can be found at the Moderate resorts (Coronado Springs, Caribbean Beach, Port Orleans) and Value resorts (All-Star, Art of Animation, and Pop Century). (The closest thing to a food court at the theme parks is **Sunshine Seasons** at Epcot.) Advance Reservations are neither required nor available at these restaurants.

COUNTER SERVICE Counter-service fast food is available in all theme parks and at Downtown Disney Marketplace, the BoardWalk, and Downtown Disney West Side. The food compares in quality with Captain D's, McDonald's, or Taco Bell but is more expensive, though often served in larger portions.

FAST CASUAL Somewhere between burgers and formal dining are the establishments in Disney's "fast casual" category,

The Cost of Counter-service Food

To help you develop your dining budget, here are prices of common counter-service items. (Sales tax isn't included.)

FOOD ITEM	PRICE
Bagel or muffin	$2.59
Brownie	$2.39–$3.29
Cake or pie	$4.00
Cereal with milk	$3.19
Cheeseburger with fries	$6.59–$9.29
Chicken-breast sandwich (grilled)	$7 ($8.59 basket)
Children's meals	$5.00
Chips	$1.50–$3.00
Cookies	$2.00
Fish basket (fried) with fries	$7.09–$9.69 (shrimp)
French fries	$2.66
Fried-chicken strips with fries	$6.89–$8.25
Fruit (whole piece)	$1.00–$2.75
Fruit cup/fruit salad	$3.00–$3.39
Hot dogs	$4.25–$7.50
Ice-cream bars	$2.50–$3.75
Nachos with cheese	$7.95
PB&J sandwich	$5.00
Pizza	$5.59–$8.69

The Cost of Counter-service Food *(cont'd.)*

FOOD ITEM	PRICE	
Popcorn	$3.25–$4.75	
Pretzel	$3.79–$4.29	
Salad (entree)	$7.79–$8.19	
Salad (side)	$3.00	
Smoked turkey leg	$7.59	
Soup/chili	$2.79–$4.49	
Sub/deli sandwich	$8.00 (cold), $9.19 (hot)	
Taco salad	$7.69	
Taco (beef) with yellow rice	$6.00	
Veggie burger (basket)	$7.09	
DRINKS	**SMALL**	**LARGE**
Beer (not available in the Magic Kingdom)	$5.50	$7.25
Bottled water	$2.50	$2.50
Cappuccino/espresso	$2.69/$3.69	$4.25/$5.25 (double)
Coffee	$2.09	$3.75
Floats/milk shakes/sundaes	$3.79	$4.59
Fruit juice	$1.69	$2.59
Hot tea and cocoa	$1.89	$2.09
Milk	$1.29	$2.19
Soft drinks, iced tea, and lemonade	$2.19	$2.49

Refillable souvenir mugs cost $14 (free refills) at Disney resorts and $10.75 at water parks; mugs sold at Disney's Animal Kingdom cost $7 (refills $1).

including three in the theme parks: **Tomorrowland Terrace** in the Magic Kingdom, **Sunshine Seasons** in Epcot, and **Studio Catering Co.** in Disney's Hollywood Studios. Fast-casual restaurants feature menu choices a cut above what you would normally find at a typical counter-service location. These eateries feature Asian or Mediterranean cuisine, something previously lacking inside the parks. Entrees cost about $2 more on average than traditional counter service, but the variety and food quality more than make up for the difference.

VENDOR FOOD Vendors abound at the theme parks, Downtown Disney Marketplace, Downtown Disney West Side, and

Disney's BoardWalk. Offerings include popcorn, ice-cream bars, churros (Mexican pastries), soft drinks, bottled water, and (in theme parks) fresh fruit. Prices include tax, and payment must be in cash.

DISNEY DINING SUGGESTIONS

FOLLOWING ARE SUGGESTIONS FOR DINING at each of the major theme parks. If you're interested in trying a theme park full-service restaurant, be aware that the restaurants continue to serve after the park's official closing time. For example, we showed up at The Hollywood Brown Derby just as Disney's Hollywood Studios closed at 8 p.m. We were seated almost immediately and enjoyed a leisurely dinner while the crowds cleared out. Incidentally, don't worry if you're depending on Disney transportation: buses, boats, and monorails run 1–3 hours after the parks close.

THE MAGIC KINGDOM

FOOD AT THE MAGIC KINGDOM HAS improved noticeably over the past several years. **The Crystal Palace** at the end of Main Street offers a good (albeit pricey) buffet chaperoned by Disney characters, while the **Liberty Tree Tavern** in Liberty Square features hearty family-style dining at dinner. **Cinderella's Royal Table,** a full-service restaurant on the second floor of the castle, delivers palatable meals in one of the World's most distinctive settings. **Tony's Town Square Restaurant** on Main Street also serves decent food. Because children love Cinderella and everyone's curious about the castle, you need to make an Advance Reservation before you leave home if you want to eat breakfast at Cinderella's Royal Table. Advance Reservations for lunch or dinner are somewhat easier to arrange.

EPCOT

FOR THE MOST PART, Epcot's restaurants have always served decent food, although World Showcase restaurants have occasionally been timid about delivering an honest representation of the host nation's cuisine. While these eateries have struggled with authenticity and have sometimes shied away from challenging the meat-and-potatoes palate of the average tourist, they are bolder now,

unofficial **TIP**
Many Epcot eateries are overpriced, most conspicuously Nine Dragons Restaurant (China) and Coral Reef Restaurant (The Seas).

erica's expanding appreciation of ethnic din-
dventuresome can still find sanitized and ho-
, but the same kitchens will serve up the real
with a spark of curiosity and daring. Represent-
od value through the combination of ambience
and we..., ...red food are **Chefs de France** (France), **Akershus Royal Banquet Hall** (Norway), **Biergarten** (Germany), and **Restaurant Marrakesh** (Morocco). Biergarten and Marrakesh also have live entertainment.

DISNEY'S ANIMAL KINGDOM

ANIMAL KINGDOM OFFERS A LOT of counter-service fast food but has converted **Tusker House** to a buffet-style restaurant and added **Yak & Yeti,** a table-service restaurant, in Asia. You'll find plenty of traditional Disney-theme-park food—hot dogs, hamburgers, deli sandwiches, and the like— but even the fast food is a cut above the average Disney fare. Our two favorites: **Flame Tree Barbecue** in Discovery Island, with its waterfront dining pavilions, and **Anandapur Local Food Cafes,** for casual Asian fare from egg rolls to crispy honey chicken. Yak & Yeti also serves above-average food (especially the seafood and duck).

unofficial **TIP**
Flame Tree Barbe-
cue in Safari Village
is our pick of the
Animal Kingdom
litter, both in terms
of food quality
and atmosphere.

The third full-service restaurant in Animal Kingdom, the **Rainforest Cafe,** has entrances both inside and outside the park (you don't have to buy park admission to eat there). Both Rainforest Cafes (the other is at Downtown Disney Marketplace) accept Advance Reservations.

DISNEY'S HOLLYWOOD STUDIOS

DINING AT DHS is more interesting than at the Magic Kingdom and less international than at Epcot. The park has five restaurants where Advance Reservations are recommended: **The Hollywood Brown Derby, 50's Prime Time Cafe, Sci-Fi Dine-In Theater Restaurant, Mama Melrose's Ristorante Italiano,** and the **Hollywood & Vine** buffet. The upscale Brown Derby is by far the best restaurant at the Studios. For simple Italian food, including pizza, Mama Melrose's is fine. At the Sci-Fi Dine-In, you eat in little cars at a simulated drive-in movie from the 1950s. Though you won't find a more entertaining restaurant in Walt Disney World, the food is quite disappointing. Somewhat better is the 50's Prime Time Cafe, where you sit in Mom's fabulous-'50s kitchen and scarf down meat loaf while watching clips of classic TV sitcoms. Hollywood & Vine features singing and dancing characters from the Disney Channel during breakfast and lunch.

WALT DISNEY WORLD RESTAURANTS:
Rated and Ranked

OVERALL RATING The overall rating represents the entire dining experience: style, service, and ambience, in addition to taste, presentation, and quality of food. Five stars is the highest rating and indicates that the restaurant offers the best of everything. Four-star restaurants are above average, and three-star restaurants offer good, though not necessarily memorable, meals. Two-star restaurants serve mediocre fare, and one-star restaurants are below average. Our star ratings don't correspond to ratings awarded by AAA, Mobil, Zagat, or other restaurant reviewers.

COST RANGE The next rating tells how much a full-service entree will cost. Appetizers, sides, soups/salads, desserts, drinks, and tips aren't included. We've rated the cost as inexpensive, moderate, or expensive.

Inexpensive	$15 or less per person
Moderate	$15–$28 per person
Expensive	More than $28 per person

QUALITY RATING The food quality is rated on a scale of one to five stars, five being the best rating attainable. The quality rating is based expressly on the taste, freshness of ingredients, preparation, presentation, and creativity of food served. There is no consideration of price. If you are a person who wants the best food available and cost is not an issue, you need look no further than the quality ratings.

VALUE RATING If, on the other hand, you are looking for both quality *and* value, then you should check the value rating, expressed as stars.

★★★★★	Exceptional value, a real bargain
★★★★	Good value
★★★	Fair value, you get exactly what you pay for
★★	Somewhat overpriced
★	Significantly overpriced

WDW Restaurants by Cuisine

CUISINE	LOCATION	OVERALL RATING	COST	QUALITY RATING	VALUE RATING
AFRICAN					
Jiko—The Cooking Place	Animal Kingdom Lodge	★★★★½	Exp	★★★★ ½	★★★½
Boma—Flavors of Africa	Animal Kingdom Lodge	★★★★	Exp	★★★★	★★★★½
Tusker House Restaurant	Animal Kingdom	★½	Mod	★	★★
AMERICAN					
California Grill	Contemporary	★★★★½	Exp	★★★★½	★★★
The Hollywood Brown Derby	DHS	★★★★	Exp	★★★★	★★★
Artist Point	Wilderness Lodge	★★★½	Exp	★★★★	★★★
Cape May Cafe	Beach Club	★★★½	Mod	★★★½	★★★★
Whispering Canyon Cafe	Wilderness Lodge	★★★	Mod	★★★½	★★★★
Captain's Grille	Yacht Club	★★★	Mod	★★★½	★★★
The Crystal Palace	Magic Kingdom	★★★	Mod	★★★½	★★★
House of Blues	West Side	★★★	Mod	★★★½	★★★
50's Prime Time Cafe	DHS	★★★	Mod	★★★	★★★
Liberty Tree Tavern	Magic Kingdom	★★★	Mod	★★★	★★★
Cinderella's Royal Table	Magic Kingdom	★★★	Exp	★★★	★★
T-REX	Downtown Disney	★★★	Mod	★★	★★
The Wave... of American Flavors	Contemporary	★★★	Mod	★★	★★
Chef Mickey's	Contemporary	★★½	Exp	★★★	★★★
ESPN Club	BoardWalk	★★½	Mod	★★★	★★★
ESPN Wide World of Sports Cafe	ESPN Wide World of Sports Complex	★★½	Mod	★★★	★★★
Hollywood & Vine	DHS	★★½	Mod	★★★	★★★
1900 Park Fare	Grand Floridian	★★½	Mod	★★★	★★★
Boatwrights Dining Hall	Port Orleans	★★½	Mod	★★★	★★
Grand Floridian Cafe	Grand Floridian	★★½	Mod	★★★	★★
Sand Trap Bar & Grill	Osprey Ridge Golf Course	★★½	Mod	★★½	★★½
Beaches & Cream Soda Shop	Beach Club	★★½	Inexp	★★½	★★½
Planet Hollywood	West Side	★★½	Mod	★★	★★
Rainforest Cafe	Animal Kingdom and Downtown Disney	★★½	Mod	★★	★★
Garden Grove	Swan	★★	Mod	★★★	★★
Olivia's Cafe	Old Key West	★★	Mod	★★½	★★
Wolfgang Puck Grand Cafe	West Side	★★	Exp	★½	★½

CUISINE	LOCATION	OVERALL RATING	COST	QUALITY RATING	VALUE RATING
AMERICAN (CONTINUED)					
Sci-Fi Dine-In Theater Restaurant	DHS	★★	Mod	★★½	★★
The Garden Grill Restaurant	Epcot	★★	Exp	★★	★★★
Big River Grille & Brewing Works	BoardWalk	★★	Mod	★★	★★
The Fountain	Dolphin	★★	Mod	★★	★★
The Plaza Restaurant	Magic Kingdom	★★	Mod	★★	★★
Trail's End Restaurant	Fort Wilderness Resort	★★	Mod	★★	★★
Turf Club Bar & Grill	Saratoga Springs	★★	Mod	★★	★★
LakeView Restaurant	Wyndham LBV	★★	Mod	★	★★★
Tusker House Restaurant	Animal Kingdom	★½	Mod	★	★★
Maya Grill	Coronado Springs	★	Exp	★	★
BUFFET					
Boma—Flavors of Africa	Animal Kingdom Lodge	★★★★	Exp	★★★★	★★★★½
Cape May Cafe	Beach Club	★★★½	Mod	★★★½	★★★★
Biergarten	Epcot	★★★½	Exp	★★★	★★★★
The Crystal Palace	Magic Kingdom	★★★	Mod	★★★½	★★★
Akershus Royal Banquet Hall	Epcot	★★★	Exp	★★★	★★★★
Chef Mickey's	Contemporary	★★½	Exp	★★★	★★★
Hollywood & Vine	DHS	★★½	Mod	★★★	★★★
1900 Park Fare	Grand Floridian	★★½	Mod	★★★	★★★
Garden Grove	Swan	★★	Mod	★★★	★★
Trail's End Restaurant	Fort Wiklerness Resort	★★	Mod	★★	★★
Tusker House Restaurant	Animal Kingdom	★½	Mod	★	★★
CHINESE					
Nine Dragons Restaurant	Epcot	★★★	Mod	★★★	★★
CUBAN					
Bongos Cuban Cafe	West Side	★★	Mod	★★	★★
ENGLISH					
Rose & Crown Dining Room	Epcot	★★★	Mod	★★★½	★★
FRENCH					
Bistro de Paris	Epcot	★★★	Exp	★★★½	★★
Les Chefs de France	Epcot	★★★	Exp	★★★	★★★

WDW Restaurants by Cuisine (cont'd.)

CUISINE	LOCATION	OVERALL RATING	COST	QUALITY RATING	VALUE RATING
GERMAN					
Biergarten	Epcot	★★★½	Exp	★★★	★★★★
GLOBAL					
Paradiso 37	Downtown Disney	★★½	Inexp	★★★	★★★
GOURMET					
Victoria & Albert's	Grand Floridian	★★★★★	Exp	★★★★★	★★★★
INDIAN/AFRICAN					
Sanaa	Animal Kingdom Lodge–Kidani Village	★★★★	Exp	★★★★	★★★★
IRISH					
Raglan Road Irish Pub & Restaurant	Downtown Disney	★★★★	Mod	★★★½	★★★
ITALIAN					
Via Napoli	Epcot	★★★★	Mod	★★½	★★½
Tutto Italia Ristorante	Epcot	★★★½	Exp	★★½	★★½
Andiamo Italian Bistro & Grille	Hilton	★★★	Exp	★★★	★★★
Il Mulino New York Trattoria	Swan	★★★	Exp	★★★	★★
Mama Melrose's Ristorante Italiano	DHS	★★½	Mod	★★★	★★
Portobello	Downtown Disney	★★½	Exp	★★★	★★
Tony's Town Square Restaurant	Magic Kingdom	★★½	Mod	★★★	★★
JAPANESE					
Kimonos	Swan	★★★★	Mod	★★★★½	★★★
Kona Island Sushi Bar	Polynesian	★★★★	Mod	★★★★	★★★★
Teppan Edo	Epcot	★★★½	Exp	★★★★	★★★
Tokyo Dining	Epcot	★★★	Mod	★★★★	★★★
Benihana	Hilton	★★★	Mod	★★★½	★★★
MEDITERRANEAN					
Kouzzina by Cat Cora	BoardWalk	★★★★	Mod	★★★★	★★★★
Cítricos	Grand Floridian	★★★½	Exp	★★★★½	★★★

CUISINE	LOCATION	OVERALL RATING	COST	QUALITY RATING	VALUE RATING
MEDITERRANEAN (CONTINUED)					
Fresh Mediterranean Market	Dolphin	★★½	Mod	★★½	★★
MEXICAN					
San Angel Inn	Epcot	★★★	Exp	★★	★★
La Hacienda de San Angel	Epcot	★★½	Exp	★★½	★★½
MOROCCAN					
Restaurant Marrakesh	Epcot	★★	Mod	★★½	★★
NORWEGIAN					
Akershus Royal Banquet Hall	Epcot	★★★	Exp	★★★	★★★★
POLYNESIAN/PAN-ASIAN					
'Ohana	Polynesian	★★★	Mod	★★★½	★★★
Kona Cafe	Polynesian	★★★	Mod	★★★	★★★★
Yak & Yeti Restaurant	Animal Kingdom	★★	Exp	★★½	★★
SEAFOOD					
Narcoossee's	Grand Floridian	★★★★½	Exp	★★★½	★★
Flying Fish Cafe	BoardWalk	★★★★	Exp	★★★★	★★★
Artist Point	Wilderness Lodge	★★★½	Exp	★★★★	★★★
Todd English's bluezoo	Dolphin	★★★	Exp	★★★	★★
Fulton's Crab House	Downtown Disney	★★½	Exp	★★★½	★★
Cap'n Jack's Restaurant	Downtown Disney	★★½	Mod	★★	★★
Coral Reef Restaurant	Epcot	★★½	Exp	★★	★★
Shutters at Old Port Royale	Caribbean Beach	★★	Mod	★★½	★★
STEAK					
Shula's Steakhouse	Dolphin	★★★★	Exp	★★★★	★★
Le Cellier Steakhouse	Epcot	★★★½	Exp	★★★½	★★★
Yachtsman Steakhouse	Yacht Club	★★★	Exp	★★★½	★★
The Outback	Buena Vista Palace	★★	Exp	★★★	★★
Shutters at Old Port Royale	Caribbean Beach	★★	Mod	★★½	★★

OPENED IN 1971, THE MAGIC KINGDOM was the first built of Walt Disney World's four theme parks. It is undoubtedly what most people think of when they think of Disney World.

ARRIVING

IF YOU DRIVE, THE MAGIC KINGDOM Ticket and Transportation Center (TTC) parking lot opens about 2 hours before the park does. After paying a fee, you are directed to a parking space, then transported by tram to the TTC, where you catch a monorail or ferry to the entrance.

If you're staying at the Contemporary–Bay Lake Tower, Polynesian, or Grand Floridian resorts, you can commute to the Magic Kingdom by monorail (guests at the Contemporary–Bay Lake Tower can walk there more quickly). If you stay at Wilderness Lodge and Villas or Fort Wilderness Campground, you can take a boat or bus. Guests at other Disney resorts can reach the park by bus. Disney lodging guests are deposited at the park's entrance, bypassing the TTC.

GETTING ORIENTED

unofficial **TIP**
If you don't already have a handout guide map of the park, get one at City Hall.

AT THE MAGIC KINGDOM, stroller and wheelchair rentals are in the train station; lockers are on the right, just inside the park entrance. On your left as you enter **Main Street, U.S.A.** is **City Hall,** the center for information, lost and found, guided tours, and entertainment schedules.

The guide map found there lists all attractions, shops, and eating places; provides information about first aid, baby care, and assistance for the disabled; and gives tips for good photos. It lists times for the day's special events, live entertainment, parades, and concerts, and it also tells when and where to find Disney characters. Often the guide map is supplemented by a daily entertainment schedule known as the *Times Guide.* In addition to listing performance times, the *Times Guide* provides info on Disney-character appearances and what Disney calls Special Hours. This term usually refers to attractions that open late or close early and to the operating hours of park restaurants.

Main Street ends at the **Central Plaza,** a hub from which branch the entrances to five other sections of the Magic Kingdom: **Adventureland, Frontierland, Liberty Square, Fantasyland,** and **Tomorrowland.**

Cinderella Castle, at the entrance to Fantasyland, is the Magic Kingdom's architectural icon and visual center. If you start in Adventureland and go clockwise around the Magic Kingdom, the castle spires will always be roughly on your right; if you start in Tomorrowland and go counterclockwise through the park, the spires will always be roughly on your left. The castle is an excellent meeting place if your group decides to split up during the day or is separated accidentally.

unofficial **TIP**
Minimize the time you spend on midway-type rides; you probably have something similar near your hometown.

STARTING THE TOUR

TAKE ADVANTAGE OF WHAT DISNEY does best: the fantasy adventures of Splash Mountain and The Haunted Mansion and the various audioanimatronic (talking-robot) attractions, including *The Hall of Presidents* and Pirates of the Caribbean. Don't burn daylight browsing the shops unless you plan to spend a minimum of 2½ days at the Magic Kingdom, and even then wait until midday or later. Eat breakfast early, and avoid lines at eateries by snacking during the day on food from vendors.

FASTPASS *at the* MAGIC KINGDOM

THE MAGIC KINGDOM OFFERS nine Fastpass attractions, the most in any Disney park. Strategies for using Fastpass at the Magic Kingdom are integrated into our touring plans.

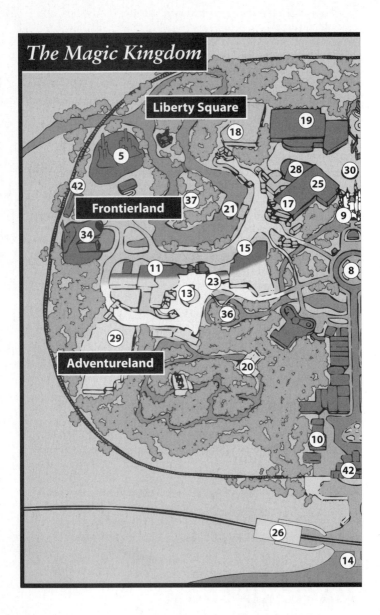

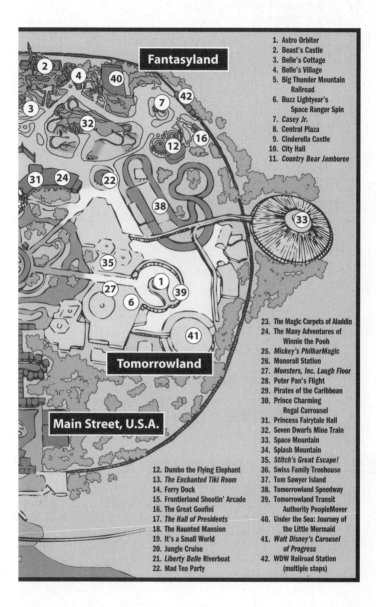

Fantasyland

Tomorrowland

Main Street, U.S.A.

1. Astro Orbiter
2. Beast's Castle
3. Belle's Cottage
4. Belle's Village
5. Big Thunder Mountain Railroad
6. Buzz Lightyear's Space Ranger Spin
7. *Casey Jr.*
8. Central Plaza
9. Cinderella Castle
10. City Hall
11. *Country Bear Jamboree*

12. Dumbo the Flying Elephant
13. *The Enchanted Tiki Room*
14. Ferry Dock
15. Frontierland Shootin' Arcade
16. The Great Goofini
17. *The Hall of Presidents*
18. The Haunted Mansion
19. It's a Small World
20. Jungle Cruise
21. *Liberty Belle* Riverboat
22. Mad Tea Party

23. The Magic Carpets of Aladdin
24. The Many Adventures of Winnie the Pooh
25. *Mickey's PhilharMagic*
26. Monorail Station
27. *Monsters, Inc. Laugh Floor*
28. Peter Pan's Flight
29. Pirates of the Caribbean
30. Prince Charming Regal Carrousel
31. Princess Fairytale Hall
32. Seven Dwarfs Mine Train
33. Space Mountain
34. Splash Mountain
35. *Stitch's Great Escape!*
36. Swiss Family Treehouse
37. Tom Sawyer Island
38. Tomorrowland Speedway
39. Tomorrowland Transit Authority PeopleMover
40. Under the Sea: Journey of the Little Mermaid
41. *Walt Disney's Carousel of Progress*
42. WDW Railroad Station (multiple stops)

MAGIC KINGDOM FASTPASS ATTRACTIONS

Adventureland	Jungle Cruise
Fantasyland	The Many Adventures of Winnie the Pooh *Mickey's PhilharMagic* (seasonally) Peter Pan's Flight Seven Dwarfs Mine Train
Frontierland	Big Thunder Mountain Railroad Splash Mountain
Tomorrowland	Buzz Lightyear's Space Ranger Spin Space Mountain

NOT TO BE MISSED AT THE MAGIC KINGDOM

Adventureland	Pirates of the Caribbean
Fantasyland	The Many Adventures of Winnie the Pooh *Mickey's PhilharMagic* Peter Pan's Flight Seven Dwarfs Mine Train Under the Sea: Journey of the Little Mermaid
Frontierland	Big Thunder Mountain Railroad Splash Mountain
Liberty Square	The Haunted Mansion
Special Events	Evening Parade *The Magic, The Memories and You!*
Tomorrowland	Space Mountain

MAIN STREET, U.S.A.

BEGIN AND END YOUR VISIT ON MAIN STREET, which may open a half hour before, and closes a half hour to an hour after, the rest of the park. The Walt Disney World Railroad stops at Main Street Station; get on to tour the park or ride to Frontierland or Fantasyland.

Main Street is a Disneyfied turn-of-the-19th-century small-town American street. Its buildings are real, not elaborate props. Attention to detail is exceptional: furnishings and fixtures are true to the period. Along the street are shops, eating places, City Hall, and a fire station. Occasionally, horse-drawn trolleys, fire engines, and horseless carriages transport visitors along Main Street to the Central Plaza.

MAIN STREET SERVICES

Most park services are centered on Main Street, including:

Baby Care Center Next to The Crystal Palace, left around the Central Plaza (toward Adventureland)

Banking Services Automated tellers (ATMs) underneath the Main Street railroad station

First Aid Next to The Crystal Palace, left around the Central Plaza (toward Adventureland)

Live Entertainment and Parade Info City Hall at the railroad-station end of Main Street

Lost and Found City Hall at the railroad-station end of Main Street

Lost Persons City Hall

Storage Lockers Underneath the Main Street railroad station; all lockers cleaned out each night

Walt Disney World and Local Attraction Information City Hall

Wheelchair, ECV, and Stroller Rentals Ground floor of the railroad station at the end of Main Street

Walt Disney World Railroad ★★½

APPEAL BY AGE	PRESCHOOL ★★★	GRADE SCHOOL ★★★★	TEENS ★★★
YOUNG ADULTS ★★★★		OVER 30 ★★★½	SENIORS ★★★

What it is Scenic railroad ride around perimeter of the Magic Kingdom, and transportation to Frontierland. **Scope and scale** Minor attraction. **When to go** Anytime. **Special comments** Main Street is usually the least congested station. **Authors' rating** Plenty to see; ★★½. **Duration of ride** About 20 minutes for a complete circuit. **Average wait in line per 100 people ahead of you** 8 minutes; assumes 2 or more trains operating. **Loading speed** Moderate.

DESCRIPTION AND COMMENTS A transportation ride blending an unusual variety of sights and experiences with an energy-saving way to get around the park. The train provides a glimpse of all lands except Adventureland.

TOURING TIPS Save the train ride until after you have seen the featured attractions, or use it when you need transportation. On busy days, lines form at the Frontierland Station but rarely at the Main Street Station. Strollers aren't allowed on the train. Wheelchair access is currently available only at the Frontierland station.

You cannot take your rental stroller on the train, but you can obtain a replacement stroller at your destination. Just take your personal belongings, your stroller name card, and your rental receipt with you on the train.

Finally, be advised that the railroad shuts down immediately preceding and during parades. Check your park guide map or *Times Guide* for parade times. Needless to say, this is not the time to queue up for the train.

Transportation Rides

DESCRIPTION AND COMMENTS Trolleys, buses, and the like that add color to Main Street.

TOURING TIPS Will save you a walk to the hub. Not worth a wait.

ADVENTURELAND

ADVENTURELAND IS THE FIRST LAND to the left of Main Street. It combines an African safari theme with an old New Orleans and Caribbean atmosphere.

The Enchanted Tiki Room ★★★½

| APPEAL BY AGE | PRESCHOOL ★★★ | GRADE SCHOOL ★★★ | TEENS ★★½ |
| YOUNG ADULTS ★★★ | OVER 30 ★★★ | | SENIORS ★★★ |

What it is Audioanimatronic Pacific-island musical-theater show. **Scope and scale** Minor attraction. **When to go** Before 11 a.m. or after 3:30 p.m. **Special comments** Frightens some preschoolers. **Authors' rating** Very, very unusual; ★★★½. **Duration of presentation** 15½ minutes. **Preshow entertainment** Talking birds. **Probable waiting time** 15 minutes.

DESCRIPTION AND COMMENTS A January 2010 fire shut down *The Enchanted Tiki Room—Under New Management!* While repairs were being made, the "management" since 1998—Iago from *Aladdin* and Zazu from *The Lion King*—was laid off, to be replaced with José, Fritz, Michael, and Pierre, the same four crooning, wisecracking parrots that hosted the original version of the attraction, which premiered at Disneyland in 1963. Despite having returned to its roots (egg?), the production remains, well, a featherweight in the Disney galaxy of attractions. Although readers like the show, they caution that it may be more frightening to younger children than it used to be.

TOURING TIPS One of the more bizarre Magic Kingdom entertainments. It's usually not too crowded. We go in the late afternoon when we especially appreciate sitting briefly in an air-conditioned theater with our brains in "park."

Jungle Cruise (Fastpass) ★★★

| APPEAL BY AGE | PRESCHOOL ★★★★ | GRADE SCHOOL ★★★★ | TEENS ★★★½ |
| YOUNG ADULTS ★★★½ | OVER 30 ★★★★ | | SENIORS ★★★★ |

What it is Outdoor safari-themed boat-ride adventure. **Scope and scale** Major attraction. **When to go** Before 10 a.m. or 2 hours before closing, or use Fastpass. **Special comments** A lot of fun to ride at night! **Authors' rating** A long-enduring Disney classic; ★★★. **Duration of ride** 8–9 minutes. **Average wait in line per 100 people ahead of you** 3½ minutes; assumes 10 boats operating. **Loading speed** Moderate.

DESCRIPTION AND COMMENTS An outdoor cruise through jungle waterways. Passengers encounter animatronic elephants, lions, hostile natives, and a menacing hippo. Boatman's spiel adds to the fun. Once one of the most grand and elaborate attractions at the Magic Kingdom, the Jungle Cruise's technology now seems dated and worn. Since the advent of Disney's Animal Kingdom, the attraction's appeal has diminished, but in its defense, you can always depend on the Jungle Cruise's robotic critters being present as you motor past.

TOURING TIPS Among the park's oldest attractions and one that occupies a good third of Adventureland. A convoluted queuing area makes it very difficult to estimate the length of the wait for the Jungle Cruise.

Fortunately, the Jungle Cruise is a Fastpass attraction. Before you obtain a Fastpass, however, ask a cast member what the estimated wait in the standby line is.

The Magic Carpets of Aladdin ★★★

APPEAL BY AGE	PRESCHOOL ★★★★½	GRADE SCHOOL ★★★★	TEENS ★★★
YOUNG ADULTS ★★½		OVER 30 ★★★	SENIORS ★★½

What it is Elaborate midway ride. **Scope and scale** Minor attraction. **When to go** Before 10 a.m. or in the hour before park closing. **Authors' rating** A visually appealing children's ride; ★★★. **Duration of ride** 1½ minutes. **Average wait in line per 100 people ahead of you** 16 minutes. **Loading speed** Slow.

DESCRIPTION AND COMMENTS The Magic Carpets of Aladdin is a midway ride like Dumbo, except with magic carpets instead of elephants. Copying the water innovation of the One Fish, Two Fish attraction at Universal's Islands of Adventure, Disney's Aladdin ride has a spitting camel positioned to spray jets of water on carpet riders. Riders can maneuver their carpets up and down to spit back and side to side to avoid getting wet.

TOURING TIPS Like Dumbo, this ride has great eye appeal but extremely limited capacity (that is, it's slow-loading). If your younger children see it, they'll probably want to ride. Try to get them on during the first 30 minutes the park is open or try just before park closing.

Pirates of the Caribbean ★★★★★

APPEAL BY AGE	PRESCHOOL ★★★½	GRADE SCHOOL ★★★★	TEENS ★★★★
YOUNG ADULTS ★★★★½	OVER 30 ★★★★½		SENIORS ★★★★½

What it is Indoor pirate-themed boat ride. **Scope and scale** Headliner. **When to go** Before noon or after 5 p.m. **Special comments** Frightens some children. **Authors' rating** Disney audioanimatronics at their best; not to be missed; ★★★★★. **Duration of ride** About 7½ minutes. **Average wait in line per 100 people ahead of you** 1½ minutes; assumes both waiting lines operating. **Loading speed** Fast.

DESCRIPTION AND COMMENTS An indoor cruise through a series of sets depicting a pirate raid on an island settlement, from bombardment of the fortress to debauchery after the victory. Regarding debauchery, Pirates of the Caribbean is one of several Disney attractions that has been administered a strong dose of political correctness. The wildly successful *Pirates of the Caribbean* movie series has boosted the ride's popularity, and guests' demands led to the addition in 2006 of animatronic figures of the movie's Captain Jack Sparrow and Captain Barbossa in key scenes.

TOURING TIPS Undoubtedly one of the park's most elaborate and timeless attractions. Engineered to move large crowds in a hurry, Pirates is a good attraction to see during late afternoon. It has two covered waiting lines.

Swiss Family Treehouse ★★★

APPEAL BY AGE	PRESCHOOL ★★★	GRADE SCHOOL ★★★	TEENS ★★★
YOUNG ADULTS ★★½	OVER 30 ★★★		SENIORS ★★★

What it is Outdoor walk-through tree house. **Scope and scale** Minor attraction. **When to go** Before 11:30 a.m. or after 5 p.m. **Special comments** Requires climbing a lot of stairs. **Authors' rating** Incredible detail and execution; ★★★. **Duration of tour** 10–15 minutes. **Average wait in line per 100 people ahead of you** 7 minutes. **Loading speed** Doesn't apply.

DESCRIPTION AND COMMENTS An immense replica of the shipwrecked family's tree house will turn your children into arboreal architects. It's the king of all tree houses, with its multiple stories and mechanical wizardry. Children enjoy the climbing and exercise; adults marvel at the ingenuity.

TOURING TIPS A self-guided walk-through tour involves a lot of stairs up and down, but no ropes, ladders, or anything fancy. People who stop for extra-long looks or to rest sometimes create bottlenecks that slow the crowd flow. Visit in late afternoon or early evening if you're on a one-day tour, or in the morning of your second day.

FRONTIERLAND

FRONTIERLAND ADJOINS ADVENTURELAND as you move clockwise around the Magic Kingdom. The focus is on the Old West, with stockade-type structures and pioneer trappings.

Big Thunder Mountain Railroad *(Fastpass)* ★★★★

APPEAL BY AGE	PRESCHOOL ★★★½	GRADE SCHOOL ★★★★½	TEENS ★★★★½
YOUNG ADULTS ★★★★		OVER 30 ★★★★½	SENIORS ★★★★

What it is Tame western-mining-themed roller coaster. **Scope and scale** Headliner. **When to go** Before 10 a.m., in the hour before closing, or use Fastpass. **Special comments** Must be 40" tall to ride; children younger than age 7 must ride with an adult. Switching-off option provided (see page 75). **Authors' rating** Great effects; relatively tame ride; not to be missed; ★★★★. **Duration of ride** About 3½ minutes. **Average wait in line per 100 people ahead of you** 2½ minutes; assumes 5 trains operating. **Loading speed** Moderate–fast.

DESCRIPTION AND COMMENTS Roller coaster through and around a Disney "mountain." The idea is that you're on a runaway mine train during the Gold Rush. This roller coaster is about 5 on a "scary scale" of 10. First-rate examples of Disney creativity are showcased: realistic mining town, falling rocks, and an earthquake, all humorously animated with swinging possums, petulant buzzards, and the like.

TOURING TIPS A superb Disney experience, but not too wild a roller coaster. Emphasis is much more on the sights than on the thrill of the ride.

   Nearby Splash Mountain affects the traffic flow to Big Thunder Mountain Railroad. Adventuresome guests ride Splash Mountain first, then go next door to ride Big Thunder. This means large crowds in Frontierland all day and long waits for Big Thunder Mountain. The best way to experience the Magic Kingdom's "mountains" is to ride Space Mountain one morning as soon as the park opens, then Splash Mountain and Big Thunder the next morning. If you only have one day, the order should be (1) Space Mountain, (2) Buzz Lightyear (optional), (3) Splash Mountain, (4) Big Thunder Mountain. If the wait exceeds 30 minutes when you arrive, use Fastpass.

Country Bear Jamboree ★★★

APPEAL BY AGE	PRESCHOOL ★★★½	GRADE SCHOOL ★★★	TEENS ★★
YOUNG ADULTS ★★½		OVER 30 ★★★	SENIORS ★★★½

What it is Audioanimatronic country-hoedown theater show. **Scope and scale** Major attraction. **When to go** Before 11:30 a.m., before a parade, or during the 2 hours before closing. **Special comments** Shows change at Christmas. **Authors' rating** Old and worn, but pure Disney; ★★★. **Duration of presentation** 15 minutes. **Preshow entertainment** None. **Probable waiting time** This attraction is moderately popular but has a comparatively small capacity. Waiting time between noon and 5:30 p.m. on a busy day will average 15–45 minutes.

DESCRIPTION AND COMMENTS A charming cast of audioanimatronic bears sing and stomp in a Western-style hoedown. Although one of the Magic Kingdom's most humorous and upbeat shows, *Country Bear Jamboree* geriatric bears have run for so long that the bears are a step away from assisted living.

TOURING TIPS During summer afternoons, rainy days, and busy times, the show draws large crowds from midmorning on.

Frontierland Shootin' Arcade ★½

APPEAL BY AGE	PRESCHOOL ★★½	GRADE SCHOOL ★★★½	TEENS ★★★
YOUNG ADULTS ★★★		OVER 30 ★★½	SENIORS ★★

What it is Electronic shooting gallery. **Scope and scale** Diversion. **When to go** Whenever convenient. **Special comments** Costs $1 per play. **Authors' rating** Very nifty shooting gallery; ★½.

DESCRIPTION AND COMMENTS Very elaborate. One of few attractions not included in Magic Kingdom admission.

TOURING TIPS Not a place to blow your time if you're on a tight schedule. If time allows, go on your second day. The fun is entirely in the target practice—no prizes can be won.

Splash Mountain *(Fastpass)* ★★★★★

APPEAL BY AGE	PRESCHOOL ★★★★†	GRADE SCHOOL ★★★★½	TEENS ★★★★★
YOUNG ADULTS ★★★★★		OVER 30 ★★★★½	SENIORS ★★★★

† Many preschoolers are too short to meet the height requirement, and others are visually intimidated when they see the ride from the waiting line. Among preschoolers who actually ride, most give the attraction high marks.

What it is Indoor/outdoor water-flume adventure ride. **Scope and scale** Super-headliner. **When to go** As soon as the park opens, during afternoon or evening parades, just before closing, or use Fastpass. **Special comments** Must be 40" tall to ride; children younger than age 7 must ride with an adult. Switching-off option provided (see page 75). **Authors' rating** A soggy delight, and not to be missed; ★★★★★. **Duration of ride** About 10 minutes. **Average wait in line per 100 people ahead of you** 3½ minutes; assumes ride is operating at full capacity. **Loading speed** Moderate.

DESCRIPTION AND COMMENTS An amusement-park flume ride Disney-style, Splash Mountain combines steep chutes and animatronics with at least one special effect for each of the

WARNING!

For Bouffants, Rug Wearers, and Elvis Impersonators

This Ride Will Muss Your 'Do

senses. The ride covers over half a mile, splashing through swamps, caves, and backwoods bayous before climaxing in a five-story plunge and Br'er Rabbit's triumphant return home. More than 100 audioanimatronic characters, including Br'er Rabbit (aka Br'er Hare), Br'er Bear, and Br'er Fox regale riders with songs, including "Zip-a-Dee-Doo-Dah."

TOURING TIPS This happy, exciting, adventuresome ride vies with Space Mountain in Tomorrowland as the park's most popular attraction. Crowds build fast in the morning, and waits of more than 2 hours can be expected once the park fills. Get in line first thing, certainly no later than 45 minutes after the park opens. Long lines will persist all day.

If you have only one day to see the Magic Kingdom, ride Space Mountain first, then Buzz Lightyear (also in Tomorrowland), then hotfoot it over to Splash Mountain. If the wait is less than 30 minutes, go ahead and ride. Otherwise, obtain a Fastpass and return later to enjoy Splash Mountain. Fastpass strategies have been incorporated into the Magic Kingdom One-day Touring Plans (see pages 162–166). If you have two mornings to devote to the Magic Kingdom, experience Space Mountain one morning and Buzz Lightyear, Splash Mountain, and Big Thunder Mountain the next. Spreading your visit over two mornings will eliminate much crisscrossing of the park as well as the backtracking that is inevitable when you use Fastpass.

As occurs with Space Mountain, when the park opens, hundreds are poised to dash to Splash Mountain. The best strategy is to go to the end of Main Street and turn left to The Crystal Palace restaurant. In front of the restaurant is a bridge that provides a shortcut to Adventureland. Stake out a position at the barrier rope. When the park opens and the rope drops, move as fast as you comfortably can and cross the bridge to Adventureland.

Here's another shortcut: Just past the first group of buildings on your right, roughly across from the Swiss Family Treehouse, is a small passageway containing restrooms and phones. Easy to overlook, it connects Adventureland to Frontierland. Go through the passageway into Frontierland and take a hard left. As you emerge along the waterfront, Splash Mountain is straight ahead. If you miss the passageway, don't fool around looking for it. Continue straight through Adventureland to Splash Mountain.

Less exhausting in the morning is to commute to Splash Mountain via the Walt Disney World Railroad. Board at Main Street Station and wait for the park to open. The train will pull out of the station a few minutes after the rope drops at the Central Plaza end of Main Street. Ride to Frontierland Station (the first stop) and disembark. As you come down the stairs at the station, the entrance to Splash Mountain will be on your left. Because of the time required to unload at the station, train passengers will arrive at Splash Mountain about the same time as the lead element from the Central Plaza.

At Splash Mountain, if you ride in the front seat, you almost certainly will get wet. Riders elsewhere get splashed, but usually not doused. Since you don't know which seat you'll be assigned, go prepared. On a cool day, carry a plastic garbage bag. Tear holes in the bottom and sides to make a water-resistant (not waterproof) sack dress. Be sure to tuck the bag under your bottom. Leave your camera with a nonriding member of your group or wrap it in plastic. An alternative to the garbage-bag getup is to store a change of clothes, including footwear, in one of the park's rental lockers. For any attraction where there's a distinct possibility of getting soaked, we recommend you wear Tevas or some other type of waterproof sandal. Change back to regular shoes after the ride.

The scariest part of this adventure ride is the steep chute you see when standing in line, but the drop looks worse than it is. Despite reassurances, however, many children wig out after watching it.

Tom Sawyer Island and Fort Langhorn ★★★

APPEAL BY AGE PRESCHOOL ★★★★ GRADE SCHOOL ★★★★ TEENS ★★★
YOUNG ADULTS ★★★   OVER 30 ★★★   SENIORS ★★★

What it is Outdoor walk-through exhibit/rustic playground. **Scope and scale** Minor attraction. **When to go** Midmorning through late afternoon. **Special comments** Closes at dusk. **Authors' rating** The place for rambunctious kids; ★★★.

DESCRIPTION AND COMMENTS Tom Sawyer Island is a getaway within the park. It has hills to climb; a cave, windmill, and pioneer stockade (Fort Langhorn) to explore; a tipsy barrel bridge to cross; and paths to follow. You can watch riverboats chug past. It's a delight for adults and a godsend for children who have been in tow and closely supervised all day.

TOURING TIPS Tom Sawyer Island isn't one of the Magic Kingdom's more celebrated attractions, but it is one of the park's better-conceived ones. Attention to detail is excellent, and kids revel in its frontier atmosphere. It's a must for families with children ages 5–15. If your group is made up of adults, visit on your second day or on your first day after you've seen the attractions you most wanted to see.

Plan on spending at least 20 minutes here, although children love the island and would likely spend a whole day playing here if left to their own devices. Access is by raft from Frontierland; two craft operate simultaneously and the trip is pretty efficient, though you may have to stand in line to board both ways.

Walt Disney World Railroad

DESCRIPTION AND COMMENTS Stops in Frontierland on its circle tour of the park. See the description under Main Street, U.S.A. (page 127), for additional details.

TOURING TIPS This is a pleasant, feet-saving link to Main Street and Fantasyland, but the Frontierland Station is usually more congested than those stations. You cannot take your rental stroller on the train. If you don't want to make a round trip to pick up your stroller, take your personal belongings, your stroller name card, and your rental receipt with you on the train. You'll be issued a replacement stroller at your Walt Disney World Railroad destination.

LIBERTY SQUARE

LIBERTY SQUARE RE-CREATES COLONIAL AMERICA at the time of the American Revolution. The architecture is Federal or Colonial. A real, 130-year-old live oak (dubbed the "Liberty Tree") lends dignity and grace to the setting.

The Hall of Presidents ★★★

APPEAL BY AGE	PRESCHOOL ★★	GRADE SCHOOL ★★★	TEENS ★★★
YOUNG ADULTS ★★★½		OVER 30 ★★★★	SENIORS ★★★★

What it is Audioanimatronic historical theater presentation. **Scope and scale** Major attraction. **When to go** Anytime. **Authors' rating** Impressive and moving; ★★★. **Duration of presentation** Almost 23 minutes. **Preshow entertainment** None. **Probable waiting time** Lines for this attraction look awesome but are usually swallowed up as the theater exchanges audiences. Your wait will probably be the remaining time of the show that's in progress when you arrive. Even during the busiest times, waits rarely exceed 40 minutes.

DESCRIPTION AND COMMENTS In 2009 Barack Obama was added and the entire show revamped, including a new narration by Morgan Freeman and a new speech by George Washington. The Father of Our Country joins Presidents Lincoln and Obama as the only chief executives with speaking parts. Although the show is revamped roughly every decade, the presentation remains strongly inspirational and patriotic, highlighting milestones in American history. A very moving show, with one of Disney's best and most ambitious audioanimatronic efforts.

TOURING TIPS Detail and costumes are masterful. If your children fidget during the show, notice that the Presidents do too. This attraction is one of the park's most popular among older visitors. Don't be put off by long lines. The theater holds more than 700 people, thus swallowing large lines at a single gulp when visitors are admitted.

The Haunted Mansion ★★★★

APPEAL BY AGE	PRESCHOOL ★★★		GRADE SCHOOL ★★★★		TEENS ★★★★½
YOUNG ADULTS ★★★★½		OVER 30 ★★★★½		SENIORS ★★★★½	

What it is Haunted-house dark ride. **Scope and scale** Major attraction. **When to go** Before 11:30 a.m. or after 8 p.m. **Special comments** Frightens some very young children. **Authors' rating** Some of Walt Disney World's best special effects; not to be missed; ★★★★. **Duration of ride** 7-minute ride plus a 1½-minute preshow. **Average wait in line per 100 people ahead of you** 2½ minutes; assumes both "stretch rooms" operating. **Loading speed** Fast.

DESCRIPTION AND COMMENTS Only slightly scarier than a whoopee cushion, The Haunted Mansion serves up some of the Magic Kingdom's best visual effects. "Doom Buggies" on a conveyor belt transport you through the house from parlor to attic, then through a graveyard. Two new scenes were added in the substantial 2007 refurbishment: an M. C. Escher–like room full of stairs heading in all directions and a montage explaining the fate of the many husbands of the mansion's mistress.

A new set of interactive elements was added to The Haunted Mansion's outdoor queue in 2011, ensuring that guests have something to occupy them when lines are long. Features include a music-playing monument, an old-fashioned pipe organ, and a ship captain's tomb that squirts water. Disneyphiles will recognize the names on many of these new elements as tributes to the mansion's designers.

TOURING TIPS Lines here ebb and flow more than those at most other Magic Kingdom hot spots because the Mansion is near *The Hall of Presidents* and the *Liberty Belle* riverboat. These two attractions disgorge 700 and 450 people, respectively, when each show or ride ends, and many of these folks head straight for the Mansion. If you can't go before 11:30 a.m. or after 8 p.m., try to slip in between crowds.

Liberty Belle Riverboat   ★★½

APPEAL BY AGE	PRESCHOOL ★★★	GRADE SCHOOL ★★★	TEENS ★★½
YOUNG ADULTS ★★★		OVER 30 ★★★	SENIORS ★★★★

What it is Outdoor scenic boat ride. **Scope and scale** Major attraction. **When to go** Anytime. **Authors' rating** Relaxing and scenic; ★★½. **Duration of ride** About 16 minutes. **Average wait to board** 10–14 minutes.

DESCRIPTION AND COMMENTS Large-capacity paddle-wheel riverboat navigates the waters around Tom Sawyer Island and Fort Langhorn, passing settler cabins, old mining paraphernalia, an Indian village, and a small menagerie of animatronic wildlife. A beautiful craft, the *Liberty Belle* provides a lofty perspective of Frontierland and Liberty Square.

TOURING TIPS The riverboat is a good attraction for the busy middle of the day. If you encounter huge crowds, chances are that the attraction has been inundated by a wave of guests coming from a just-concluded performance of *The Hall of Presidents*.

FANTASYLAND

FANTASYLAND IS THE HEART OF THE MAGIC KINGDOM, an enchanting place spread gracefully like a miniature Alpine village beneath the steepled towers of Cinderella Castle.

Much of Fantasyland will be undergoing construction through 2013. While most of the work will be occurring behind existing attractions, you'll almost certainly see construction walls or exterior refurbishment all through Fantasyland until the expansion is complete. Check **touringplans.com** for the latest developments.

The expanded Fantasyland is divided into three distinct new sections. Directly behind Cinderella Castle and set upon a snowcapped mountain is **Beast's Castle,** part of a *Beauty and the Beast*–themed area. Most of this section will host dining and shopping, such as the **Be Our Guest** restaurant (see page 503); **Gaston's Tavern,** a small quick-service restaurant; and a gift shop. The far-right corner of Fantasyland—including the new **Dumbo** attraction, the **Great Goofini** kiddie coaster, and the Fantasyland train station—is called **Storybook Circus** as a homage to Disney's *Dumbo* film. These are low-capacity amusement-park rides appropriate for younger children. Finally, the middle of the new Fantasyland territory holds the headliners, including the new Little Mermaid and Seven Dwarfs attractions. Placing these in the middle of the new land should allow good traffic flow either to the left (toward Beast's Castle) for dining, to the right for attractions geared to smaller children, or back to the original part of Fantasyland for classic attractions such as **Peter Pan's Flight** and **The Many Adventures of Winnie the Pooh.**

Dumbo the Flying Elephant ★★★

APPEAL BY AGE	PRESCHOOL ★★★★★	GRADE SCHOOL ★★★★	TEENS ★★½
YOUNG ADULTS ★★½		OVER 30 ★★★	SENIORS ★★½

What it is Disneyfied midway ride. **Scope and scale** Minor attraction. **When to go** Before 10 a.m. or after 9 p.m. **Authors' rating** Disney's signature ride for children; ★★★. **Duration of ride** 1½ minutes. **Average wait in line per 100 people ahead of you** 20 minutes. **Loading speed** Slow.

DESCRIPTION AND COMMENTS A tame, happy children's ride based on the lovable flying pachyderm. Parents and children sit inside small fiberglass "elephants" mounted on long metal arms, which spin around a central axis. Controls inside each vehicle allow you to raise the arm, making you spin higher off the ground. Despite being little different from rides at state fairs and amusement parks, Dumbo is the favorite Magic Kingdom attraction of many younger children.

As part of the Fantasyland expansion, Dumbo will move to the upper-right corner of the land. Once there, the attraction's capacity will be doubled with the addition of a second ride—a clone of the first. "Double Dumbo" will also include a covered queue featuring interactive elements (read: things your kids can play with to pass the time in line). Disney hasn't said whether it's going to move the existing ride or just build two entirely new sets of ride vehicles; if the latter turns out to be true, the old ride can continue to run in its current location while the other is being assembled.

TOURING TIPS If Dumbo is essential to your child's happiness, make it your first stop, preferably within 15 minutes of park opening. If you don't make it, however, Disney is installing new games and interactive features at the new queuing area, thus helping keep your antsy ones occupied.

The Great Goofini ★★

APPEAL BY AGE	PRESCHOOL ★★★★	GRADE SCHOOL ★★★★	TEENS ★★½
YOUNG ADULTS ★★½		OVER 30 ★★★	SENIORS ★★

What it is Small roller coaster. **Scope and scale** Minor attraction. **When to go** Before 10:30 a.m., during parades, or in the evening just before the park closes. **Special comments** Must be 35" or taller to ride. **Authors' rating** Great for little ones, but not worth the wait for adults; ★★. **Duration of ride** About 53 seconds. **Average wait in line per 100 people ahead of you** 7 minutes. **Loading speed** Slow.

DESCRIPTION AND COMMENTS The Great Goofini is a very small roller coaster. Formerly known as The Barnstormer at Goofy's Wiseacre Farm, it was rethemed as part of the Fantasyland expansion, with minimal changes. The ride is zippy but super-short. In fact, of the 53 seconds the ride is in motion, 32 seconds are consumed in leaving the loading area, being ratcheted up the first hill, and braking into the off-loading area. The actual time you spend careering around the track is 21 seconds.

The Great Goofini is a fairly benign introduction to the roller-coaster genre and a predictably positive way to help your children step up to more adventuresome rides. Simply put, a few circuits on Goofini will increase your little one's confidence and improve his or her chances for enjoying Disney's more adult attractions. As always, be sensitive and encouraging, but respect your child's decision whether or not to ride.

TOURING TIPS The cars of this dinky coaster are too small for most adults and tend to whiplash taller people. This, plus the limited capacity, equals an engineering marvel along the lines of Dumbo. Parties without children should skip this one. If you're touring with children, you have a problem: like Dumbo, the ride is visually appealing, and all kids want to ride, subjecting the whole family to slow-moving lines. If Goofini is high on your children's hit parade, try to ride as soon as Fantasyland opens.

It's a Small World   ★★★

APPEAL BY AGE	PRESCHOOL ★★★★½	GRADE SCHOOL ★★★★	TEENS ★★★
YOUNG ADULTS ★★★	OVER 30 ★★★½	SENIORS ★★★★	

What it is World-brotherhood-themed indoor boat ride. **Scope and scale** Major attraction. **When to go** Anytime. **Authors' rating** Exponentially cute; ★★★. **Duration of ride** Approximately 11 minutes. **Average wait in line per 100 people ahead of you** 11 minutes; assumes busy conditions with 30 or more boats operating. **Loading speed** Fast.

DESCRIPTION AND COMMENTS Small World is a happy, upbeat indoor attraction with a mind-numbing tune that only a backhoe can remove from your brain. Small boats carry visitors on a tour around the world, with singing and dancing dolls showcasing the dress and culture of each nation. One of Disney's oldest entertainment offerings, It's a Small World first unleashed its brainwashing song and lethally cute ethnic dolls on the real world at the 1964 New York World's Fair. Though it bludgeons you with its sappy redundancy, almost everyone enjoys It's a Small World (at least the first time). It stands, however, along with the *Enchanted Tiki Room* in the "What were they smokin'?" category.

TOURING TIPS Cool off here during the heat of the day. With two waiting lines, It's a Small World loads fast and usually is a good bet between 11 a.m. and 5 p.m. If you wear a hearing aid, turn it off.

Mad Tea Party ★★

APPEAL BY AGE	PRESCHOOL ★★★★	GRADE SCHOOL ★★★★	TEENS ★★★★
YOUNG ADULTS ★★★		OVER 30 ★★★	SENIORS ★★

What it is Midway-type spinning ride. **Scope and scale** Minor attraction. **When to go** Before 11 a.m. or after 5 p.m. **Special comments** You can make the teacups spin faster by turning the wheel in the center of the cup. **Authors' rating** Fun but not worth the wait; ★★. **Duration of ride** 1½ minutes. **Average wait in line per 100 people ahead of you** 7½ minutes. **Loading speed** Slow.

Motion Sickness

DESCRIPTION AND COMMENTS Riders whirl feverishly in big teacups. Alice in Wonderland's Mad Hatter provides the theme. A version of this ride without Disney characters can be found at every local carnival. Teenagers like to lure adults onto the teacups, then turn the wheel in the middle (making the cup spin faster), until the adults are plastered against the sides and on the verge of throwing up. Unless your life's ambition is to be the test subject in a human centrifuge, don't even consider getting on this ride with anyone younger than 21.

TOURING TIPS This ride, well done but not unique, is notoriously slow-loading. Skip it on a busy schedule—if the kids will let you. Ride the morning of your second day if your schedule is more relaxed.

The Many Adventures of Winnie the Pooh ★★★½
(Fastpass)

APPEAL BY AGE   PRESCHOOL ★★★★½   GRADE SCHOOL ★★★★   TEENS ★★★
YOUNG ADULTS ★★★   OVER 30 ★★★½   SENIORS ★★★½

What it is Indoor track ride. **Scope and scale** Minor attraction. **When to go** Before 10 a.m., in the 2 hours before closing, or use Fastpass. **Authors' rating** Cute as the Pooh Bear himself; ★★★½. **Duration of ride** About 4 minutes. **Average wait in line per 100 people ahead of you** 4 minutes. **Loading speed** Moderate.

DESCRIPTION AND COMMENTS Opened in the summer of 1998, this addition to Fantasyland replaced the alternately praised and maligned Mr. Toad's Wild Ride (Toadsters are still p.o.'d). Pooh is sunny, upbeat, and fun—more in the image of Peter Pan's Flight or Splash Mountain. You ride a "Hunny Pot" through the pages of a huge picture book into the Hundred Acre Wood, where you encounter Pooh, Piglet, Eeyore, Owl, Rabbit, Tigger, Kanga, and Roo as they contend with a blustery day. There's even a dream sequence with Heffalumps and Woozles.

TOURING TIPS Because of its relatively small capacity, the daily allocation of Fastpasses for The Many Adventures of Winnie the Pooh is often distributed by early afternoon. For the same reason, your scheduled return time to enjoy the ride might be hours away. It's not unusual to pick up a Fastpass for Winnie the Pooh at 12:30 p.m. with a scheduled return time of 5 p.m. or later.

Mickey's PhilharMagic (Fastpass seasonally) ★★★★

APPEAL BY AGE PRESCHOOL ★★★★ GRADE SCHOOL ★★★★½ TEENS ★★★★
YOUNG ADULTS ★★★★½   OVER 30 ★★★★½   SENIORS ★★★★★

What it is 3-D movie. **Scope and scale** Major attraction. **Special comments** Not to be missed. **When to go** Before 11 a.m., during parades, or use Fastpass. **Authors' rating** A zany masterpiece; ★★★★. **Duration of presentation** About 20 minutes. **Probable waiting time** 12–30 minutes.

DESCRIPTION AND COMMENTS With *Mickey's PhilharMagic*, there is a 3-D movie attraction at each of the four Disney theme parks. The *PhilharMagic* features an odd collection of Disney characters, mixing Mickey and Donald with Simba, Ariel (from the *Little Mermaid*), as well as Jasmine and Aladdin. Presented in a theater large enough to accommodate a 150-foot-wide screen—huge by 3-D movie standards, the 3-D movie is augmented by an arsenal of special effects built into the theater. The plot involves Mickey as the conductor of the *PhilharMagic*, leaving the theater to solve a mystery. In his absence, Donald appears and attempts to take charge, with disastrous results.

The attraction is one of Disney's best 3-D efforts. Brilliantly conceived, furiously paced, and laugh-out-loud funny, *Philhar-Magic* incorporates a hit parade of Disney's most beloved characters in a production that will leave you grinning.

TOURING TIPS While the other 3-D movies are loud, in-your-face affairs, *Mickey's PhilharMagic* is much softer and cuddlier. Things still pop out of the screen, but they're really not scary. Most children are enthusiastic and astonished instead of quaking in their Crocs. You should still proceed cautiously if you have kids under age 5 in your group, but it's the rare child who is frightened. The show is very popular, but on the other hand, the theater is very large. This is a seasonal Fastpass attraction, but except on the busiest of days you shouldn't wait more than 25 minutes (usually less) without Fastpass.

Peter Pan's Flight *(Fastpass)* ★★★★

APPEAL BY AGE	PRESCHOOL ★★★★½	GRADE SCHOOL ★★★★	TEENS ★★★½
YOUNG ADULTS ★★★★	OVER 30 ★★★★		SENIORS ★★★★

What it is Indoor track ride. **Scope and scale** Minor attraction. **When to go** Before 10 a.m., or use Fastpass after 6 p.m. **Authors' rating** Nostalgic, mellow, and well done; ★★★★. **Duration of ride** A little over 3 minutes. **Average wait in line per 100 people ahead of you** 5½ minutes. **Loading speed** Moderate–slow.

DESCRIPTION AND COMMENTS Though not considered a major attraction, Peter Pan's Flight is superbly designed and absolutely delightful, with a happy theme uniting some favorite Disney characters, beautiful effects, and charming music. An indoor attraction, Peter Pan's Flight offers a relaxing ride in a "flying pirate ship" over old London and thence to Never-Never Land, where Peter saves Wendy from walking the plank and Captain Hook rehearses for *Dancing with the Stars* on the snout of the ubiquitous crocodile. Unlike some dark rides, there's nothing here that will jump out at you or frighten young children.

TOURING TIPS Because Peter Pan's Flight is very popular, count on long lines all day. Fortunately, Disney has redesigned much of the queue to run under the roof of the building, out of direct sun and rain. Ride before 10 a.m., during a parade, just before the park closes, or use Fastpass.

If you use Fastpass, pick up your pass as early in the day as possible. Sometimes Peter Pan exhausts its whole day's supply of Fastpasses by 2 p.m.

Prince Charming Regal Carrousel ★★★

APPEAL BY AGE	PRESCHOOL ★★★★	GRADE SCHOOL ★★★½	TEENS ★★
YOUNG ADULTS ★★★	OVER 30 ★★★		SENIORS ★★★

What it is Merry-go-round. **Scope and scale** Minor attraction. **When to go** Before 11 a.m. or after 8 p.m. **Special comments** Adults enjoy the beauty and nostalgia of this ride. **Authors' rating** A beautiful children's ride; ★★★. **Duration of ride** About 2 minutes. **Average wait in line per 100 people ahead of you** 5 minutes. **Loading speed** Slow.

DESCRIPTION AND COMMENTS One of the most elaborate and beautiful merry-go-rounds you'll ever see, especially when its lights are on.

TOURING TIPS Unless young children in your party insist on riding, appreciate this attraction from the sidelines. While lovely to look at, the carousel loads and unloads very slowly.

Princess Fairytale Hall *(opens 2012)* ★★

APPEAL BY AGE NOT YET OPEN

What it is Character-greeting venue. **Scope and scale** Minor attraction. **When to go** Before 10:30 a.m. or after 4 p.m. **Authors' rating** You want princesses? We got 'em! ★★. **Duration of ride** 7–10 minutes (estimated). **Average wait in line per 100 people ahead of you** 35 minutes (estimated). **Loading speed** Slow.

DESCRIPTION AND COMMENTS Scheduled to open in 2012 on the site of Snow White's Scary Adventures, Princess Fairytale Hall will be the central location for meeting Disney princesses in the Magic Kingdom. While Disney has not yet released details, we think the meet-and-greet process will work similarly to those of other Magic Kingdom character convos: The princesses will occupy a greeting room where 15–20 guests at a time are admitted. They'll be allowed to visit 7–10 minutes—long enough for a photo, an autograph, and a hug from each princess.

TOURING TIPS With all the new attractions in Fantasyland, it's possible that this one will be overlooked in the morning as guests head for the new rides. Check the line on your way out of Fantasyland to see if it's worth a quick stop.

Seven Dwarfs Mine Train *(opens 2012)* ★★

APPEAL BY AGE NOT YET OPEN

What it is Indoor/outdoor roller coaster. **Scope and scale** Major attraction. **When to go** Before 10 a.m., during parades, or in the evening. **Special comments** Height requirement (not yet available). **Authors' rating** N/A. **Duration of ride** N/A. **Average wait in line per 100 people ahead of you** N/A. **Loading speed** N/A.

DESCRIPTION AND COMMENTS The land on which the Mine Train sits was originally supposed to be character-greeting areas for Disney princesses and fairies, according to the first press release announcing the project. A legion of parents must have convinced Disney that having a land composed entirely of princesses, fairies, and amusement-park kiddie rides offered nothing to grade-school boys, however, and Disney soon announced changes. (One, the renaming of Cinderella's Golden Carrousel to Prince Charming Regal Carrousel, is laughably transparent.) The Mine Train, however, looks to appeal to the entire family. Although the attraction had not opened as we went to press, the concept art shows a set of small mine trains running through the Seven Dwarfs' workplace and around the forest above the ground. From what we can make out, the experience looks relatively tame—there are no loops, inversions, or rolls in the track, with no massive hills or steep drops. The attraction seems geared to tweens and those slightly younger.

We've also heard that the ride vehicles will "swing" back and forth around the track. We suspect this means your seats pitch left and right while your ride vehicle barrels along—making the ride's tight turns all the more fun.

TOURING TIPS Under the Sea may be the big draw, but we'd bet that the Mine Train will have longer lines throughout the day. If your vacation won't be complete without a comprehensive tour of Fantasyland, see Dumbo and the Great Goofini first, then the Mine Train and Under the Sea. We think the Mine Train will have Fastpass, in which case use it if the line exceeds 30 minutes.

Snow White's Scary Adventures ★★½

APPEAL BY AGE PRESCHOOL ★★★ GRADE SCHOOL ★★★ TEENS ★★★ YOUNG ADULTS ★★★ OVER 30 ★★★ SENIORS ★★★

What it is Indoor track ride. **Scope and scale** Minor attraction. **When to go** Before 11 a.m. or after 6 p.m. **Special comments** Terrifying to many young children. **Authors' rating** Worth seeing if the wait isn't long; ★★½. **Duration of ride** Almost 2½ minutes. **Average wait in line per 100 people ahead of you** 6¼ minutes. **Loading speed** Moderate–slow.

DESCRIPTION AND COMMENTS Mine cars travel through a spook house showing Snow White as she narrowly escapes harm at the hands of the wicked witch. Action and effects are not as good as Peter Pan's Flight or Winnie the Pooh.

The ride is scheduled for demolition as part of the Fantasyland expansion, to be replaced by Princess Fairytale Hall, a Disney-princess meet-and-greet area (see previous page). We don't yet know when Snow White will be gone for good, so we've left the description here for now.

TOURING TIPS *Parents, take note:* This attraction scares the bejeepers out of many children age 6 and younger. Though a 1994 upgrade gave Snow White a larger role, the witch (who is relentless and ubiquitous) continues to be the focal character. Many readers tell us their children have refused to ride any attraction that operates in the dark after having experienced Snow White's Scary Adventures.

Ride Snow White if lines aren't too long or on a second day at the theme park.

Under the Sea: Journey of the Little Mermaid (*opens 2012*)

APPEAL BY AGE   NOT YET OPEN

What it is Indoor dark ride retelling the film's story. **Scope and scale** Major attraction. **When to go** Before 11 a.m., during parades, or in the evening. **Authors' rating** N/A. **Duration of ride** About 5½ minutes. **Average wait in line per 100 people ahead of you** 3 minutes. **Loading speed** Fast.

DESCRIPTION AND COMMENTS The centerpiece of the Fantasyland expansion, Under the Sea takes riders through almost a dozen scenes retelling the story of *The Little Mermaid,* this time with audioanimatronics, video effects, and a vibrant 3-D set the size of a small theater.

Guests board a clamshell-shaped ride vehicle running along a continuously moving track (similar to The Haunted Mansion's). Then the ride "descends" under water, past Ariel's grotto and on to King Triton's undersea kingdom. The detailed animatronics include Ariel, a school of singing lobsters, octopi, and a conga line of cod. Other scenes hit the film's highlights, including Ariel meeting Prince Eric, her deal with Ursula to become human, and, of course, the couple's happy ending.

TOURING TIPS We estimate that Under the Sea will have a capacity of around 2,000 riders per hour, making it one of the most efficient attractions in the Magic Kingdom. Disney is so sure of its ability to move guests that it isn't making Under the Sea a Fastpass attraction. While we expect long lines in the first few months the attraction is open, the attraction's sheer capacity means that early mornings, after dinner, and evening Extra Magic Hours should afford shorter waits.

Walt Disney World Railroad

DESCRIPTION AND COMMENTS Stops in Fantasyland on its circle tour of the park. See the description under Main Street, U.S.A. (page 127), for additional details.

TOURING TIPS Pleasant, feet-saving link to Main Street and Frontierland . . . but so crowded in the afternoon during times of peak attendance that you'll almost certainly find it faster to walk anywhere in the park.

◄█I TOMORROWLAND

TOMORROWLAND IS A MIX OF rides and experiences relating to technological development and what life will be like in the future. If this sounds like Epcot's theme, it's because Tomorrowland was a breeding ground for ideas that spawned Epcot. Yet, Tomorrowland and Epcot are very different in more than scale. Epcot is more educational. Tomorrowland is more for fun, depicting the future as envisioned in science fiction.

Exhaustive renovation of Tomorrowland was completed in 1995. Before refurbishing, Tomorrowland's 24-year-old buildings resembled 1970s motels more than anyone's vision of the future. The current design is ageless, revealing the future as imagined by dreamers and scientists in the 1920s and 1930s. Today's Tomorrowland conjures visions of Buck Rogers, fanciful mechanical rockets, and metallic cities spread beneath towering obelisks. Disney calls the renovated Tomorrowland the "Future That Never Was," while *Newsweek* dubbed it "retro-future."

Astro Orbiter ★★

APPEAL BY AGE	PRESCHOOL ★★★½	GRADE SCHOOL ★★★½	TEENS ★★★
YOUNG ADULTS ★★		OVER 30 ★★½	SENIORS ★

Motion Sickness

What it is Buck Rogers–style rockets revolving around a central axis. **Scope and scale** Minor attraction. **When to go** Before 11 a.m. or after 5 p.m. **Special comments** This attraction is not as innocuous as it appears. **Authors' rating** Not worth the wait; ★★. **Duration of ride** 1½ minutes. **Average wait in line per 100 people ahead of you** 13½ minutes. **Loading speed** Slow.

DESCRIPTION AND COMMENTS Though visually appealing, the Astro Orbiter is still a slow-loading carnival ride. The fat little rocket ships simply fly in circles. The best thing about the Astro Orbiter is the nice view when you're aloft.

TOURING TIPS Expendable on any schedule. If you ride with preschoolers, seat them first, then board. The Astro Orbiter flies higher and faster than Dumbo and frightens some young children. It also apparently messes with some adults.

Buzz Lightyear's Space Ranger Spin *(Fastpass)* ★★★★

APPEAL BY AGE	PRESCHOOL ★★★★	GRADE SCHOOL ★★★★½	TEENS ★★★★
YOUNG ADULTS ★★★★		OVER 30 ★★★★	SENIORS ★★★★

What it is Whimsical space travel–themed indoor ride. **Scope and scale** Minor attraction. **When to go** Before 10:30 a.m., after 6 p.m., or use Fastpass. **Authors' rating** Surreal shooting gallery; ★★★★. **Duration of ride** About 4½ minutes. **Average wait in line per 100 people ahead of you** 3 minutes. **Loading speed** Fast.

DESCRIPTION AND COMMENTS This attraction is based on the space-commando character of Buzz Lightyear from the film *Toy Story*. The marginal story line has you and Buzz Lightyear trying to save the universe from the evil Emperor Zurg. The indoor ride is interactive to the extent that you can spin your car and shoot simulated "laser cannons" at Zurg and his minions.

TOURING TIPS Each car is equipped with two laser cannons and a scorekeeping display. Each scorekeeping display is independent, so you can compete with your riding partner. A joystick allows you to spin the car to line up the various targets. Each time you pull the trigger you'll release a red laser beam that you can see hitting or missing the target. Most folks' first ride is occupied with learning how to use the equipment (fire off individual shots as opposed to keeping the trigger depressed) and figuring out how the targets work. The next ride (like certain potato chips, one is not enough), you'll surprise yourself by how much better you do. *Unofficial* readers are unanimous in their praise of Buzz Lightyear. Some, in fact, spend several hours on it, riding again and again.

Experience Buzz Lightyear after riding Space Mountain first thing in the morning or use Fastpass.

Monsters, Inc. Laugh Floor   ★★★½

APPEAL BY AGE	PRESCHOOL ★★★½	GRADE SCHOOL ★★★★½	TEENS ★★★★★
YOUNG ADULTS ★★★★★	OVER 30 ★★★★		SENIORS ★★★★★

What it is Interactive animated comedy routine. **Scope and scale** Major attraction. **When to go** Before 11 a.m. or after 4 p.m. **Authors' rating** Good concept, but jokes are hit-or-miss; ★★★½. **Duration of presentation** About 15 minutes.

DESCRIPTION AND COMMENTS We learned in Disney/Pixar's *Monsters, Inc.* that children's screams could be converted into electricity, which was used to power a town inhabited by monsters. During the film, the monsters discovered that children's laughter was an even better source of energy. In this attraction, the monsters have set up a comedy club to capture as many laughs as possible. Mike Wazowski, the one-eyed character from the film, emcees the club's three comedy acts. Each consists of an animated monster (most not seen in the film) trying out various bad puns, knock-knock jokes, and Abbott and Costello–like routines. Using the same cutting-edge technology as Epcot's popular *Turtle Talk with Crush,* behind-the-scenes

Disney cast members voice the characters and often interact with audience members during the skits. Disney has shown a willingness to try new routines and jokes, so the show should remain fresh to repeat visitors.

TOURING TIPS The theater holds several hundred people, so there's no need to rush here first thing in the morning. Try to arrive late in the morning after you've visited other Tomorrowland attractions, or after the afternoon parade when guests start leaving the park.

Space Mountain *(Fastpass)*   ★★★★

APPEAL BY AGE	PRESCHOOL ★★½†	GRADE SCHOOL ★★★★½	TEENS ★★★★½
YOUNG ADULTS ★★★★½		OVER 30 ★★★★½	SENIORS ★★★

†*Some preschoolers love Space Mountain; others are frightened by it.*

What it is Roller coaster in the dark. **Scope and scale** Super-headliner. **When to go** When the park opens, between 6 and 7 p.m., during the hour before closing, or use Fastpass. **Special comments** Great fun and action; much wilder than Big Thunder Mountain Railroad. 44" minimum height requirement; children younger than age 7 must be accompanied by an adult. Switching-off option provided (see page 75). **Authors' rating** An unusual roller coaster with excellent special effects; not to be missed; ★★★★. **Duration of ride** Almost 3 minutes. **Average wait in line per 100 people ahead of you** 3 minutes; assumes 2 tracks, with 1 dedicated to Fastpass riders, dispatching at 21-second intervals. **Loading speed** Moderate–fast.

Motion Sickness

DESCRIPTION AND COMMENTS Totally enclosed in a mammoth futuristic structure, Space Mountain has always been the Magic Kingdom's most popular attraction. The theme is a space flight through dark recesses of the galaxy. Effects are superb, and the ride is the fastest and wildest in the Magic Kingdom. As a roller coaster, Space Mountain is much zippier than Big Thunder Mountain Railroad, but much tamer than the Rock 'n' Roller Coaster at Disney's Hollywood Studios or Expedition Everest at Disney's Animal Kingdom.

Refurbished in 2009, Space Mountain got larger ride vehicles, new lighting and effects, an improved sound system, and a completely redesigned queuing area with interactive games to help pass the time in line. The track was replaced as well but retains the same paths as the old. Then in 2010, a soundtrack was added to the ride that accented high-octane music with sounds of speeding rockets ships and other intergalactic occurrences. It is difficult to know if it's just because of hearing asteroids whiz past your vehicle, but we think the new ride is slightly faster than it was. Roller-coaster aficionados will tell you (correctly) that Space Mountain is a designer version of the Wild Mouse, a midway ride that's been around for at least 50 years. There are no long drops or swooping hills as there are on a traditional roller coaster—only quick, unexpected turns and small drops. Disney's contribution essentially was to add a space theme to the Wild Mouse and put it in the dark. And this does indeed make the Mouse seem wilder.

TOURING TIPS People who can handle a fairly wild roller-coaster ride will take Space Mountain in stride. What sets Space Mountain apart is that cars plummet through darkness, with only occasional lighting. Half the fun of Space Mountain is not knowing where the car will go next.

Space Mountain is a favorite of many Magic Kingdom visitors ages 7–60. Each morning before opening, particularly during summer and holiday periods, several hundred Space Mountain "junkies" crowd the rope barriers at the Central Plaza, awaiting the signal to head to the ride's entrance. To get ahead of the competition, be one of the first in the park. Proceed to the end of Main Street and wait at the entrance to Tomorrowland.

Couples touring with children too small to ride Space Mountain can both ride without waiting twice in line by taking advantage of "switching off." Here's how it works: When you enter the Space Mountain line, tell the first Disney attendant (Greeter One) that you want to switch off. The attendant will allow you, your spouse, and your small child (or children) to continue together, phoning ahead to tell Greeter Two to expect you. When you reach Greeter Two (at the turnstile near the boarding area), you'll be given specific directions. One of you will proceed to ride, while the other stays with the kids. Whoever rides will be admitted by the unloading attendant to stairs leading back up to the boarding area. Here you switch off. The second parent rides, and the first parent takes the kids down the stairs to the unloading area where everybody is reunited and exits together. Switching off is also available at Big Thunder Mountain Railroad and Splash Mountain, and for Fastpass users.

Seats are one behind another, as opposed to side by side. Parents whose children meet the height and age requirements for Space Mountain can't sit next to their kids.

If you don't catch Space Mountain first in the morning, use Fastpass or try again during the hour before closing. Often, would-be riders are held in line outside the entrance until all those previously in line have ridden, thus emptying the attraction. The appearance from the outside is that the line is enormous when, in fact, the only people waiting are those visible. This crowd-control technique, known as "stacking," discourages visitors from getting in line. Stacking is used at several Disney rides and attractions during the hour before closing to ensure that the ride will be able to close on schedule. It is also used to keep the number of people who are waiting inside from overwhelming the air-conditioning. Despite the apparently long line, the wait is usually no longer than if you had been allowed to queue inside.

Stitch's Great Escape!   ★★

APPEAL BY AGE PRESCHOOL ★½   GRADE SCHOOL ★★½   TEENS ★★½
YOUNG ADULTS ★★   OVER 30 ★★   SENIORS ★½

What it is Theater-in-the-round sci-fi adventure show. **Scope and scale** Major attraction. **When to go** Before 11 a.m. or after 6 p.m.; try during parades. **Special comments** Frightens children of all ages. 40" minimum height requirement. **Authors' rating** A cheap coat of paint on a broken car; ★★. **Duration of presentation** About 12 minutes. **Preshow entertainment** About 6 minutes. **Probable waiting time** 12–35 minutes.

DESCRIPTION AND COMMENTS *Stitch's Great Escape!* is a virtual clone of the oft-maligned *Alien Encounter* attraction. Same theater, same teleportation theme, but this time starring the havoc-wreaking little alien from the feature film *Lilo & Stitch*. In *Great Escape,* Stitch is a prisoner of the galactic authorities and is being transferred to a processing facility en route to his final place of incarceration. He manages to escape by employing an efficient though gross trick, knocking out power to the facility in the process. At this juncture Stitch lumbers around in the dark in much the same way as the theater's previous resident Alien. One wonders why an alien civilization smart enough to master teleportation hasn't yet invented a backup power source.

The pitch-black darkness in the ride was changed to dim lighting and several scenes have been reworked in an attempt to make it less frightening. Even these measures may not have been enough, as Disney has raised the height requirement from 35 inches to 40 inches (the same as Big Thunder Mountain Railroad) in an attempt to keep out smaller children. The fact that Big Thunder is a roller coaster and this ride doesn't move should be a warning to parents about its fright potential. In our opinion, tinkering at the margins will be futile when it comes to resuscitating this puppy. We think Disney will keep *Stitch* around only long enough to save face.

TOURING TIPS Disney's press release touting *Stitch* as a child-friendly attraction was about as accurate as Enron's book-keeping. As in *Alien Encounter,* you're held in your seat by overhead restraints and subjected to something weird clambering around you and whispering to you in a theater darker than a stack of black cats. The *Stitch* version is perhaps slightly less frightening to small children than *Alien Encounter,* but more than enough to scare the pants off many kids ages 6 and younger. *Parents, take note:* The overhead restraints will prevent you from leaving your seat to comfort your child if the need arises.

Tomorrowland Speedway ★★

APPEAL BY AGE PRESCHOOL ★★★★ GRADE SCHOOL ★★★★ TEENS ★★★½
YOUNG ADULTS ★★★★   OVER 30 ★★½   SENIORS ★★★★

What it is Drive-'em-yourself miniature cars. **Scope and scale** Major attraction. **When to go** Before 11 a.m. or after 5 p.m. **Special comments** Kids must be 54" tall to drive unassisted. **Authors' rating** Boring for adults (★★); great for preschoolers. **Duration of ride** About 4½ minutes. **Average wait in line per 100 people ahead of you** 4½ minutes; assumes 285-car turnover every 20 minutes. **Loading speed** Slow.

DESCRIPTION AND COMMENTS An elaborate miniature raceway with gasoline-powered cars that travel up to 7 mph. The raceway, with sleek cars and racing noises, is quite alluring. Unfortunately, the cars poke along on a guide rail, leaving the driver little to do. Pretty ho-hum for most adults and teenagers. The height requirement excludes small children who would enjoy the ride.

TOURING TIPS This ride is visually appealing but definitely one adults can skip. The 9-and-under crowd, however, love it. If your child is too short to drive, ride along and allow the child to steer the car while you work the foot pedal.

The line for the Tomorrowland Indy Speedway snakes across a pedestrian bridge to the loading areas. For a shorter wait, turn right off the bridge to the first loading area (rather than continuing to the second).

Tomorrowland Transit Authority
PeopleMover ★★★

APPEAL BY AGE   PRESCHOOL ★★★★ GRADE SCHOOL ★★★½ TEENS ★★★½
YOUNG ADULTS ★★★★   OVER 30 ★★★★   SENIORS ★★★★

What it is Scenic tour of Tomorrowland. **Scope and scale** Minor attraction. **When to go** Anytime, but especially during hot, crowded times of day (11:30 a.m.–4:30 p.m.). **Special comments** A good way to check out the Fastpass line at Space Mountain. **Authors' rating** Scenic and relaxing; ★★★. **Duration of ride** 10 minutes. **Average wait in line per 100 people ahead of you** 1½ minutes; assumes 39 trains operating. **Loading speed** Fast.

DESCRIPTION AND COMMENTS A once-unique prototype of a linear-induction-powered mass-transit system, the PeopleMover's tramlike cars carry riders on a leisurely tour of Tomorrowland, including a peek inside Space Mountain. In ancient times, the attraction was called the WEDway PeopleMover ("WED" being the initials of one Walter Elias Disney).

TOURING TIPS A relaxing ride where lines move quickly and you seldom have to wait. It's a good choice during busier times of day.

Walt Disney's Carousel of Progress ★★★

APPEAL BY AGE	PRESCHOOL ★★★	GRADE SCHOOL ★★★	TEENS ★★★
YOUNG ADULTS ★★★½		OVER 30 ★★★½	SENIORS ★★★★

What it is Audioanimatronic theater production. **Scope and scale** Major attraction. **When to go** Anytime. **Authors' rating** Nostalgic, warm, and happy; ★★★. **Duration of presentation** 18 minutes. **Preshow entertainment** Documentary on the attraction's long history. **Probable waiting time** Less than 10 minutes.

DESCRIPTION AND COMMENTS Updated and improved during the Tomorrowland renovation, *Walt Disney's Carousel of Progress* offers a nostalgic look at how technology and electricity have changed the lives of an audioanimatronic family over several generations. The family is easy to identify with, and a cheerful, sentimental tune bridges the generations.

TOURING TIPS This attraction is a great favorite among repeat visitors and is included on all of our one-day touring plans. *The Carousel* handles big crowds effectively and is a good choice during busier times of day.

LIVE ENTERTAINMENT *in* the MAGIC KINGDOM

FOR SPECIFIC EVENTS THE DAY YOU VISIT, check the live-entertainment schedule in your Disney guide map (free as you enter the park or at City Hall) or the *Times Guide*, available along with the guide map.

Our one-day touring plans exclude live performances in favor of seeing as much of the park as time permits. This tactical decision is based on the fact that some parades and performances siphon crowds away from the more popular rides, thus shortening lines. Nonetheless, the color and pageantry of live events are integral to the Magic Kingdom and a persuasive argument for a second day of touring. Here's a list and description of some performances and events.

BAY LAKE AND SEVEN SEAS LAGOON FLOATING ELECTRICAL PAGEANT Usually performed at nightfall (9 p.m. at the Polynesian Resort, 9:15 at the Grand Floridian, and 10:15 at the Contemporary Resort) on Seven Seas Lagoon and Bay Lake, this is a stunning electric-light show aboard small barges and set to electronic music. Take the monorail to the Contemporary, Grand Floridian, or Polynesian.

CAPTAIN JACK SPARROW'S PIRATE TUTORIAL Meet the legendary pirate and his crew in Adventureland. Check the *Times Guide* for schedules.

CASTLE FORECOURT STAGE A 20-minute show called *Dream-Along with Mickey* is built around the premise that—*quelle horreur!*—Donald doesn't believe in the power of dreams. Crisis is averted through a frenetic whirlwind of song and dance. The show is performed several times a day according to the season, with showtimes listed in the *Times Guide*.

DISNEY CHARACTER SHOWS AND APPEARANCES Most days, a character is on duty for photos and autographs from 9 a.m. to 10 p.m. next to City Hall. Mickey and Minnie (and, for a time, the Disney princesses) can be found in the Town Square Theater, to the right as you enter the park. Your best bet is to check the daily *Times Guide* for character-greeting locations and times..

ENCHANTED TALES WITH BELLE (OPENS 2012) Disney hasn't promoted this interactive storytelling session as much as other parts of the Fantasyland expansion, but something similar was held in another part of Fantasyland for years. Belle and several helpers would select children from the audience and dress them as characters from *Beauty and the Beast*. As Belle would tell the story, the children would act out the roles. Photo and autograph opportunities would follow. We expect Disney to retain many of these details when Enchanted Tales opens near Beast's Castle in 2012.

FANTASYLAND PAVILION Site of various concerts.

FLAG RETREAT At 4:45 p.m. daily at Town Square (Walt Disney World Railroad end of Main Street). Sometimes performed with large college marching bands, sometimes with a smaller Disney band.

MAGIC KINGDOM BANDS Banjo, Dixieland, steel drum, marching, and fife-and-drum bands roam the park.

THE MAGIC, THE MEMORIES AND YOU! In one of the most imaginative shows yet, videos and photos of guests in the park are set to music and projected nightly on Cinderella Castle. The special effects are tremendous—in one vignette, the entire castle appears to shimmer and sway; in another, flames appear throughout the castle's windows to emulate a scene from the Pirates of the Caribbean ride. Throughout the show, images of guests who visited the park that day are displayed. We rate this as not to be missed.

MOVE IT! SHAKE IT! CELEBRATE IT! PARADE Starting at the train-station end of Main Street, U.S.A., and working toward the Central Plaza, this short walk incorporates around a dozen guests with a handful of floats, Disney characters, and entertainers. Music is provided by one of Disney's latest artists (Miley Cyrus currently), and there's a good amount of interaction between the entertainers and the crowd.

TINKER BELL'S FLIGHT This nice special effect in the sky above Cinderella Castle heralds the beginning of *Wishes* fireworks (when the park is open late).

WISHES FIREWORKS SHOW Memorable vignettes and music from beloved Disney films combine with a stellar fireworks display while Jiminy Cricket narrates a lump-in-your-throat story about making wishes come true. For an uncluttered view and lighter crowds, watch from the end of Main Street between The Plaza Restaurant and Tomorrowland Terrace. Another good viewing area is the second story of the Main Street railroad station. The spot we'd previously recommended, in the Tomorrowland Terrace area, was apparently so good that Disney decided they could charge for it. To view *Wishes* from this location now costs $27.68 per adult and $14.90 per child. The viewing comes with a dessert buffet and nonalcoholic beverages. Reservations can be made 180 days in advance by calling ☎ 407-WDW-DINE (939-3463).

WISHES FIREWORKS CRUISE For a different view, you can watch the fireworks from Seven Seas Lagoon aboard a chartered pontoon boat. The charter costs $346 and accommodates up to 10 people. Chips, soda, and water are provided; sandwiches and more-substantial food items may be arranged through reservations. Your Disney captain will take you for a little cruise and then position the boat in a perfect place to watch the fireworks. Because this is a private charter rather than a tour, only your group will be aboard. Life jackets are provided, but wearing them is at your discretion. To reserve a charter, call ☎ 407-WDW-PLAY (939-7529) at exactly 7 a.m. about 180 days before the day you want to cruise. We recommend phoning about 95 days out to have a Disney agent specify the morning to call for reservations.

PARADES

PARADES AT THE MAGIC KINGDOM ARE full-fledged spectaculars with dozens of Disney characters and amazing special effects. We rate the afternoon parade as outstanding and the evening parade as not to be missed.

In addition to providing great entertainment, parades lure guests away from the attractions. If getting on rides appeals to you more than watching a parade, you'll find substantially shorter lines just before and during parades. Because the parade route doesn't pass through Adventureland, Tomorrowland, or Fantasyland, attractions in these lands are particularly good bets. Be forewarned: parades disrupt traffic in the Magic Kingdom. It's nearly impossible, for example, to get to Adventureland from Tomorrowland, or vice versa, during one.

unofficial **TIP**
Be advised that the Walt Disney World Railroad shuts down during parades, making it impossible to access other lands by train.

AFTERNOON PARADE

USUALLY STAGED AT 3 P.M., THE PARADE features bands, floats, and marching Disney characters. A new afternoon parade is introduced every year or two. While some elements, such as Disney characters, remain constant, the theme, music, and float design change. Seasonal parades during major holidays round out the mix.

EVENING PARADE(S)

THE EVENING PARADE IS A HIGH-TECH AFFAIR employing electroluminescent and fiber-optic technologies, light-spreading thermoplastics (don't try this at home!), and clouds of underlit liquid-nitrogen smoke. Don't worry, you won't need a gas mask or lead underwear to watch. The parade also offers music, Mickey Mouse, and twinkling lights. The evening parade is staged once or twice each evening, depending on the time of year. During less busy times of year, the evening parade is held only on weekends, and sometimes not even then. We rate it as not to be missed.

The **Main Street Electrical Parade** returned to the Magic Kingdom in 2010 after running there from 1977 to 1991. It replaces—temporarily, we hear—the popular SpectroMagic parade. There's no word on how long the Electrical Parade will last in its current run, but the soundtrack, a synthesizer-tinged ode to country music, is a classic. In our opinion, the Magic Kingdom's nighttime parade is always the best in Walt Disney World, and the Electrical Parade is the standard against which everything else is judged. If you're at Disney World while the parade is running, make a special trip to see it.

PARADE ROUTE AND VANTAGE POINTS

MAGIC KINGDOM PARADES CIRCLE TOWN SQUARE, head down Main Street, go around the Central Plaza, and cross the bridge to Liberty Square. In Liberty Square, they follow the waterfront and end in Frontierland. Sometimes they begin in Frontierland and run the route in the opposite direction. Most guests watch from the Central Plaza, or from Main Street. One of the best and most popular vantage points is the upper platform of the Walt Disney World Railroad station at the Town Square end of Main Street. Problem is, you have to stake out your position 30–45 minutes before the events begin.

Because most spectators pack Main Street and the Central Plaza, we recommend watching the parade from Liberty Square or Frontierland. Great vantage points frequently overlooked are as follows:

1. Sleepy Hollow snack-and-beverage shop, immediately to your right as you cross the bridge into Liberty Square. You'll have a perfect view of the parade as it crosses Liberty Square Bridge, but only when the parade begins on Main Street.

2. The pathway on the Liberty Square side of the moat from Sleepy Hollow snack-and-beverage shop to Cinderella Castle. Any point along this path offers a clear and unobstructed view as the parade crosses Liberty Square Bridge. Once again, this spot works only for parades coming from Main Street.

3. The covered walkway between Liberty Tree Tavern and The Diamond Horseshoe Saloon. This elevated vantage point is perfect (particularly on rainy days).

4. Elevated wooden platforms in front of the Frontierland Shootin' Arcade, Frontier Trading Post, and the building with the sign reading FRONTIER MERCANTILE. These spots usually get picked off 10–12 minutes before parade time.

5. Benches on the perimeter of the Central Plaza, between the entrances to Liberty Square and Adventureland.

Usually unoccupied until after the parade begins, they offer a comfortable resting place and unobstructed (though somewhat distant) view of the parade as it crosses Liberty Square Bridge.

6. Liberty Square and Frontierland dockside areas.

7. The elevated porch of Tony's Town Square Restaurant on Main Street provides an elevated viewing platform and an easy path to the park exit when the fireworks are over.

Assuming it starts on Main Street (evening parades normally do), the parade takes 16–20 minutes to reach Liberty Square or Frontierland. On evenings when the parade runs twice, the first parade draws a huge crowd, siphoning guests from attractions. Many folks leave the park after the early parade, with many more departing following the fireworks (which are scheduled on the hour between the two parades).

Continue to tour after the fireworks. This is a particularly good time to ride Space Mountain and enjoy attractions in Adventureland. If you're touring Adventureland and the parade begins on Main Street, you won't have to assume your viewing position in Frontierland until 15 minutes after the parade kicks off. If you watch from the Splash Mountain side of the street and head for the attraction as the last float passes, you'll be able to ride with only a couple minutes' wait.

MAGIC KINGDOM TOURING PLANS

OUR STEP-BY-STEP TOURING PLANS ARE field-tested for seeing *as much as possible* in one day with a minimum of time wasted in lines. They're designed to help you avoid crowds and bottlenecks on days of moderate–heavy attendance. Understand, however, that there's more to see in the Magic Kingdom than can be experienced in one day. Since we first began covering the Magic Kingdom, four headliner attractions and an entire new land have been added. Today, even if you could experience every attraction without any wait, it would still be virtually impossible to see all of the park in a single day.

On days of lighter attendance (see "Selecting the Time of Year for Your Visit," page 12), our plans will save you time, but they won't be as critical to successful touring as on busier days. Don't worry that other people will be following the plans and render them useless. Fewer than 1 in every 350 people in the park will have been exposed to this information.

CHOOSING THE APPROPRIATE TOURING PLAN

WE PRESENT FIVE MAGIC KINGDOM TOURING PLANS:

- Magic Kingdom One-day Touring Plan for Adults
- Authors' Selective Magic Kingdom One-day Touring Plan for Adults
- Magic Kingdom One-day Touring Plan for Parents with Young Children
- Magic Kingdom Dumbo-or-Die-in-a-Day Touring Plan for Parents with Young Children
- Magic Kingdom Two-day Touring Plan

unofficial **TIP**
No matter when the park closes, our two-day plan guarantees the most efficient touring and the least time in lines.

If you have two days (or two mornings) at the Magic Kingdom, the Two-day Touring Plan is *by far* the most relaxed and efficient. The two-day plan takes advantage of early morning, when lines are short and the park hasn't filled with guests. This plan works well year-round and eliminates much of the extra walking required by the one-day plans. The plan is perfect for guests who wish to sample both the attractions and the atmosphere of the Magic Kingdom.

If you only have one day but wish to see as much as possible, use the One-day Touring Plan for Adults. It's exhausting, but it packs in the maximum. If you prefer a more relaxed visit, use the Authors' Selective One-day Touring Plan. It includes the best the park has to offer (in the author's opinion), eliminating some less impressive attractions.

If you have children younger than age 8, adopt the One-day Touring Plan for Parents with Young Children. It's a compromise, blending the preferences of younger children with those of older siblings and adults. The plan includes many children's rides in Fantasyland but omits roller coaster rides and other attractions that frighten young children or are off-limits because of height requirements. Or, use the One-day Touring Plan for Adults or the Authors' Selective One-day Touring Plan and take advantage of switching off, a technique where children accompany adults to the loading area of a ride with age and height requirements but don't board (see page 75). Switching off allows adults to enjoy the more adventuresome attractions while keeping the group together.

The Dumbo-or-Die-in-a-Day Touring Plan for Parents with Young Children is designed for parents who will withhold no sacrifice for the children. On the Dumbo-or-Die plan, adults generally stand around, sweat, wipe noses, pay for stuff, and watch the children enjoy themselves. It's great!

Two-day Touring Plan for Families with Young Children

If you have young children and are looking for a two-day itinerary, combine the Magic Kingdom One-day Touring Plan for Parents with Young Children with the second day of the Magic Kingdom Two-day Touring Plan.

Two-day Touring Plan for Early Morning Touring on Day One and Afternoon–Evening Touring on Day Two

Many of you enjoy an early start at the Magic Kingdom on one day, followed by a second day with a lazy, sleep-in morning, resuming your touring in the afternoon and/or evening. If this appeals to you, use the Magic Kingdom One-day Touring Plan for Adults or the Magic Kingdom One-Day Touring Plan for Parents with Young Children on your early day. Adhere to the touring plan for as long as feels comfortable (many folks leave after the afternoon parade). On the second day, pick up where you left off. If you intend to use Fastpass on your second day, try to arrive at the park by 1 p.m., or the Fastpasses may be gone. Customize the remaining part of the touring plan to incorporate parades, fireworks, and other live performances according to your preferences.

"NOT A TOURING PLAN" TOURING PLANS

FOR THE TYPE-B READER, these touring plans avoid detailed step-by-step strategies for saving every last minute in line. To paraphrase one of our favorite movies, they're more guidelines than actual rules. Use these to avoid the longest waits in line while having maximum flexibility to see whatever interests you in a particular part of the park.

FOR PARENTS OF SMALL CHILDREN WITH ONE DAY TO TOUR, ARRIVING AT PARK OPENING See Fantasyland first. See Frontierland and some of Adventureland, then take a midday break. Return to the park and complete your tour of Adventureland. Next see Liberty Square and Tomorrowland. End on Main Street for parades and fireworks.

FOR ADULTS WITH ONE DAY TO TOUR, ARRIVING AT PARK OPENING First see Space Mountain and Buzz Lightyear in Tomorrowland, then Fantasyland, Frontierland, Adventureland, Liberty Square, and the rest of Tomorrowland. End on Main Street for parades and fireworks.

FOR PARENTS AND ADULTS WITH TWO DAYS TO TOUR *Note:*
Day One works great for Disney resort guests on Extra
Magic Hour mornings. Start Day One in Fantasyland, then
tour Frontierland and Pirates of the Caribbean in Adventureland. Take a midday break and return to Adventureland.
Next see Liberty Square and the evening parade. See fireworks from Main Street. Begin Day Two in Tomorrowland.
See any missed Adventureland or Frontierland attractions
before leaving the park around midday.

**FOR PARENTS AND ADULTS WITH AN AFTERNOON AND A FULL
DAY** For the afternoon, get Fastpasses, if possible, for any
Frontierland and Adventureland headliners you can; save
other headliners for later in the evening. Tour Liberty
Square, Adventureland, and Frontierland, then see the eve-
ning parade and fireworks. On your full day of touring, see
Fantasyland, and Tomorrowland (use Fastpass for Space
Mountain), then catch any missed attractions from the pre-
vious afternoon.

THE SINGLE-DAY TOURING CONUNDRUM

TOURING THE MAGIC KINGDOM IN A DAY is complicated
by the fact that the premier attractions are at almost opposite
ends of the park: Splash Mountain and Big Thunder Mountain Railroad in Frontierland, Space Mountain and Buzz
Lightyear in Tomorrowland, and Under the Sea: Journey of
the Little Mermaid in the top center. It's virtually impossible
to ride all five without encountering lines at one or another. If
you ride Space Mountain and see Buzz Lightyear immediately
after the park opens, for example, you won't have much of a
wait, if any. By the time you leave Tomorrowland and hurry to
Frontierland, however, the line for Splash Mountain will be
substantial. The same situation prevails if you ride the Frontierland duo first: Splash Mountain and Big Thunder Mountain
Railroad, no problem; Space Mountain and Buzz Lightyear,
fair-sized lines. From 10 minutes after opening until just before
closing, lines are long at these headliners.

The best way to ride all five without long waits is to tour
the Magic Kingdom over two mornings: ride Space Mountain first thing one morning, then ride Buzz Lightyear; then
ride Under the Sea, Splash Mountain, and Big Thunder
Mountain first thing on the other. If you have only one day,
be present at opening time. Speed immediately to Space
Mountain, then take in Buzz Lightyear. After Buzz Lightyear, rush to Frontierland and scope out the situation at
Splash Mountain. If the posted wait time is 30 minutes or

less, go ahead and hop in line. If the wait exceeds 30 minutes, get a Fastpass for Splash Mountain, then ride Big Thunder Mountain Railroad. Save Under the Sea for last.

PRELIMINARY INSTRUCTIONS FOR ALL MAGIC KINGDOM TOURING PLANS

ON DAYS OF MODERATE–HEAVY ATTENDANCE, follow your chosen touring plan exactly, deviating only:

1. When you aren't interested in an attraction it lists. For example, the plan may tell you to go to Tomorrowland and ride Space Mountain, a roller coaster. If you don't enjoy roller coasters, skip this step and proceed to the next.

2. When you encounter a very long line at an attraction the touring plan calls for. Crowds ebb and flow at the park, and an unusually long line may have gathered at an attraction to which you're directed. For example, you arrive at The Haunted Mansion and find extremely long lines. It's possible that this is a temporary situation caused by several hundred people arriving en masse from a recently concluded performance of *The Hall of Presidents* nearby. If this is the case, skip The Haunted Mansion and go to the next step, returning later to retry The Haunted Mansion.

PARK-OPENING PROCEDURES

YOUR SUCCESS DURING YOUR FIRST HOUR of touring will be affected somewhat by the opening procedure Disney uses that day:

A. All guests are held at the turnstiles until the entire park opens (which may or may not be at the official opening time). If this happens on the day you visit, blow past Main Street and head for the first attraction on the touring plan you're following.

B. Guests are admitted to Main Street a half hour to an hour before the remaining lands open. Access to other lands will be blocked by a rope barrier at the Central Plaza end of Main Street. Once admitted, stake out a position at the rope barrier as follows:

If you're going to Frontierland first (Splash Mountain and Big Thunder Mountain Railroad), stand in front of The Crystal Palace restaurant, on the left at the Central Plaza end of Main Street. Wait next to the rope barrier blocking the walkway to Adventureland. When the rope is dropped, move quickly to Frontierland by way of Adventureland. This is also the place to line up if your first stop is Adventureland.

If you're going to Buzz Lightyear and Space Mountain first, wait at the entrance of the bridge to Tomorrowland.

Then, when the rope drops, walk quickly across into Tomorrowland.

If you're going to Fantasyland or Liberty Square first, go to the end of Main Street and line up left of center at the rope.

BEFORE YOU GO

1. Call ☎ 407-824-4321 the day before you go to check the official opening time.
2. Purchase admission before you arrive.
3. Familiarize yourself with park-opening procedures (above) and reread the touring plan you've chosen.

THE TOURING PLANS

Magic Kingdom One-day Touring Plan for Adults

FOR Adults without young children.

ASSUMES Willingness to experience all major rides (including roller coasters) and shows.

THIS PLAN REQUIRES CONSIDERABLE WALKING and some backtracking; this is necessary to avoid long lines. Extra walking plus some morning hustle will spare you 2–3 hours of standing in line. You might not complete the tour. How far you get depends on how quickly you move from ride to ride, how many times you rest or eat, how quickly the park fills, and what time the park closes.

1. Arrive at the entrance to the Magic Kingdom 50 minutes (Disney resort guests) to 70 minutes (non–Disney resort guests) prior to opening. Get guide maps and the daily entertainment schedule.
2. In Tomorrowland, ride Space Mountain.
3. Ride Buzz Lightyear.
4. In Fantasyland, ride Winnie the Pooh.
5. Ride Peter Pan's Flight.
6. Ride It's a Small World.
7. In Liberty Square, see The Haunted Mansion.
8. In Frontierland, ride Splash Mountain if wait is 20 minutes or less. If not, obtain Fastpass.
9. Ride Big Thunder Mountain Railroad.
10. In Adventureland, ride Pirates of the Caribbean.
11. If you missed it earlier, ride Splash Mountain using Fastpass.
12. Eat lunch.
13. In Adventureland, ride the Jungle Cruise if wait is 20 minutes or less. If not, obtain Fastpass.
14. See *The Enchanted Tiki Room*.

15. In Frontierland, see *Country Bear Jamboree.*
16. If you missed it earlier, take the Jungle Cruise in Adventureland using Fastpass.
17. Explore the Swiss Family Treehouse.
18. In Liberty Square, ride the *Liberty Belle* Riverboat.
19. Experience *The Hall of Presidents.*
20. In Fantasyland, see *Mickey's PhilharMagic.*
21. Ride Under the Sea: Journey of the Little Mermaid (opens 2012).
22. Eat dinner.
23. In Tomorrowland, see *Monsters, Inc. Laugh Floor.*
24. Ride the Tomorrowland Transit Authority PeopleMover.
25. See *Walt Disney's Carousel of Progress.*
26. Tour Main Street, U.S.A., and take a round-trip on the Walt Disney World Railroad, if time permits.
27. Meet any characters that interest you. Check the *Times Guide* for greeting locations and times.
28. See the evening parade on Main Street.
29. See the evening fireworks on Main Street. A good viewing spot is to the right of the Central Plaza, between The Plaza Restaurant and Tomorrowland Terrace.

Authors' Selective Magic Kingdom One-day Touring Plan for Adults

FOR Adults touring without young children.
ASSUMES Willingness to experience all major rides (including roller coasters) and shows.

THIS PLAN INCLUDES ONLY THOSE ATTRACTIONS the author believes are the best in the Magic Kingdom. It requires a lot of walking and some backtracking to avoid long lines. Extra walking and morning hustle will spare you 3 or more hours of standing in line. You might not complete the tour. How far you get depends on how quickly you move from ride to ride, how many times you rest or eat, how quickly the park fills, and what time the park closes.

1. Arrive at the entrance to the Magic Kingdom 50 minutes (Disney resort guests) to 70 minutes (non–Disney resort guests) prior to opening. Get guide maps and the daily entertainment schedule.
2. In Tomorrowland, ride Space Mountain.
3. Ride Buzz Lightyear.
4. In Fantasyland, ride Winnie the Pooh.
5. Ride Peter Pan's Flight.
6. Ride It's a Small World.
7. In Liberty Square, see The Haunted Mansion.

8. In Frontierland, ride Splash Mountain if wait is 20 minutes or less. If not, obtain Fastpass.
9. Ride Big Thunder Mountain Railroad.
10. In Adventureland, ride Pirates of the Caribbean.
11. If you missed it earlier, ride Splash Mountain using Fastpass.
12. Eat lunch.
13. In Adventureland, ride the Jungle Cruise if wait is 20 minutes or less. If not, obtain Fastpass.
14. See *The Enchanted Tiki Room.*
15. If you missed it earlier, take the Jungle Cruise in Adventureland using Fastpass.
16. Explore the Swiss Family Treehouse.
17. In Liberty Square, ride the *Liberty Belle* Riverboat.
18. Experience *The Hall of Presidents.*
19. In Fantasyland, see *Mickey's PhilharMagic.*
20. Also in Fantasyland, ride Under the Sea: Journey of the Little Mermaid (opens 2012).
21. Eat dinner.
22. In Tomorrowland, see *Monsters, Inc. Laugh Floor.*
23. See *Walt Disney's Carousel of Progress.*
24. Tour Main Street, U.S.A., and meet any characters that i nterest you. Check the daily entertainment schedule for greeting locations and times.
25. See the evening parade on Main Street.
26. See the evening fireworks on Main Street. A good viewing spot is to the right of the Central Plaza, between The Plaza Restaurant and Tomorrowland Terrace.

Magic Kingdom One-day Touring Plan for Parents with Young Children

FOR Parents with children younger than age 8.
ASSUMES Periodic stops for rest, restrooms, and refreshments.

THIS PLAN REPRESENTS A COMPROMISE between the observed tastes of adults and those of younger children. Included are many rides that children may have the opportunity to experience at fairs and amusement parks back home. Omit them if possible—these cycle-loading rides in particular often have long lines, consuming valuable touring time:

Mad Tea Party	Dumbo the Flying Elephant
The Magic Carpets of Aladdin	Prince Charming Regal Carrousel

This time could be better spent experiencing the many attractions that better demonstrate the Disney creative genius and are found only in the Magic Kingdom. Instead of this plan, try either of the one-day plans for adults and take advantage of "switching off." This allows parents and young children to enter the ride together. At the boarding area, one parent watches the children while the other rides.

Before entering the park, decide whether you will return to your hotel for a midday rest. You won't see as much, but everyone will be more relaxed and happy.

This touring plan requires a lot of walking and some backtracking to avoid long lines. A little extra walking and some morning hustle will spare you 2–3 hours of standing in line. You probably won't complete the tour. How far you get depends on how quickly you move from ride to ride, how many times you rest or eat, how quickly the park fills, and what time the park closes.

1. Arrive at the entrance to the Magic Kingdom 50 minutes (Disney resort guests) to 70 minutes (non–Disney resort guests) prior to opening. Get guide maps and the daily entertainment schedule. Rent strollers (if necessary).
2. In Fantasyland, ride Dumbo.
3. Ride Winnie the Pooh. Unless the wait exceeds 30 minutes, do not use Fastpass.
4. Ride the Seven Dwarfs Mine Train (opens 2012).
5. Ride Peter Pan's Flight. Unless the wait exceeds 30 minutes, do not use Fastpass.
6. Ride It's a Small World.
7. In Liberty Square, see The Haunted Mansion.
8. In Adventureland, take the Jungle Cruise. Obtain Fastpasses for your entire family if wait exceeds 30 minutes
9. Ride Pirates of the Caribbean.
10. In Frontierland, take the raft over to Tom Sawyer Island. Allow at least 30 minutes to explore the island.
11. Obtain Fastpasses for Splash Mountain. If the wait is 20 minutes or less, ride now instead of using Fastpass.
12. Ride train to Main Street. Leave the park for lunch and a nap.
13. Return to the park and send one member of your family to obtain Fastpasses for Buzz Lightyear.
14. See *Monsters, Inc. Laugh Floor.*
15. Explore the Swiss Family Treehouse in Adventureland.
16. If you obtained Fastpasses for Jungle Cruise earlier, ride now.
17. See *Country Bear Jamboree.*
18. Eat dinner.
19. Ride Splash Mountain using Fastpass.
20. See *Mickey's PhilharMagic* in Fantasyland.
21. Ride Under the Sea: Journey of the Little Mermaid (opens 2012).

22. Meet Mickey, Minnie, and the Disney princesses at the Town Square Theater on Main Street. Check the *Times Guide* for locations and times for other character meet-and-greets
23. Ride Buzz Lightyear using Fastpass.
24. See the evening parade on Main Street near the Central Plaza.
25. See the evening fireworks on Main Street. A good viewing spot is to the right of the Central Plaza, between The Plaza Restaurant and Tomorrowland Terrace.

TO CONVERT THIS ONE-DAY TOURING PLAN INTO A TWO-DAY TOURING PLAN Follow Steps 1–13 on Day One, skipping Step 12. Begin Day Two with Step 14, then Step 12, then Steps 16 and 15 and then 17–25. Day One works great when morning Extra Magic Hours are offered at the Magic Kingdom.

Magic Kingdom Dumbo-or-Die-in-a-Day Touring Plan for Parents with Young Children

FOR Adults compelled to devote every waking moment to the pleasure and entertainment of their young children, or rich people who are paying someone else to take their children to the theme park.

unofficial **TIP**
We strongly recommend that you break from touring and return to your hotel for a swim and a nap (even if you aren't lodging in Walt Disney World).

PREREQUISITE This plan is designed for days when the Magic Kingdom doesn't close until 9 p.m. or later.

ASSUMES Frequent stops for rest, restrooms, and refreshments.

Note: Name aside, this touring plan is not a joke. Regardless of whether you're loving, guilty, masochistic, selfless, insane, or saintly, this itinerary will provide a young child with about as perfect a day as is possible at the Magic Kingdom.

THIS PLAN IS A CONCESSION to adults determined to give their young children the ultimate Magic Kingdom experience. It addresses the preferences, needs, and desires of young children to the virtual exclusion of those of adults or older siblings. If you left the kids with a sitter yesterday or wouldn't let little Marvin eat barbecue for breakfast, this plan will expiate your guilt. It is also a wonderful itinerary if you're paying a sitter, nanny, or chauffeur to take your children to the Magic Kingdom.

1. Arrive at the entrance to the Magic Kingdom 50 minutes (Disney resort guests) to 70 minutes (non–Disney

resort guests) prior to opening. Get guide maps and the daily entertainment schedule. Rent strollers (if necessary).

2. In Fantasyland, ride Dumbo.
3. Ride Dumbo again. *Tip:* Have one parent stand in line 24 people behind the other parent and child. When first parent is done riding, hand child to second parent in line.
4. Ride Winnie the Pooh. Unless wait exceeds 30 minutes, do not use Fastpass.
5. Ride the Seven Dwarfs Mine Train (opens 2012).
6. Ride Peter Pan's Flight. Unless wait exceeds 30 minutes, do not use Fastpass.
7. In Tomorrowland, ride the Speedway.
8. Ride the Astro Orbiter.
9. Ride Buzz Lightyear. Use Fastpass if the wait exceeds 30 minutes.
10. Leave the park for lunch and a nap.
11. Return to the park and take the train to Frontierland.
12. Take the raft to Tom Sawyer Island. Allow at least 30 minutes to explore.
13. See *Country Bear Jamboree.*
14. In Liberty Square, see The Haunted Mansion.
15. In Fantasyland, ride It's a Small World.
16. See *Mickey's PhilharMagic.*
17. Ride the Prince Charming Regal Carrousel.
18. Ride Under the Sea: Journey of the Little Mermaid (opens 2012).
19. Eat dinner.
20. Meet Mickey, Minnie, and the Disney princesses at the Town Square Theater on Main Street. Check the *Times Guide* for locations and times for other character meet-and-greets.
21. In Adventureland, explore the Swiss Family Treehouse.
21. See the evening parade on Main Street.
22. See *The Enchanted Tiki Room.*
23. Ride The Magic Carpets of Aladdin.
24. Ride the Jungle Cruise.
25. Ride Pirates of the Caribbean.
26. See the evening parade on Main Street near the Central Plaza.
28. See the evening fireworks on Main Street. A good viewing spot is to the right of the Central Plaza, between The Plaza Restaurant and Tomorrowland Terrace.

TO CONVERT THIS ONE-DAY TOURING PLAN INTO A TWO-DAY TOURING PLAN Follow Steps 1–12 on Day One. Begin Day Two with Step 13, then Steps 21–24, 14–20, and 25–27. Day One works great when morning Extra Magic Hours are offered at the Magic Kingdom.

Magic Kingdom Two-day Touring Plan

FOR Parties wishing to spread their Magic Kingdom visit over two days.

ASSUMES Willingness to experience all major rides (including roller coasters) and shows.

THIS TWO-DAY TOURING PLAN takes advantage of early-morning touring. Each day, you should complete the structured part of the plan by about 4 p.m. This leaves plenty of time for live entertainment. If the park is open late (after 8 p.m.), consider returning to your hotel at midday for a swim and a nap. Eat an early dinner outside Walt Disney World and return refreshed to enjoy the park's nighttime festivities.

DAY ONE

1. Arrive at the entrance to the Magic Kingdom 50 minutes (Disney resort guests) to 70 minutes (non–Disney resort guests) prior to opening. Get guide maps and the daily entertainment schedule.
2. In Fantasyland, ride Winnie the Pooh.
3. Ride Peter Pan's Flight.
4. Ride Under the Sea: Journey of the Little Mermaid (opens 2012).
5. In Liberty Square, see The Haunted Mansion.
6. In Frontierland, obtain Fastpasses for Splash Mountain.
7. Ride Big Thunder Mountain Railroad.
8. Experience Pirates of the Caribbean in Adventureland.
9. Eat lunch.
10. Explore Tom Sawyer Island.
11. See *Country Bear Jamboree*.
12. Ride the *Liberty Belle* Riverboat.
13. See *The Hall of Presidents*.
14. In Fantasyland, see It's a Small World.
15. See *Mickey's PhilharMagic*.
16. Tour Main Street, U.S.A., and meet any characters that interest you. Check the daily entertainment schedule for greeting locations and times.
17. Shop, see live entertainment, or revisit favorite attractions.
18. See the evening parade on Main Street.
19. See the evening fireworks on Main Street. A good viewing spot is to the right of the Central Plaza, between The Plaza Restaurant and Tomorrowland Terrace.

DAY TWO

1. Arrive at the entrance to the Magic Kingdom 50 minutes (Disney resort guests) to 70 minutes (non–Disney

resort guests) prior to opening. Get guide maps and the daily entertainment schedule.

2. In Tomorrowland, ride Space Mountain.
3. Ride Buzz Lightyear. Ride again if desired.
4. If you want to reride Splash Mountain or Big Thunder Mountain Railroad, send a member of your party to obtain Fastpasses for those now.
5. Take the Jungle Cruise (use Fastpass if needed).
6. See *The Enchanted Tiki Room*.
7. In Adventureland, explore the Swiss Family Treehouse.
8. Return to Tomorrowland and see *Monsters, Inc. Laugh Floor*.
9. Ride the Tomorrowland Transit Authority PeopleMover.
10. Eat lunch.
11. See *Walt Disney's Carousel of Progress*.
12. Tour Main Street and meet any characters that interest you. Check the daily entertainment schedule for greeting locations and times.
13. Shop, see live entertainment, or revisit favorite attractions.

PART TEN

EPCOT

EDUCATION, INSPIRATION, AND CORPORATE IMAGERY are the focus at Epcot, the most adult of the Disney theme parks. Some people find the attempts at education to be superficial, while others want more entertainment and less education. Most visitors, however, find plenty of both.

Epcot is more than twice as big as either the Magic Kingdom or Disney's Hollywood Studios and, though smaller than Disney's Animal Kingdom, has more territory to be covered on foot. Epcot rarely sees the congestion so common to the Magic Kingdom, but it has lines every bit as long as those at the Jungle Cruise or Space Mountain. Visitors must come prepared to do considerable walking among attractions and a comparable amount of standing in line.

Epcot's size means you can't see it all in one day without skipping an attraction or two and giving others a cursory glance. A major difference between Epcot and the other parks, however, is that some Epcot attractions can be savored slowly or skimmed, depending on personal interests. For example, the first section of General Motors' Test Track is a thrill ride, the second a collection of walk-through exhibits. Nearly all visitors take the ride, but many people, lacking time or interest, bypass the exhibits.

OPERATING HOURS

EPCOT HAS TWO THEMED AREAS: **Future World** and **World Showcase.** Each has its own operating hours. Though schedules change throughout the year, Future World always opens before World Showcase in the morning and usually closes before World Showcase in the evening. Most of the year,

World Showcase opens 2 hours later than Future World. For exact hours during your visit, call ☎ 407-824-4321.

ARRIVING

PLAN TO ARRIVE AT THE TURNSTILES 30–40 minutes prior to official opening time. Give yourself an extra 10 minutes or so to park and make your way to the entrance.

If you are a guest at one of the Epcot resorts, it will take you about 20–30 minutes to walk from your hotel to the Future World section of Epcot via the International Gateway (back entrance of Epcot). Instead of walking, you can catch a boat from your resort to the International Gateway and walk about 8 minutes to the Future World section. To reach the front (Future World) entrance of Epcot from the resorts, take a boat from your hotel to Disney's Hollywood Studios and transfer to an Epcot bus, take a bus to Downtown Disney and transfer to an Epcot bus, or best of all, take a cab.

Arriving by car is easy. Walk or take a tram from the parking lot to the front gate. Monorail service connects Epcot with the Transportation and Ticket Center, the Magic Kingdom (transfer required), and Magic Kingdom resorts (transfer required).

unofficial **TIP**
Epcot has its own parking lot and, unlike at the Magic Kingdom, there's no need to take a monorail or ferry to reach the entrance.

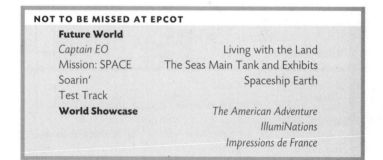

NOT TO BE MISSED AT EPCOT

Future World

Captain EO	Living with the Land
Mission: SPACE	The Seas Main Tank and Exhibits
Soarin'	Spaceship Earth
Test Track	

World Showcase

The American Adventure
IllumiNations
Impressions de France

GETTING ORIENTED

EPCOT'S THEMED AREAS ARE DISTINCTLY DIFFERENT. Future World combines Disney creativity and major corporations' technological resources to examine where mankind has come from and where it's going. World Showcase features

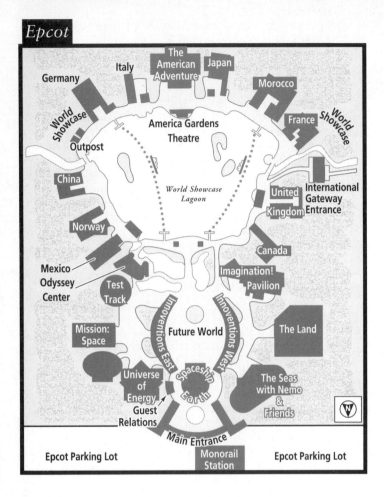

Epcot

Germany
Italy
The American Adventure
Japan
Morocco

World Showcase

Outpost

America Gardens Theatre

France

World Showcase

China

World Showcase Lagoon

United Kingdom

International Gateway Entrance

Norway

Canada

Mexico
Odyssey Center

Imagination! Pavilion

Test Track

Innoventions East
Innoventions West

Future World

The Land

Mission: Space

Universe of Energy

Spaceship Earth

The Seas with Nemo & Friends

Guest Relations

Main Entrance

Epcot Parking Lot

Monorail Station

Epcot Parking Lot

landmarks, cuisine, and culture of almost a dozen nations and is meant to be a sort of permanent World's Fair.

At Epcot, the architectural symbol is **Spaceship Earth.** This shiny, 180-foot geosphere is visible from almost everywhere in the park. Like Cinderella Castle at the Magic Kingdom, Spaceship Earth can help you keep track of where you are in Epcot. But it's in a high-traffic area and isn't centrally located, so it isn't a good meeting place.

Any of the distinctive national pavilions in World Showcase makes a good meeting place, but be specific. "Hey, let's meet in Japan!" sounds fun, but each pavilion is a mini-town with buildings, monuments, gardens, and plazas. You could wander awhile without finding your group. Pick a specific place in Japan—the sidewalk side of the pagoda, for example.

FUTURE WORLD

GLEAMING, FUTURISTIC STRUCTURES OF immense proportions define the first themed area you encounter at Epcot. Broad thoroughfares are punctuated with billowing fountains—all reflected in shining, space-age facades. Everything, including landscaping, is sparkling clean and seems bigger than life. Pavilions dedicated to mankind's past, present, and future technological accomplishments form the perimeter of Future World. Front and center is **Spaceship Earth,** flanked by **Innoventions East and West.** Most Epcot services are concentrated in Future World's Entrance Plaza, near the main gate.

FUTURE WORLD SERVICES

Baby Care Center On the World Showcase side of the Odyssey Center

Banking Services Automated tellers (ATMs) outside the main entrance, on the Future World bridge, and in World Showcase at the Germany Pavilion

Dining Reservations At Guest Relations

First Aid Next to the Baby Care Center on the World Showcase side of the Odyssey Center

Live Entertainment Information At Guest Relations, to the left of Spaceship Earth

Lost and Found At the main entrance at the gift shop

Lost Persons At Guest Relations and the Baby Care Center on the World Showcase side of the Odyssey Center

Storage Lockers Turn right at Spaceship Earth (lockers cleaned out nightly)

Walt Disney World and Local Attraction Information At Guest Relations

Wheelchair, ECV, and Stroller Rental Inside the main entrance and to the left, toward the rear of the Entrance Plaza

GUEST RELATIONS

GUEST RELATIONS, LEFT OF THE GEODESIC sphere, is Epcot's equivalent of the Magic Kingdom's City Hall. It serves as park headquarters and as Epcot's primary information center. Attendants staff information booths and take same-day Advance Reservations for Epcot restaurants. If you wish to eat in one of Epcot's sit-down restaurants, you can make your Advance Reservations at Guest Relations.

Spaceship Earth ★★★★

APPEAL BY AGE	PRESCHOOL ★★★★	GRADE SCHOOL ★★★★	TEENS ★★★★
YOUNG ADULTS ★★★★		OVER 30 ★★★★	SENIORS ★★★★½

What it is Educational dark ride through past, present, and future. **Scope and scale** Headliner. **When to go** Before 10 a.m. or after 4 p.m. **Special comments** If lines are long when you arrive, try again after 4 p.m. **Authors' rating** One of Epcot's best; not to be missed; ★★★★. **Duration of ride** About 16 minutes. **Average wait in line per 100 people ahead of you** 3 minutes. **Loading speed** Fast.

DESCRIPTION AND COMMENTS This ride spirals through the 18-story interior of Epcot's premier landmark, taking visitors past audioanimatronic scenes depicting mankind's developments in communications, from cave painting to printing to television to space communications and computer networks. The ride shows an amazing use of the geodesic sphere's interior.

    Scenes are periodically redone to keep things fresh. Interactive video screens on the ride vehicles allow you to customize the ride's ending animated video. A postshow area with games and interactive exhibits rounds out the attraction.

TOURING TIPS Because it's near Epcot's main entrance, Spaceship Earth is inundated with arriving guests throughout the morning. If you're interested in riding Test Track, postpone Spaceship Earth until, say, after 4 p.m. Spaceship Earth loads continuously and quickly. If the line runs only along the right side of the sphere, you'll board in less than 15 minutes.

Innoventions East and West ★★★½

APPEAL BY AGE	PRESCHOOL ★★★½	GRADE SCHOOL ★★★★	TEENS ★★★½
YOUNG ADULTS ★★★		OVER 30 ★★★	SENIORS ★★★

What it is Static and hands-on exhibits relating to products and technologies of the near future. **Scope and scale** Major diversion. **When to go** On your second day at Epcot or after seeing all major attractions. **Special comments** Most exhibits demand time and participation to be rewarding; not much gained here by a quick walk-through. **Authors' rating** Something for everyone; ★★★½.

DESCRIPTION AND COMMENTS Innoventions, a huge, busy collection of hands-on walk-through exhibits sponsored by corporations, consists of two huge, crescent-shaped, glass-walled structures separated by a central plaza. Dynamic, interactive, and forward-looking, the area resembles a high-tech trade show. Electronics and entertainment technology exhibits play a prominent role, as do ecology and "how things work" displays.

Our favorite attraction is Raytheon's **Sum of All Thrills,** a roller-coaster simulator in which you design the coaster track on a computer, then climb aboard a giant robotic arm to experience your creation. We've given it its own attraction review and added a step devoted to it in our Epcot touring plans.

TOURING TIPS Spend time at Innoventions on your second day at Epcot. If you have only one day, visit late if you have the time and endurance. (The one exception to this is Sum of All Thrills, which you should visit in the morning after Soarin', Test Track, and Mission: SPACE).

Although many of these productions are worthwhile, the guest capacity of each theater is so small that long lines form. Skip exhibits with waits of more than 10 minutes, or experience them first thing in the morning on your second day, when there are no lines.

Club Cool

DESCRIPTION AND COMMENTS Attached to the fountain side of Innoventions West is a retail space–soda fountain called Club Cool. It doesn't look like much, but inside, this Coca-Cola–sponsored exhibit provides free unlimited samples of soft drinks from around the world. Because it's centrally located in Future World, it makes a good meeting or break place.

Sum of All Thrills

DESCRIPTION AND COMMENTS Sum of All Thrills is a design-your-own-roller-coaster simulator in which you use a computer program to specify the drops, curves, and loops of a coaster track before boarding an industrial robotic arm to experience your creation. Three vehicle options are available: bobsled, roller coaster, and jet aircraft. It's possible to program actual loops into both the coaster and jet courses, and the robot arm will swing you upside down.

In addition to the vehicle, you also select the kinds of turns, loops, and hills in your track design. Using computer-design tools, you can further customize these components by changing the height and width of each piece as you go. *Note:* Sum of All Thrills has a 48-inch height requirement, which increases to 54 inches if your track design includes an upside-down segment.

TOURING TIPS Not a high-capacity attraction, but also not on most guests' radar. Ride as early in the morning as possible.

Universe of Energy: *Ellen's Energy Adventure* ★★★★

APPEAL BY AGE	PRESCHOOL ★★★	GRADE SCHOOL ★★★½	TEENS ★★★
YOUNG ADULTS ★★★		OVER 30 ★★★½	SENIORS ★★★½

What it is Combination ride–theater presentation about energy. **Scope and scale** Major attraction. **When to go** Before 11:15 a.m. or after 4:30 p.m. **Special comments** Don't be dismayed by long lines; 580 people enter the pavilion each time the theater changes audiences. **Authors' rating** The most unique theater in Walt Disney World; ★★★★. **Duration of presentation** About 26½ minutes. **Preshow entertainment** 8 minutes. **Probable waiting time** 20–40 minutes.

DESCRIPTION AND COMMENTS Audioanimatronic dinosaurs and the unique traveling theater make this Exxon pavilion one of Future World's most popular. Because this is a theater with a ride component, the line doesn't move while the show is in progress. When the theater empties, however, a large chunk of the line will disappear as people are admitted for the next show. Visitors are seated in what appears to be an ordinary theater while they watch a film about energy sources. Then the theater seats divide into six 97-passenger traveling cars that glide among the swamps and reptiles of a prehistoric forest. Special effects include the feel of warm, moist air from the swamp, and the smell of sulphur from an erupting volcano. The accompanying film is a humorous and upbeat flick starring Ellen DeGeneres and Bill Nye that sugarcoats the somewhat ponderous discussion of energy. Kids of all ages lose the thread during the educational segments, plus the dinosaurs frighten some preschoolers, .

TOURING TIPS This attraction draws large crowds beginning early in the morning. Because Universe of Energy can operate more than one show at a time, lines are generally tolerable.

Mission: SPACE *(Fastpass)* ★★★★

APPEAL BY AGE	PRESCHOOL ★★★	GRADE SCHOOL ★★★★	TEENS ★★★★½
YOUNG ADULTS ★★★★		OVER 30 ★★★★	SENIORS ★★★

What it is Space-flight-simulation ride. **Scope and scale** Super-headliner. **When to go** First hour the park is open, or use Fastpass. **Special comments** Not recommended for pregnant women or people prone to motion sickness or claustrophobia; 44" minimum height requirement; a gentler nonspinning version is also available. **Authors' rating** Impressive; ★★★★. **Duration of ride** About 5 minutes plus preshow. **Average wait in line per 100 people ahead of you** 4 minutes.

Motion Sickness

DESCRIPTION AND COMMENTS Mission: SPACE, among other things, is Disney's reply to all the cutting-edge attractions introduced over the past few years by crosstown rival Universal. The first truly groundbreaking Disney attraction since The Twilight Zone Tower of Terror, Mission: SPACE was one of the hottest tickets at Walt Disney World until two guests died after riding it in 2005 and 2006. While neither death was linked directly to the attraction, the negative publicity caused many guests to skip it entirely. In response, Disney added a tamer nonspinning version of Mission: SPACE in 2006.

Guests for both versions of the attraction enter the NASA Mission: SPACE Training Center, where they are introduced to the deep-space exploration program and then divided into groups for flight training. After orientation, they are strapped into space capsules for a simulated flight, where, of course, the unexpected happens. Each capsule accommodates a crew consisting of a group commander, pilot, navigator, and engineer, with a guest functioning in each role. The crew's skill and finesse (or, more often, lack thereof) in handling their respective responsibilities have no effect on the outcome of the flight. The capsules are small, and both ride versions are amazingly realistic. The nonspinning version does not subject your body to g-forces, but it does bounce and toss you around in a manner roughly comparable to other Disney motion simulators.

TOURING TIPS In minutes, Disney can reconfigure the ride's four centrifuges to either version of the attraction based on guest demand. In general, the kinder, gentler version has a wait time of about half that of its more harrowing counterpart.

Having experienced the industrial-strength version of Mission: SPACE under a variety of circumstances, we've always felt icky when riding it on an empty stomach, especially first thing in the morning. We came up with a number of potential explanations for this phenomenon, involving everything from low blood sugar and inner-ear disorders to some of us just not being astronaut material. Understandably disturbed by the latter possibility, we looked around for an expert opinion to explain what we were feeling. The number of organizations with experience studying the effects of high-g (high-gravity) forces on humans is limited to a select few: NASA, the Air Force, and Mad Tea Party cast members were the first to come to mind. As NASA is a codeveloper of Mission: SPACE, we called them. Amazingly, a spokesman told us that NASA no longer does much high-g training these days. And the agency was reluctant to pass along anything resembling medical advice to the general public.

Make a restroom stop before you get in line; you'll think your bladder has been to Mars and back for real before you get out of this attraction. Fastpass is generally needed only during times of peak attendance, and then only if you intend to ride during the middle of the day; mornings and dinner-times should have shorter waits.

TEST TRACK PAVILION

DESCRIPTION AND COMMENTS Test Track, presented by General Motors, contains the Test Track ride and Inside Track, a col-lection of transportation-themed stationary exhibits and multimedia presentations. The pavilion is the last on the left before crossing into the World Showcase.

Many readers tell us that Test Track is "one big commer-cial" for General Motors. We agree that promotional hype is more heavy-handed here than in most other business-spon-sored attractions. But Test Track is one of the most creatively conceived and executed attractions in Walt Disney World.

Test Track *(Fastpass)*   ★★★½

APPEAL BY AGE	PRESCHOOL ★★★★	GRADE SCHOOL ★★★★½	TEENS ★★★★★
YOUNG ADULTS ★★★★½		OVER 30 ★★★★½	SENIORS ★★★★

What it is Automobile test-track simulator ride. **Scope and scale** Super-headliner. **When to go** The first 30 minutes the park is open, just before closing, or use Fastpass. **Special comments** 40" height mini-mum. **Authors' rating** Not to be missed; ★★★½. **Duration of ride** About 4 minutes. **Average wait in line per 100 people ahead of you** 4½ minutes. **Loading speed** Moderate–fast.

DESCRIPTION AND COMMENTS Visitors test a future-model car at high speeds through hairpin turns, up and down steep hills, and over rough terrain. The six-guest vehicle is a motion simulator that rocks and pitches. But unlike the Star Tours simulator at Dis-ney's Hollywood Studios, for example, the Test Track model is affixed to a track and actually travels.

TOURING TIPS Great technology is at work here. Test Track is so complex, in fact, that keeping it running is a constant chal-lenge. When it works, it's one of the park's better attractions.

If you use Fastpass, be aware that the daily allocation of passes is often distributed by 12:30 or 1 p.m. If all the Fast-passes are gone, another time-saving technique is to join the singles line, a separate line for individuals who are alone or who do not object to riding alone. The objective of the singles line is to fill the odd spaces left by groups that don't fill up the ride vehicle. Because there are not many singles, and because most groups are unwilling to split up, singles lines are usually much shorter than regular lines and can save you a bunch of time if you don't mind riding by yourself.

IMAGINATION! PAVILION

DESCRIPTION AND COMMENTS Multiattraction pavilion on the west side of Innoventions West and down the walk from The Land. Outside is an "upside-down waterfall" and one of our favorite Future World landmarks, the "jumping water," a fountain that hops over the heads of unsuspecting passersby.

TOURING TIPS We recommend early-morning or late-evening touring. See the individual attractions for specifics.

Honey, I Shrunk the Audience ★★★★½
Captain EO ★★★★

APPEAL BY AGE	PRESCHOOL ★★★★½	GRADE SCHOOL ★★★★	TEENS ★★★
YOUNG ADULTS ★★	OVER 30 ★★½		SENIORS ★★

What they are 3-D films with special effects. **Scope and scale** Headliners. **When to go** Before noon or after 4 p.m. **Special comments** Adults shouldn't be put off by the sci-fi theme of either film (or rock music, for *Captain EO*). The high decibels and *Honey*'s tactile effects frighten some young children. **Authors' rating** *Honey:* An absolute hoot! Not to be missed; ★★★★½. *EO:* ★★★★. **Duration of presentation** About 17 minutes. **Preshow entertainment** 8 minutes. **Probable waiting time** 15 minutes (at suggested times).

DESCRIPTION AND COMMENTS In response to Michael Jackson's death in 2009, Disney has brought back his 3-D space-themed musical film presentation *Captain EO* for a "limited engagement" in its theme parks; at Epcot, it has temporarily supplanted *Honey, I Shrunk the Audience. Captain EO* originally ran here from 1986 to 1994; there's no telling how long it'll last on its second run, but we've heard Disney will yank the film as soon as its audience numbers begin to drop. Both films share exceptionally loud soundtracks and a propensity to frighten young kids.

HONEY, I SHRUNK THE AUDIENCE A 3-D offshoot of Disney's feature film *Honey, I Shrunk the Kids, Honey, I Shrunk the Audience* features an array of special effects, including simulated explosions, smoke, fiber optics, lights, water spray, and moving seats. This attraction is played strictly for laughs—a commodity that's in short supply when it comes to Epcot entertainment.

CAPTAIN EO The ultimate music video. Starring the late Michael Jackson and directed by Francis Ford Coppola, this 3-D space fantasy is more than a film; it's a happening. Action on the screen is augmented by lasers, fiber optics, cannons, and a host of other special effects in the theater, as well as by some audience participation. There's not much of a story, but there's plenty of music and dancing performed by some of the most unlikely creatures ever to shake a tail feather.

TOURING TIPS Shows usually begin on the hour and half hour. The sound level is earsplitting, frightening some young children. Many adults report that the loud soundtrack is distracting, even uncomfortable. While *Honey, I Shrunk the Audience* is a huge hit, it overwhelms some preschoolers.

Journey into Imagination with Figment ★★½

APPEAL BY AGE	PRESCHOOL ★★★½	GRADE SCHOOL ★★★½	TEENS ★★★
YOUNG ADULTS ★★★		OVER 30 ★★★	SENIORS ★★★

What it is Dark fantasy-adventure ride. **Scope and scale** Major-attraction wannabe. **When to go** Anytime. **Authors' rating** ★★½. **Duration of ride** About 6 minutes. **Average wait in line per 100 people ahead of you** 2 minutes. **Loading speed** Fast.

DESCRIPTION AND COMMENTS This attraction replaced its dull and vacuous predecessor in the fall of 1999 and was retooled again in 2002 to add the ever-popular purple dragon, Figment. Drawing on the Imagination Institute theme from *Honey, I Shrunk the Audience* (in the same pavilion), the attraction takes you on a tour of the zany institute. Sometimes you're a passive observer and sometimes you're a test subject as the ride provides a glimpse of the fictitious lab's inner workings. Stimulating all of your senses and then some, you are hit with optical illusions, an experiment where noise generates colors, a room that defies gravity, and other brain teasers. All along the way, Figment makes surprise appearances. After the ride, you can adjourn to an interactive exhibit area offering the latest in unique, hands-on imagery technology.

TOURING TIPS The standby wait for this attraction rarely exceeds 15 minutes. You can enjoy the interactive exhibit without taking the ride, so save it for later in the day.

THE LAND PAVILION

DESCRIPTION AND COMMENTS The Land is a huge pavilion that contains three attractions and several restaurants. Its emphasis has shifted from farming to environmental concerns.

TOURING TIPS This is a good place to grab a fast-food lunch. If you're there to see the attractions, however, don't go during mealtimes.

The Circle of Life ★★★½

APPEAL BY AGE	PRESCHOOL ★★★	GRADE SCHOOL ★★★	TEENS ★★★
YOUNG ADULTS ★★★		OVER 30 ★★★	SENIORS ★★★½

What it is Film exploring man's relationship with his environment. **Scope and scale** Minor attraction. **When to go** Before 11 a.m. or after 2 p.m. **Authors' rating** Highly interesting and enlightening; ★★★½.

Duration of presentation About 12½ minutes. **Preshow entertainment** Ecological slide show and trivia. **Probable waiting time** 10–15 minutes.

DESCRIPTION AND COMMENTS This playful yet educational film, starring Pumbaa, Simba, and Timon from *The Lion King,* spotlights the environmental interdependency of all creatures, demonstrating how easily the ecological balance can be upset. The message is sobering, but one that enlightens.

TOURING TIPS Every visitor should see this film. To stay ahead of the crowd, see it in late afternoon. Long lines usually occur at mealtimes.

Living with the Land (Fastpass seasonally)   ★★★★

APPEAL BY AGE	PRESCHOOL ★★★½	GRADE SCHOOL ★★★½	TEENS ★★★½
YOUNG ADULTS ★★★★		OVER 30 ★★★★	SENIORS ★★★★

What it is Indoor boat-ride adventure chronicling the past, present, and future of farming and agriculture in the United States. **Scope and scale** Major attraction. **When to go** Before 10:30 a.m. or after 5 p.m, or use Fastpass if available. **Special comments** Go early in the morning and save other Land attractions (except for Soarin') for later in the day. The ride is located on the pavilion's lower level. **Authors' rating** Interesting, fun, and not to be missed; ★★★★. **Duration of ride** About 12 minutes. **Average wait in line per 100 people ahead of you** 3 minutes; assumes 15 boats operating. **Loading speed** Moderate.

DESCRIPTION AND COMMENTS This boat ride takes visitors through swamps, past inhospitable farm environments, and through a futuristic greenhouse where real crops are grown using the latest agricultural technologies.

TOURING TIPS See this attraction before the lunch crowd hits The Land restaurants, or use Fastpass. If you really enjoy Living with the Land or you have a special interest in the agricultural techniques demonstrated, take the **Behind the Seeds** tour. It's a 1-hour guided walk behind the scenes that examines advanced and experimental growing methods in-depth. The tour costs $19 for adults and $15 for children ages 3–9. Reservations are made on a space-available basis at the guided-tour waiting area near the entrance to Soarin'. This tour can also be reserved in advance by calling ☎ 407-WDW-TOUR.

Soarin' (Fastpass)   ★★★★½

APPEAL BY AGE	PRESCHOOL ★★★★	GRADE SCHOOL ★★★★★	TEENS ★★★★★
YOUNG ADULTS ★★★★★		OVER 30 ★★★★★	SENIORS ★★★★★

What it is Flight-simulation ride. **Scope and scale** Super-headliner. **When to go** First 30 minutes the park is open, or use Fastpass. **Special comments** Entrance on the lower level of the Land Pavilion. May induce motion sickness; 40" minimum height requirement; switching off available (see page 75). **Authors' rating** Exciting and mellow at the same time; ★★★★½. Not to be missed. **Duration of ride** 5½ minutes. **Average wait in line per 100 people ahead of you** 4 minutes; assumes 2 concourses operating. **Loading speed** Moderate.

DESCRIPTION AND COMMENTS   Soarin' is a thrill ride for all ages, exhilarating as a hank on the wing and as mellow as swinging in a hammock. If you are fortunate enough to have experienced "flying dreams" in your sleep, you'll have a sense of how Soarin' feels.

Once you enter the main theater, you are secured in a seat not unlike those on inverted roller coasters (where the coaster is suspended from above). When everyone is in place, the rows of seats swing into position and you are suspended with your legs dangling. Thus hung out to dry, you embark on a simulated hang-glider tour with IMAX-quality images projected all around you, and with the flight simulator moving in sync with the movie. The IMAX images are well chosen and drop-dead beautiful. Special effects include wind, sound, and even olfactory stimulation. The ride itself is thrilling but perfectly smooth. We think Soarin' is a must-experience for guests of any age who meet the height requirement. And yes, we interviewed senior citizens who tried the ride and were crazy about it.

TOURING TIPS   Soarin' joins Test Track and Mission: SPACE as an Epcot super-headliner attraction. Its addition to the Epcot lineup will undoubtedly boost attendance but also take some of the pressure off the park's other two big attractions. Keep in mind, however, that Test Track and Mission: SPACE serve up a little too much thrill for some guests. Soarin', conversely, is an almost platonic ride for any age. Expressed differently, guests of all ages will want to ride. For that reason, and because it's new, we predict it will rise quickly to the top of the hit parade. Our advice: See it before 10:30 a.m. or use Fastpass. If you opt for the latter, don't expect any to be left after 12:30 p.m. or so. Another strategy, if your group doesn't mind splitting up, is to use the singles line.

THE SEAS WITH NEMO & FRIENDS PAVILION

THIS AREA ENCOMPASSES one of America's top marine aquariums, a ride that tunnels through the aquarium, an interactive animated film, and a number of first-class educational walk-through exhibits. It's a stunning package, one we rate as not to be missed. A comprehensive makeover featuring characters from Disney/Pixar's *Finding Nemo* has brought whimsy and much-needed levity to what theretofore was educationally brilliant but somewhat staid.

The Seas Main Tank and Exhibits ★★★½

What it is A huge saltwater aquarium, plus exhibits on oceanography, ocean ecology, and sea life. **Scope and scale** Major attraction. **When to go** Before 11:30 a.m. or after 5 p.m. **Authors' rating** An excellent marine exhibit; ★★★½. **Average wait in line per 100 people ahead of you** 3½ minutes. **Loading speed** Fast.

DESCRIPTION AND COMMENTS The Seas is among Future World's most ambitious offerings. Scientists and divers conduct actual marine experiments in a 200-foot-diameter, 27-foot-deep main tank containing fish, mammals, and crustaceans in a simulation of an ocean ecosystem. Visitors can watch the activity through 8-inch-thick windows below the surface (including some in the Coral Reef Restaurant). On entering The Seas, you're directed to the loading area for The Seas with Nemo & Friends, an attraction that conveys you via a Plexiglas tunnel through The Seas' main tank. Following the ride, you disembark at Sea Base Alpha, where you can enjoy the attractions mentioned previously. (If the wait for the ride is too long, it's possible to head straight for the exhibits by going through the pavilion's exit, around back, and to the left of the main entrance.)

    The Seas' fish population is substantial, but the strength of this attraction lies in the dozen or so exhibits offered after the ride. Visitors can view fish-breeding experiments, watch short films about sea life, and more. A delightful exhibit showcases clownfish (Nemo), regal blue tang (Dory), and other species featured in *Finding Nemo*. Other highlights include a haunting, hypnotic jellyfish tank; a sea horse aquarium; a stingray exhibit; and a manatee tank.

    About two-thirds of the main aquarium is home to reef species, including sharks, rays, and a number of fish that you've seen in quiet repose on your dinner plate. The other third, separated by an inconspicuous divider, houses bottle-nosed dolphins and sea turtles. As you face the main aquarium, the most glare-free viewing windows for the dolphins are on the ground floor to the left by the escalators. For the reef species, it's the same floor on the right by the escalators. Stay as long as you wish.

TOURING TIPS With *Turtle Talk with Crush* and The Seas with Nemo & Friends, The Seas has become one of Epcot's most popular venues. We recommend that you experience the ride and *Turtle Talk* in the morning before the park gets crowded and save the excellent exhibits for later in the day, when you can linger over them.

The Seas with Nemo & Friends ★★★

APPEAL BY AGE PRESCHOOL ★★★★ GRADE SCHOOL ★★★★ TEENS ★★★
YOUNG ADULTS ★★★   OVER 30 ★★★½   SENIORS ★★★½

What it is Ride through a tunnel in The Seas' main tank. **Scope and scale** Major attraction. **When to go** Before 11 a.m. or after 5 p.m. **Authors' rating** ★★★. **Duration of ride** 4 minutes. **Average wait in line per 100 people ahead of you** 3½ minutes. **Loading speed** Fast.

DESCRIPTION AND COMMENTS The Seas with Nemo & Friends is a high-tech ride featuring characters from the animated hit Finding Nemo. The ride likewise deposits you at the heart of The Seas, where the exhibits, Turtle Talk with Crush, and viewing platforms for the main aquarium are.

Upon entering The Seas, you're given the option of experiencing the ride or proceeding directly to the exhibit area. If you choose the ride, you'll be ushered to its loading area, where you'll be made comfortable in a "clamobile" for your journey through the aquarium. The attraction features technology that makes it seem as if the animated characters are swimming with live fish. Very cool. Almost immediately you meet Mr. Ray and his class and learn that Nemo is missing. The remainder of the odyssey consists of finding Nemo with the help of Dory, Bruce, Marlin, Squirt, and Crush, all characters from the animated feature. Unlike the film, however, the ride ends with a musical finale.

TOURING TIPS The earlier you experience the ride the better; ditto for *Turtle Talk with Crush*. If waits are intolerable, come back after 5 p.m. or so.

Turtle Talk with Crush ★★★★

APPEAL BY AGE PRESCHOOL ★★★★½ GRADE SCHOOL ★★★★½ TEENS ★★★★
YOUNG ADULTS ★★★★   OVER 30 ★★★★   SENIORS ★★★★

What it is An interactive animated film. **Scope and scale** Minor attraction. **When to go** Before 11 a.m. or after 5 p.m. **Authors' rating** A real spirit lifter; ★★★★. **Duration of presentation** 17 minutes. **Preshow entertainment** None. **Probable waiting time** 10–20 minutes before 11 a.m. and after 5 p.m.; as much as 40–60 minutes during the more crowded part of the day.

DESCRIPTION AND COMMENTS *Turtle Talk with Crush* is an interactive theater show starring the 153-year-old surfer-dude turtle from *Finding Nemo*. Although it starts like a typical Disney-theme-park movie, *Turtle Talk* quickly turns into a surprise interactive encounter as the on-screen Crush begins to have actual conversations with guests in the audience. Real-time computer graphics are used to accurately move Crush's mouth when forming words, and he's voiced by a guy who went to the *Fast Times at Ridgemont High* school of diction.

TOURING TIPS The interactive technology behind *Turtle Talk* proved so successful in drawing crowds that a follow-up attraction, *Monsters, Inc. Laugh Floor,* debuted in the Magic Kingdom's Tomorrowland in 2007. Turtle Talk has also moved to a new, larger theater in an attempt to shorten waits, which sometimes exceeded an hour. Still, the attraction's capacity is relatively small, so you'll want to get here as early as you can to avoid long lines.

The "Mom, I Can't Believe It's Disney!" Fountain ★★★★

APPEAL BY AGE	PRESCHOOL ★★★★★	GRADE SCHOOL ★★★★★	TEENS ★★★★
YOUNG ADULTS ★★★★	OVER 30 ★★★★		SENIORS ★★★★★

What it is Combination fountain and shower. **When to go** When it's hot. **Scope and scale** Diversion. **Special comments** Secretly installed by Martians during *IllumiNations*. **Authors' rating** YES! ★★★★. **Duration of experience** Indefinite. **Probable waiting time** None.

DESCRIPTION AND COMMENTS This simple fountain on the walkway linking Future World to World Showcase isn't much to look at, but it offers a truly spontaneous experience—rare in Walt Disney World, where everything is controlled, from the snow peas in your stir-fry to how frequently the crocodile yawns in the Jungle Cruise.

Spouts of water erupt randomly from the sidewalk. You can frolic in the water or let it cascade down on you or blow up your britches. On a broiling Florida day, when you think you might suddenly combust, fling yourself into the fountain and do decidedly un-Disney things. Dance, skip, sing, jump, splash, cavort, roll around, stick your toes down the spouts, or catch the water in your mouth as it descends. You can do all of this with your clothes on or, depending on your age, with your clothes off. It's hard to imagine so much personal freedom at Disney World and almost unthinkable to contemplate soggy people slogging and squishing around the park, but there you have it. Hurrah!

TOURING TIPS We don't know if the fountain's creator has been drummed out of the corps by the Disney Tribunal of People Who Sit on Sticks, but we're all grateful for his courage in introducing one thing that's not super-controlled. We do know your kids will be right in the middle of this thing before your brain sounds the alert. Our advice: pack a pair of dry shorts and turn the kids loose. You might even want to bring a spare pair for yourself. Or maybe not—so much advance planning would stifle the spontaneity.

WORLD SHOWCASE

WORLD SHOWCASE, EPCOT'S SECOND themed area, is a sort of ongoing World's Fair that encircles a picturesque 40-acre lagoon. The cuisine, culture, history, and architecture of almost a dozen countries are permanently displayed in individual national pavilions spaced along a 1.2-mile promenade. The pavilions replicate familiar landmarks and present representative street scenes from the host countries.

World Showcase features some of the most lovely gardens in the United States. Located in Germany, France, England, Canada, and, to a lesser extent, China, they are sometimes tucked away and out of sight of pedestrian traffic on the World Showcase promenade.

unofficial **TIP**
To get your kids interested in World Showcase, buy them a Passport Kit and let them collect stamps from each Epcot country.

Most adults enjoy World Showcase, but many children find it boring. To make it more interesting to children, most Epcot retail shops sell **Passport Kits** for about $10. Each kit contains a blank passport and stamps for every World Showcase country. As kids accompany their folks to each country, they tear out the appropriate stamp and stick it in the passport. The kit also contains basic information on the nations and a Mickey Mouse button. Disney has built a lot of profit into this little product, but we guess that isn't the issue. More important, parents tell us the Passport Kit helps get the kids through World Showcase with a minimum of impatience, whining, and tantrums.

Children also enjoy **Kidcot Fun Stops,** a program Disney designed to make World Showcase more interesting for the 5- to 12-year-old crowd. So simple and uncomplicated that you can't believe Disney people thought it up, the Fun Stops usually are nothing more than a large table on the sidewalk at each pavilion. Each table is staffed by a Disney cast member who stamps passports and supervises children in modest craft projects relating to the host country. Reports from parents about the Fun Stops have been uniformly positive.

Kim Possible World Showcase Adventure ★★★★

APPEAL BY AGE	PRESCHOOL ★★★½	GRADE SCHOOL ★★★★½	TEENS ★★★
YOUNG ADULTS ★★★		OVER 30 ★★★½	SENIORS ★★

What it is Interactive scavenger hunt in select World Showcase pavilions. **Scope and scale** Minor attraction. **When to go** Anytime. **Authors' rating** One of our favorite additions to the Disney World theme parks; ★★★★. **Duration of presentation** Allow 30 minutes per adventure. **Preshow entertainment** None. **Probable waiting time** None.

DESCRIPTION AND COMMENTS Disney Channel's Kim Possible show follows a teen heroine as she battles the forces of evil in exotic locations. In the Kim Possible World Showcase Adventure, you play the part of Kim and are given a cell phone–like Kimmunicator before being dispatched on a mission to your choice of seven World Showcase pavilions. Once you arrive at the pavilion, the Kimmunicator's video screen and audio provide various clues about the adventure. As you discover each clue, you'll find special effects such as talking statues and flaming lanterns, plus live "secret agents" stationed in the pavilions just for this game.

Kim Possible makes static World Showcase pavilions more interactive and kid-friendly. The adventures have relatively simple clues, fast pacing, and neat rewards for solving the puzzles. Since the experience debuted in early 2009, reader reviews have been uniformly positive.

TOURING TIPS Playing the game is free, and no deposit is required for the Kimmunicator. You'll need a valid theme park ticket to sign up before you play, and you can choose both the time and location of your adventure. Register at Future World's Innoventions East or Innoventions West buildings, or along the Odyssey Bridge connecting Future World to World Showcase. Report to the Italy, Norway, or United Kingdom Pavilion to pick up your Kimmunicator before heading off to your chosen country.

Each group can have up to three Kimmunicators for the same adventure. Because you're working with a device about the size of a cell phone, it's best to have one Kimmunicator for every two people in your group.

NOW, MOVING CLOCKWISE around the World Showcase promenade, here are the nations represented and their attractions.

MEXICO PAVILION

DESCRIPTION AND COMMENTS Pre-Columbian pyramids dominate the architecture of this exhibit. One forms the pavilion's facade, and the other overlooks the restaurant and plaza alongside the boat ride, Gran Fiesta Tour, inside the pavilion.

TOURING TIPS A romantic and exciting testimony to Mexico's charms, the pyramids contain a large number of authentic and valuable artifacts. Many people zip past these treasures without stopping to look. The village scene inside the pavilion is beautiful and exquisitely detailed. A retail shop occupies most of the left half of the inner pavilion, while Mexico's Kidcot stop is in the first entryway inside the pyramid. On the opposite side of the main floor is **La Cava de Tequila,** a bar serving more than 70 varieties of tequila as well as margaritas and appetizers.

Gran Fiesta Tour Starring The Three Caballeros ★★½

APPEAL BY AGE	PRESCHOOL ★★★★	GRADE SCHOOL ★★★½	TEENS ★★★
YOUNG ADULTS ★★★		OVER 30 ★★★	SENIORS ★★★

What it is Indoor scenic boat ride. **Scope and scale** Minor attraction. **When to go** Before noon or after 5 p.m. **Authors' rating** Visually appealing, light and relaxing; ★★½. **Duration of ride** About 7 minutes (plus 1½-minute wait to disembark). **Average wait in line per 100 people ahead of you** 4½ minutes. **Assumes** 16 boats in operation. **Loading speed** Moderate.

DESCRIPTION AND COMMENTS The Gran Fiesta Tour replaces this pavilion's first boat ride, El Río del Tiempo. The new incarnation adds animated versions of Donald Duck, José Carioca, and Panchito—an avian singing group called The Three Caballeros, from Disney's 1944 film of the same name—to spice up what was often characterized as a slower-paced Mexican "It's a Small World."

The ride's premise is that the Caballeros are scheduled to perform at a fiesta, but Donald has gone missing. Large video screens show Donald enjoying Mexico's pyramids, monuments, and water sports while José and Panchito search other Mexican points of interest. Everyone is reunited in time for a rousing concert near the end of the ride. Along the way, guests are treated to detailed scenes in eye-catching colors, and an improved music system. At the risk of sounding like the Disney geeks we are, we must point out that Panchito is technically the only Mexican Caballero; José Carioca is from Brazil, and Donald is from Burbank. Either way, more of the ride's visuals seem to be on the left side of the boat. Have small children sit nearer the left to keep their attention, and listen for Donald's humorous monologue as you wait to disembark at the end of the ride.

TOURING TIPS The attraction tends to get busier during early afternoon.

NORWAY PAVILION

DESCRIPTION AND COMMENTS The Norway Pavilion is complex, beautiful, and architecturally diverse. Surrounding a courtyard is an assortment of traditional Scandinavian buildings, including a replica of the 14th-century Akershus Castle, a wooden stave church (go inside—the doors open!), red-tiled cottages, and replicas of historic buildings representing the traditional designs of Bergen, Alesund, and Oslo. Attractions include an adventure boat ride in the mold of Pirates of the Caribbean, a movie about Norway, and a gallery of art and artifacts. The pavilion houses Akershus Royal Banquet Hall, a sit-down eatery that hosts princess character meals for breakfast, lunch, and dinner; breakfast here is one of the most popular character meals in the World. An open-air cafe attached to a bakery caters to those on the run. Shoppers find abundant native handicrafts.

Maelstrom *(Fastpass)* ★★★

APPEAL BY AGE	PRESCHOOL ★★★	GRADE SCHOOL ★★★½	TEENS ★★★½
YOUNG ADULTS ★★★½		OVER 30 ★★★½	SENIORS ★★★½

What it is Indoor adventure boat ride. **Scope and scale** Major attraction. **When to go** Before noon, after 4:30 p.m., or use Fastpass. **Authors' rating** Too short, but has its moments; ★★★. **Duration of ride** 4½ minutes, followed by a 5-minute film with a short wait in between; about 14 minutes for the whole show. **Average wait in line per 100 people ahead of you** 4 minutes. **Assumes** 12 or 13 boats operating. **Loading speed** Fast.

DESCRIPTION AND COMMENTS In one of Disney World's shorter water rides, guests board dragon-headed ships for a voyage through the fabled rivers and seas of Viking history and legend. They brave trolls, rocky gorges, waterfalls, and a storm at sea. A second-generation Disney water ride, the Viking voyage assembles an impressive array of special effects, combining visual, tactile, and auditory stimuli in a fast-paced and often humorous odyssey. Afterward, guests see a 5-minute film on Norway. We don't have any major problems with Maelstrom, but a vocal minority of our readers consider the ride too brief and resent having to sit through what they characterize as a travelogue.

TOURING TIPS Sometimes, several hundred guests from a recently concluded screening of *Reflections of China* arrive at Maelstrom en masse. Should you encounter this horde, postpone Maelstrom. If you don't want to see the Norway film, not to worry. You will be given the opportunity to exit before the film begins.

CHINA PAVILION

DESCRIPTION AND COMMENTS A half-sized replica of the Temple of Heaven in Beijing identifies this pavilion. Gardens and reflecting ponds simulate those found in Suzhou, and an art gallery features a lotus-blossom gate and formal saddle roof line. The China Pavilion offers two restaurants: a quick service eatery and a full-service establishment (Advance Reservations recommended) that serves lamentably lackluster Chinese food in a lovely setting. **The Joy of Tea,** a tea stand and specialty-drink vendor, feeds your caffeine addiction until you can get to Morocco's espresso bar.

The pavilion also hosts regularly updated exhibits on Chinese history, culture, or trend-setting developments. The current exhibit features a look at Chinese funeral sculptures, including miniature clay warriors who protect the tombs' occupants.

Reflections of China   ★★★½

APPEAL BY AGE	PRESCHOOL ★★½	GRADE SCHOOL ★★★	TEENS ★★★
YOUNG ADULTS ★★★		OVER 30 ★★★½	SENIORS ★★★½

What it is Film about the Chinese people and country. **Scope and scale** Major attraction. **When to go** Anytime. **Special comments** Audience stands throughout the performance. **Authors' rating** A beautifully produced film; ★★★½. **Duration of presentation** About 14 minutes. **Preshow entertainment** None. **Probable waiting time** 10 minutes.

DESCRIPTION AND COMMENTS Pass through the Hall of Prayer for Good Harvest to view the Circle-Vision 360 film *Reflections of China*. Warm and appealing, it's a brilliant (albeit politically sanitized) introduction to the people and natural beauty of China.

TOURING TIPS The pavilion is truly beautiful—serene yet exciting. *Reflections of China* plays in a theater where guests must stand, but the film can usually be enjoyed anytime without much waiting. If you're touring World Showcase in a counterclockwise rotation and plan next to go to Norway and ride Maelstrom, position yourself on the far left of the theater (as you face the attendant's podium). After the show, be one of the first to exit. Hurry to Maelstrom as fast as you can to arrive ahead of the several hundred other *Reflections of China* patrons who will be right behind you.

GERMANY PAVILION

DESCRIPTION AND COMMENTS A clock tower adorned with boy and girl figures rises above the *platz* (plaza) marking the Germany pavilion. Dominated by a fountain depicting St. George's victory over the dragon, the platz is encircled by buildings done in traditional German architecture. The main attraction is the Biergarten, a buffet restaurant (Advance Reservations required) serving German food and beer. Yodeling, folk dancing, and oompah-band music are included during mealtimes.

The latest addition to the Germany Pavilion is **Karamell-Küche** ("Caramel Kitchen"), offering small caramel-covered sweets including apples, fudge, and cupcakes. We love coming here for a midday snack to tide us over before dinner. Also be sure to check out the large and elaborate model railroad just beyond the restrooms as you walk from Germany toward Italy.

TOURING TIPS The pavilion is pleasant and festive. Anytime is good for touring.

ITALY PAVILION

DESCRIPTION AND COMMENTS The entrance to Italy is marked by an 83-foot-tall campanile (bell tower) said to mirror the tower in St. Mark's Square in Venice. Left of the campanile is a replica of the 14th-century Doge's Palace, also in the famous square. The pavilion has a waterfront on the lagoon where gondolas are tied to striped moorings.

TOURING TIPS Streets and courtyards in the Italy Pavilion are among the most realistic in World Showcase. For a quick lunch, **Via Napoli** occasionally offers pizza by the slice—eat it on the go for complete authenticity. Because there's no film or ride, tour the rest of the pavilion at any hour.

UNITED STATES PAVILION

The American Adventure ★★★★

APPEAL BY AGE	PRESCHOOL ★★½	GRADE SCHOOL ★★★	TEENS ★★★
YOUNG ADULTS ★★★★	OVER 30 ★★★★		SENIORS ★★★½

What it is Patriotic mixed-media and audioanimatronic theater presentation on U.S. history. **Scope and scale** Headliner. **When to go** Anytime. **Authors' rating** Disney's best historic/patriotic attraction; not to be missed; ★★★★. **Duration of presentation** About 29 minutes. **Preshow entertainment** Voices of Liberty chorale singing. **Probable waiting time** 16 minutes.

DESCRIPTION AND COMMENTS The United States Pavilion, generally referred to as The American Adventure, consists (not surprisingly) of a fast-food restaurant and a patriotic show, also called *The American Adventure*.

The presentation is a composite of everything Disney does best. Located in an imposing brick structure reminiscent of Colonial Philadelphia, the 29-minute production is a stirring, but sanitized, rendition of American history narrated by an audioanimatronic Mark Twain (who carries a smoking cigar) and Ben Franklin (who climbs a set of stairs to visit Thomas Jefferson). Behind a stage (almost half the size of a football field) is a 28-by-55-foot rear-projection screen (the largest ever used) on which motion-picture images are interwoven with action on stage.

TOURING TIPS Architecturally, the United States Pavilion isn't as interesting as most other pavilions. But the presentation, our researchers believe, is the very best patriotic attraction in the Disney repertoire (some find it overstated and boring, however). It usually plays to capacity audiences from around 1:30–3:30 p.m., but it isn't hard to get into. Because of the theater's large capacity, the wait during busy times of day seldom approaches an hour and averages 25–40 minutes.

JAPAN PAVILION

DESCRIPTION AND COMMENTS The five-story, blue-roofed pagoda, inspired by a 17th-century shrine in Nara, sets this pavilion apart. A hill garden behind it features waterfalls, rocks, flowers, lanterns, paths, and rustic bridges. The building on the right (as one faces the entrance) was inspired by the ceremonial and coronation hall at the Imperial Palace at Kyoto. It contains restaurants and a large retail store. Through the center entrance and to the left is the **Bijutsu-kan Gallery,** exhibiting colorful displays from Japanese pop culture.

TOURING TIPS Tasteful and elaborate, the pavilion creatively blends simplicity, architectural grandeur, and natural beauty. Tour anytime.

MOROCCO PAVILION

DESCRIPTION AND COMMENTS The bustling market, winding streets, lofty minarets, and stuccoed archways re-create the romance and intrigue of Marrakesh and Casablanca. Attention to detail makes Morocco one of the most exciting World Showcase pavilions. It also has a museum of Moorish art and **Restaurant Marrakesh,** which serves some unusual and difficult-to-find North African specialties.

TOURING TIPS Morocco has neither a ride nor theater, so tour it anytime.

FRANCE PAVILION

DESCRIPTION AND COMMENTS Naturally, a replica of the Eiffel Tower (a big one) is this pavilion's centerpiece. In the foreground, streets recall *la belle époque,* France's "beautiful time" between 1870 and 1910. The sidewalk cafe and restaurant are very popular, as is the pastry shop. You won't be the first visitor to buy a croissant to tide you over until your next real meal.

Impressions de France ★★★½

APPEAL BY AGE	PRESCHOOL ★★	GRADE SCHOOL ★★★	TEENS ★★★
YOUNG ADULTS ★★★½		OVER 30 ★★★½	SENIORS ★★★★

What it is Film essay on the French people and country. **Scope and scale** Major attraction. **When to go** Anytime. **Authors' rating** Exceedingly beautiful film; not to be missed; ★★★½. **Duration of presentation** About 18 minutes. **Preshow entertainment** None. **Probable waiting time** 12 minutes (at suggested times).

DESCRIPTIONS AND COMMENTS *Impressions de France* is an 18-minute movie projected over 200 degrees onto five screens. Unlike at China and Canada, the audience sits to view this well-made film introducing France's people, cities, and natural wonders.

TOURING TIPS Detail and the evocation of a bygone era enrich the atmosphere of this pavilion. Streets are small and become quite congested when visitors queue for the film.

UNITED KINGDOM PAVILION

DESCRIPTION AND COMMENTS A variety of period architecture attempts to capture Britain's city, town, and rural atmospheres. One street alone has a thatched-roof cottage, a four-story timber-and-plaster building, a pre-Georgian plaster building, a formal Palladian exterior of dressed stone, and a city square with a Hyde Park bandstand (whew!).

The pavilion is mostly shops. The **Rose & Crown Pub and Dining Room** is the only World Showcase full-service restaurant with dining on the water side of the promenade. For fast food, try the **Yorkshire County Fish Shop.**

TOURING TIPS There are no attractions, hence minimal congestion; tour anytime. Alice in Wonderland, and/or Pooh can occasionally be found in the character-greeting area; check the *Times Guide* for a schedule. Advance Reservations aren't required to enjoy the pub section of the Rose & Crown, making it a nice place to stop for a beer. (If you can't make up your mind, an "Imperial Sampler" of seven different brews—including Bass, Harp, Boddingtons, and Guinness—is available for about $11.)

CANADA PAVILION

Canada's cultural, natural, and architectural diversity are reflected in this large and impressive pavilion. Thirty-foot-tall totem poles embellish a Native American village at the foot of a magnificent château-style hotel. Nearby is a rugged stone building said to be modeled after a famous landmark near Niagara Falls and reflecting Britain's influence on Canada. **Le Cellier,** a steakhouse on the pavilion's lower level, is incredibly popular, although it can't hurt to try for a walk-in spot.

O Canada! ★★★½

APPEAL BY AGE	PRESCHOOL ★★½	GRADE SCHOOL ★★★	TEENS ★★★½
YOUNG ADULTS ★★★½		OVER 30 ★★★★	SENIORS ★★★★

What it is Film essay on the Canadian people and their country. **Scope and scale** Major attraction. **When to go** Anytime. **Special comments** Audience stands during performance. **Authors' rating** Makes you want to catch the first plane to Canada; ★★★½. **Duration of presentation** About 18 minutes. **Preshow entertainment** None. **Probable waiting time** 10 minutes.

DESCRIPTION AND COMMENTS *O Canada!* showcases Canada's natural beauty and population diversity and demonstrates the immense pride Canadians have in their country. Visitors leave the theater through Victoria Gardens, which was inspired by the famed Butchart Gardens of British Columbia.

TOURING TIPS *O Canada!,* a large-capacity theater attraction (guests must stand), gets fairly heavy late-morning attendance because Canada is the first pavilion encountered as one travels counterclockwise around World Showcase Lagoon.

LIVE ENTERTAINMENT *in* EPCOT

LIVE ENTERTAINMENT IN EPCOT IS MORE diverse than it is in the Magic Kingdom. In World Showcase, it reflects the nations represented. Future World provides a perfect setting for new and experimental offerings. Information about live entertainment on the day you visit is contained in the Epcot guide map you obtain upon entry or at Guest Relations.

Here are some performers and performances you're apt to encounter:

AMERICA GARDENS THEATRE This large amphitheater, near The American Adventure, faces World Showcase Lagoon. International talent plays limited engagements there. Many shows spotlight the music, dance, and costumes of the performer's home country. Other programs feature Disney characters.

AROUND THE WORLD SHOWCASE Impromptu performances take place in and around the World Showcase pavilions.

They include a strolling mariachi group in Mexico; street actors in Italy; a fife-and-drum corps or singing group (The Voices of Liberty) at The American Adventure; traditional songs, drums, and dances in Japan; street comedy in the United Kingdom; white-faced mimes in France; and bagpipes in Canada, among other offerings. Street entertainment occurs about every half hour.

DINNER AND LUNCH SHOWS Restaurants in World Showcase serve healthy portions of live entertainment to accompany the victuals. Find folk dancing and an oompah band in Germany, singing waiters in Italy, and belly dancers in Morocco. Shows are performed only at dinner in Italy, but at both lunch and dinner in Germany and Morocco. Advance Reservations are required.

DISNEY CHARACTERS Once believed to be inconsistent with Epcot's educational focus, Disney characters have now been imported in significant numbers. Characters appear throughout Epcot (see page 81) and in live shows at the America Gardens Theatre and the Showcase Plaza between Mexico and Canada. Times are listed in the *Times Guide* available upon entry and at Guest Relations. Finally, The Garden Grill Restaurant in the Land Pavilion and Akershus Royal Banquet Hall in Norway offer character meals.

IN FUTURE WORLD A musical crew of drumming janitors works near the front entrance and at Innoventions Plaza (between the two Innoventions buildings and by the fountain) according to the daily entertainment schedule. They're occasionally complemented by an electric-keyboard band playing oldies tunes.

INNOVENTIONS FOUNTAIN SHOW Numerous times each day, the fountain situated between the two Innoventions buildings comes alive with pulsating, arching plumes of water synchronized to a musical score.

KIDCOT FUN STOPS World Showcase pavilions have areas called Kidcot Fun Stops, where younger children can hear a story or make some small craft representative of the host nation. The Fun Stops are informal, usually set up right on the walkway. During busy times of the year, you'll find Fun Stops at each country in World Showcase; at slower times, only a couple of zones operate. Many parents who thought Epcot would be a drag for their kids are pleasantly surprised by the Fun Stops experience.

THE BEST WAYS TO SEE *ILLUMINATIONS*

ILLUMINATIONS IS EPCOT'S GREAT OUTDOOR spectacle, integrating fireworks, laser lights, neon, and music in a stirring tribute to the nations of the world. It's the climax of every Epcot day when the park is open late. Don't miss it.

Getting out of Epcot after *IllumiNations* (Read This before Selecting a Viewing Spot)

Decide how quickly you want to leave the park after the show, then pick your vantage point. *IllumiNations* ends the day at Epcot. When it's over, only a couple of gift shops remain open. Because there's nothing to do, everyone leaves at once. This creates a great snarl at Package Pick-Up, the Epcot monorail station, and the Disney bus stop. It also pushes to the limit the tram system hauling guests to their cars in the parking lot. Stroller return, however, is extraordinarily efficient and doesn't cause any delay.

If you're staying at an Epcot resort (Swan, Dolphin, Yacht & Beach Club Resorts, and BoardWalk Inn & Villas), watch the show from somewhere on the southern (American Adventure) half of World Showcase Lagoon and then leave through the International Gateway between France and the United Kingdom. You can walk or take a boat back to your hotel from the International Gateway. If you have a car and you're visiting Epcot in the evening for dinner and *IllumiNations,* park at the Yacht or Beach Club. After the show, duck out the International Gateway and be on the road to your hotel in 15 minutes. We should warn you that there's a manned security gate at the entrances to most of the Epcot resorts, including the Yacht and Beach clubs. You will, of course, be admitted if you have legitimate business, such as dining at one of the hotel restaurants, or, if you park at the BoardWalk Inn & Villas (requiring a slightly longer walk to Epcot), going to the clubs and restaurants at the BoardWalk. If you're staying at any other Disney hotel and you don't have a car, the fastest way home is to join the mass exodus through the main gate after *IllumiNations* and catch a bus or the monorail.

Those who have a car in the Epcot lot have a more problematic situation. To beat the crowd, find a viewing spot at the end of World Showcase Lagoon nearest Future World (and the exits). Leave as soon as *IllumiNations* concludes, trying to exit ahead of the crowd (note that thousands of people will be doing exactly the same thing). To get a good vantage point between Mexico and Canada on the northern end of the lagoon, stake out your spot 60–100 minutes before the show (45–90 minutes during less-busy periods). Conceivably, you may squander more time holding your spot before

IllumiNations than you would if you watched from the less-congested southern end of the lagoon and took your chances with the crowd upon departure.

More groups get separated, and more children lost, after *IllumiNations* than at any other time. In summer you will be walking in a throng of up to 30,000 people. If you're heading for the parking lot, anticipate this congestion and preselect a point in the Epcot entrance area where you can meet in the event that someone gets separated from the group. We recommend the fountain just inside the main entrance. It can be a nightmare if the group gets split up and you don't know whether the others are inside or outside the park.

For those with a car, the main problem is reaching it. Once there, traffic leaves the parking lot pretty well. If you paid close attention to where you parked, consider skipping the tram and walking. If you walk, watch your children closely and hang on to them for all you're worth. The parking lot is pretty wild at this time of night, with hundreds of moving cars.

> **unofficial TIP**
> Everyone in your party should be told not to exit through the turnstiles until all noses have been counted.

Good Locations for Viewing *IllumiNations* and Other World Showcase Lagoon Performances

The best place to be for any presentation on World Showcase Lagoon is in a seat on the lakeside veranda of **La Cantina de San Angel** in Mexico. Come early (*at least* 90 minutes before *IllumiNations*) and relax with a cold drink or snack while you wait for the show.

La Hacienda de San Angel in Mexico and the **Rose & Crown Pub** in the United Kingdom also have lagoon-side seating. Because of a small wall at the Rose & Crown, however, the view isn't quite as good as from the Cantina. If you want to combine dinner at either location with *IllumiNations*, make a dinner reservation for about 1 hour and 15 minutes before showtime. Report a few minutes early for your seating and tell the host that you want a table outside where you can view *IllumiNations* during or after dinner. Our experience is that the staff will bend over backward to accommodate you. If you aren't able to obtain a table outside, eat inside, then hang out until showtime. When the lights dim, indicating the start of *IllumiNations*, you'll be allowed to join the diners to watch the show.

> **unofficial TIP**
> It's important not to position yourself under a tree, an awning, or anything else that blocks your overhead view.

Because most guests run for the exits after a presentation, and because islands in the southern (American Adventure) half of the lagoon block the view from some places, the most popular spectator positions are along the northern waterfront from Norway and Mexico to Canada and the United Kingdom. It's usually necessary to claim a spot 60–100 minutes before *IllumiNations* begins. If you're late finishing dinner or you don't want to spend an hour-plus standing by a rail, here are some good viewing spots along the southern perimeter (moving counterclockwise from the U.K. to Germany) that often go unnoticed until 10–30 minutes before showtime:

1. **International Gateway Island** The pedestrian bridge across the canal near International Gateway spans an island that offers great viewing. This island normally fills 30 minutes or more before showtime.

2. **Second-floor (Restaurant-level) Deck of the Mitsuko-shi Building in Japan** An Asian arch slightly blocks your sightline, but this covered deck offers a great vantage point, especially if the weather is iffy. Only the Hacienda de San Angel in Mexico is more protected.

3. **Gondola Landing at Italy** An elaborate waterfront promenade offers excellent viewing positions. Claim your spot at least 30 minutes before showtime.

4. **The Boat Dock Opposite Germany** Another good vantage point, the dock generally fills 30 minutes before *IllumiNations*.

5. **Waterfront Promenade by Germany** Views are good from the 90-foot-long lagoonside walkway between Germany and China.

None of the above viewing locations are reserved for *Unofficial Guide* readers, and on busier nights, good spots go early. But we still won't hold down a slab of concrete for 2 hours before *IllumiNations* as some people do. Most nights, you can find an acceptable vantage point 15–30 minutes before the show. Because most of the action is significantly above ground level, you don't need to be right on the rail or have an unobstructed view of the water. If *IllumiNations* is a top priority for you and you want to be absolutely certain of getting a good viewing position, claim your place an hour or more before showtime.

IllumiNations Cruise

For a really good view, you can charter a pontoon boat for $346 with tax. Captained by a Disney cast member, the boat holds up to 10 guests. Your captain will take you for a little cruise and then position the boat in a perfect place to watch *IllumiNations*. Chips, soda, and water are provided; sandwiches and more-substantial food items may be arranged through Disney reservations or Yacht Club Private Dining (☎ 407-934-3160.) Cruises depart from Bayside Marina. A major indirect benefit of the charter is that you can enjoy *IllumiNations* without fighting the mob afterward. Because this is a private charter rather than a tour, only your group will be aboard. Life jackets are provided, but you can wear them at your discretion. Because there are few boats, charters sell out fast. To reserve, call ☎ 407-WDW-PLAY (939-7529) at exactly 7 a.m. 180 days before the day you want to charter. We recommend phoning about 185 days out to have a Disney agent specify the exact morning to call for reservations. Similar charters are available on the Seven Seas Lagoon to watch the Magic Kingdom fireworks.

unofficial **TIP**
Although the northern end of the lagoon offers unquestionably excellent viewing, we advise that you claim a spot 40–60 minutes before *IllumiNations* begins.

EPCOT TOURING PLANS

OUR EPCOT TOURING PLANS ARE FIELD-TESTED, step-by-step itineraries for seeing all major attractions at Epcot with a minimum of waiting in line. They're designed to keep you ahead of the crowds while the park is filling in the morning, and to place you at the less crowded attractions during Epcot's busier hours. They assume you would be happier doing a little extra walking rather than a lot of extra standing in line.

unofficial **TIP**
Unlike the Magic Kingdom, Epcot has no effective in-park transportation; wherever you want to go, it's always quicker to walk.

Touring Epcot is much more strenuous and demanding than touring the other theme parks. Epcot requires about twice as much walking. Our plans will help you avoid crowds and bottlenecks on days of moderate–heavy attendance, but they can't shorten the distance you have to walk. (Wear comfortable shoes.) On days of lighter attendance, when the crowd conditions aren't a critical factor, the plans will help you organize your tour. We offer four touring plans:

EPCOT ONE-DAY TOURING PLAN This plan packs as much as possible into one long day and requires a lot of hustle and stamina.

AUTHORS' SELECTIVE EPCOT ONE-DAY TOURING PLAN This plan eliminates some lesser attractions (in the author's opinion) and offers a somewhat more relaxed tour if you have only one day.

EPCOT TWO-DAY SUNRISE–STARLIGHT TOURING PLAN This plan combines the easy touring of early morning on one day with Epcot's festivity and live pageantry at night on the second day. The first day requires some backtracking and hustle but is much more laid-back than either one-day plan.

EPCOT TWO-DAY EARLY-RISER TOURING PLAN This is the most efficient Epcot touring plan, eliminating 90% of the backtracking and extra walking required by the others while still providing a comprehensive tour.

"NOT A TOURING PLAN" TOURING PLANS

FOR PARENTS AND ADULTS WITH ONE DAY TO TOUR, ARRIVING AT PARK OPENING Obtain Fastpasses for Soarin' first, then see Test Track and Mission: SPACE. See remaining Future World West attractions, then tour Future World East. Tour World Showcase clockwise, starting in Mexico.

FOR PARENTS AND ADULTS WITH ONE DAY TO TOUR, ARRIVING LATE MORNING Try to obtain Fastpasses for Soarin', Test Track, or Mission: SPACE (in that order). See Future World East attractions, then Future World West. Tour World Showcase counterclockwise, starting in Canada.

FOR PARENTS AND ADULTS WITH TWO DAYS TO TOUR On Day One, see Future World East attractions and Mexico through the United States in World Showcase. On Day Two, tour Future World West and Canada through Japan.

PRELIMINARY INSTRUCTIONS FOR ALL EPCOT TOURING PLANS

1. Call ☎ 407-824-4321 in advance for the hours of operation on the day of your visit.
2. Make Advance Reservations at the Epcot full-service restaurant(s) of your choice before your visit.

THE TOURING PLANS

Epcot One-day Touring Plan

FOR Adults and children ages 8 or older.
ASSUMES Willingness to experience all major rides and shows.

THIS PLAN REQUIRES A LOT OF WALKING and some backtracking in order to avoid long waits in line. A little extra walking and some early-morning hustle will spare you 2–3 hours of standing in line. You might not complete the tour. How far you get depends on how quickly you move from attraction to attraction, how many times you rest and eat, how quickly the park fills, and what time it closes.

This plan is not recommended for families with very young children. If you're touring with young children and have only one day, use the Authors' Selective Epcot One-day Touring Plan. Break after lunch and then relax at your hotel, returning to the park in late afternoon. If you can allocate two days to Epcot, use one of the Epcot two-day touring plans.

1. Arrive 40 minutes before official opening time. Pick up a guide map and daily entertainment schedule when entering the park.
2. Obtain Fastpasses for Soarin'.
3. In Future World East, ride Test Track.
4. Ride Mission: SPACE. Do not use Fastpass.
5. In Innoventions East, ride Sum of All Thrills.
6. Ride Living with the Land in the Land Pavilion.
7. Now might be a good time to pick up a second Fastpass for Soarin', if available.
8. See The Seas with Nemo & Friends and *Turtle Talk with Crush.*
9. Ride Journey into Imagination with Figment.
10. See *Honey, I Shrunk the Audience* or *Captain EO,* depending on which is showing.
11. Return to the Land Pavilion and see *The Circle of Life.*
12. Ride Soarin' using the Fastpasses obtained in Step 2.
13. Eat lunch.
14. Ride Spaceship Earth.
15. Ride Universe of Energy in Future World East.
16. Tour the remaining exhibits in Innoventions East.
17. If you have children, sign up for the Kim Possible World Showcase Adventure on the walk to World Showcase.
18. Take the Gran Fiesta Tour boat ride at Mexico.
19. Ride Maelstrom and tour the stave church in Norway.
20. See *Reflections of China.*
21. Tour Germany.
22. Visit Italy.
23. See *The American Adventure.*
24. Explore Japan.
25. Visit Morocco, including the small museum on the left side of the pavilion.
26. See *Impressions de France.*
27. Eat dinner.
28. Visit the United Kingdom.

29. Tour Canada and see *O Canada!*
30. See *Illuminations.* Prime viewing spots are along the lagoon between Canada and France.

Authors' Selective Epcot One-day Touring Plan

FOR All parties.
ASSUMES Willingness to experience major rides and shows.

THIS TOURING PLAN INCLUDES only what the authors believes is the best Epcot has to offer. However, exclusion of an attraction doesn't mean it isn't worthwhile.

Families with children younger than age 8 using this touring plan should review Epcot attractions in the Small-child Fright-potential Chart (pages 76–80). Rent a stroller for any child small enough to fit in one, and take your young children back to the hotel for a nap after lunch. If you can allocate two days to seeing Epcot, try one of the Epcot two-day touring plans.

1. Arrive 40 minutes before official opening time. Pick up a guide map and daily entertainment schedule when entering the park.
2. Obtain Fastpasses for Soarin'.
3. In Future World East, ride Test Track.
4. Ride Mission: SPACE. Do not use Fastpass.
5. In Innoventions East, ride Sum of All Thrills.
6. Ride Living with the Land in the Land Pavilion.
7. If you want a second Fastpass for Soarin', get it now.
8. See The Seas with Nemo & Friends and *Turtle Talk with Crush.*
9. Ride Journey into Imagination with Figment.
10. See *Honey, I Shrunk the Audience* or *Captain EO,* depending on which is showing.
11. Return to The Land and ride Soarin' using the Fastpasses obtained in Step 2.
12. Eat lunch.
13. Ride Spaceship Earth.
14. Visit the Universe of Energy.
15. Tour Canada and see *O Canada!*
16. See *Impressions de France.*
17. Visit Morocco, including the small museum on the left side of the pavilion.
18. Explore Japan.
19. See *The American Adventure.*
20. Visit Italy.

21. Tour Germany.
22. See *Reflections of China.*
23. Ride Maelstrom and tour the stave church in Norway.
24. Take the Gran Fiesta Tour boat ride in Mexico.
25. Eat dinner.
26. See *Illuminations.* Prime viewing spots are at Mexico and at the front of World Showcase lagoon.

Epcot Two-day Sunrise–Starlight Touring Plan

FOR All parties.

THIS TOURING PLAN is for visitors who want to tour Epcot comprehensively over two days. Day One takes advantage of early morning touring opportunities. Day Two begins in late afternoon and continues until closing.

Many readers spend part of their Disney World arrival day traveling, checking into their hotel, and unpacking. They aren't free to go to the theme parks until the afternoon. The second day of the Epcot Two-day Sunrise–Starlight Touring Plan is ideal for people who want to commence their Epcot visit later in the day.

Families with children younger than age 8 who use this plan should review Epcot attractions listed in the Small-child Fright-potential Chart (pages 76–80). Rent a stroller for any child small enough to fit into one. Break off Day One no later than 2:30 p.m., and return to your hotel to get some rest. If you missed any attractions on Day One, add them to your itinerary on Day Two.

DAY ONE

1. Arrive 40 minutes before official opening time. Pick up a guide map and daily entertainment schedule when entering the park.
2. Obtain Fastpasses for Soarin'.
3. In Future World East, ride Test Track.
4. Ride Mission: SPACE.
5. Experience Sum of All Thrills in Innoventions East.
6. Make dinner reservations at Guest Relations or by calling ☎ 407WDW-DINE.
7. In the Land Pavilion, ride Living with the Land.
8. If you want a second Fastpass for Soarin', get it now.
9. Ride Journey into Imagination with Figment.
10. See *Honey, I Shrunk the Audience* or *Captain EO,* depending on which is showing.
11. Ride Soarin' using the Fastpasses obtained in Step 2.

12. Eat lunch.
13. Take the Gran Fiesta Tour boat ride in Mexico.
14. Ride Maelstrom at Norway. Use Fastpass if wait exceeds 20 minutes.
15. See *Reflections of China.*
16. Visit Germany.
17. Tour Italy.
18. See *The American Adventure.*
19. Visit Japan.
20. If you have kids, try the Kim Possible World Showcase Adventure in Japan.

DAY TWO

1. Arrive at Epcot at 1 p.m. Get a guide map and daily entertainment schedule.
2. Make dinner reservations at Guest Relations or by calling ☎ 407-WDW-DINE.
3. Ride Spaceship Earth.
4. See the Universe of Energy.
5. See The Seas with Nemo & Friends and *Turtle Talk with Crush.*
6. At the Land Pavilion, see *The Circle of Life.*
7. Tour Innoventions West.
8. See *O Canada!*
9. Visit the United Kingdom.
10. See *Impressions de France.*
11. Visit Morocco and tour the museum on the left side of the pavilion.
12. Eat dinner.
13. See *Illuminations.* Good viewing spots are along the waterway between France and Canada.

Epcot Two-day Early-riser Touring Plan

FOR All parties.

THIS IS THE MOST EFFICIENT Epcot touring plan, eliminating much of the backtracking and crisscrossing required by the other plans. Most folks will complete each day of the plan by midafternoon. While the plan doesn't include *IllumiNations* or other evening festivities, these activities, along with dinner at an Epcot restaurant, can be added to the itinerary at your discretion.

Families with children younger than age 8 using this plan should review Epcot attractions in the Small-child Fright-potential Chart (pages 76–80). Rent a stroller for any child small enough to fit.

DAY ONE

1. Arrive 40 minutes before official opening time. Pick up a guide map and daily entertainment schedule.
2. At the Land Pavilion, ride Soarin'.
3. Ride Living with the Land. If you want to ride Soarin' again, get Fastpasses now.
4. See *The Circle of Life.*
5. Make dinner reservations at Guest Relations or by calling ☎ 407-WDW-DINE.
6. See The Seas with Nemo & Friends and *Turtle Talk with Crush.*
7. Ride Journey into Imagination with Figment.
8. See *Honey, I Shrunk the Audience* or *Captain EO,* depending on which is showing.
9. If you have small children, sign up for the Kim Possible World Showcase Adventure on the way to World Showcase. Ask for a mission in either the United Kingdom or France.
10. Start a counterclockwise tour of World Showcase with the film *O Canada!* at Canada.
11. Explore the United Kingdom.
12. See *Impressions de France.*
13. Continue around the lagoon, or tour Innoventions West.

DAY TWO

1. Arrive 40 minutes before official opening time. Pick up a guide map and daily entertainment schedule.
2. Ride Test Track. Use Fastpass if wait exceeds 30 minutes.
3. Ride Mission: SPACE.
4. Tour Innoventions East and ride Sum of All Thrills.
5. See the Universe of Energy.
6. Ride Spaceship Earth.
7. Take the Gran Fiesta Tour boat ride in Mexico.
8. Ride Maelstrom at Norway. Use Fastpass if wait exceeds 20 minutes.
9. See *Reflections of China.*
10. Visit Germany.
11. Visit Italy.
12. See *The American Adventure.*
13. Visit Japan.
14. Visit Morocco and tour the museum on the left side of the pavilion.
15. If you have kids, try the *Kim Possible* World Showcase Adventure in Japan.
16. Eat dinner and enjoy *IllumiNations.*

DISNEY'S ANIMAL KINGDOM

AT 500 ACRES, DISNEY'S ANIMAL KINGDOM is five times the size of the Magic Kingdom and more than twice the size of Epcot. But as at Disney's Hollywood Studios, most of Animal Kingdom's vast geography is accessible only on guided tours or as part of attractions. Animal Kingdom comprises six sections, or "lands": **The Oasis, Discovery Island, DinoLand U.S.A., Camp Minnie-Mickey, Africa,** and **Asia.** (A seventh section, **Rafiki's Planet Watch,** is touted as a land by Disney but doesn't really qualify as such in our eyes.)

Its size notwithstanding, Disney's Animal Kingdom features a limited number of attractions: seven rides, several walk-through exhibits, an indoor theater, four amphitheaters, a conservation exhibit, and a children's playground.

With more than a decade under its belt, Animal Kingdom has received mixed reviews. Guests complain loudly about the park layout and the necessity of backtracking through Discovery Island in order to access the various themed areas. However, most of the attractions (with one or two notable exceptions) have been well received. Also praised are the natural-habitat animal exhibits as well as the park architecture and landscaping.

ARRIVING

DISNEY'S ANIMAL KINGDOM IS OFF OSCEOLA PARKWAY in the southwest corner of Walt Disney World and is not too far from Blizzard Beach, the Coronado Springs Resort, and the All-Star Resorts. Animal Kingdom Lodge is about a mile away from the park on its northwest side. From Interstate 4, take Exit

64B, US 192, to the so-called Walt Disney World main entrance (World Drive) and follow the signs to Animal Kingdom. The park has its own 6,000-car pay parking lot with close-in parking for the disabled. Once parked, you can walk to the entrance or catch a ride on one of Disney's trademark trams. Animal Kingdom is connected to other Walt Disney World destinations by the Disney bus system. If you're staying at a Disney resort and plan to arrive at Animal Kingdom entrance before park opening, use Disney transportation rather than taking your own car. The Animal Kingdom parking lot often opens only 15 minutes before the park, causing long lines and frustration for drivers.

unofficial **TIP**
Be sure to mark the location of your car on your parking receipt and tuck it in a safe place (preferably on your person rather than in your car).

OPERATING HOURS

ANIMAL KINGDOM, NOT UNEXPECTEDLY, hosted tremendous crowds during its early years. Consequently, Disney management has done a fair amount of fiddling and experimenting with operating hours and opening procedures. Animal Kingdom's opening time now roughly corresponds to that of the other parks. Thus, you can expect a 9 a.m. opening during less busy times of the year and an 8 a.m. opening during holidays and high season. Animal Kingdom usually closes well before the other parks—as early as 5 p.m., in fact, during off-season. More common is a 6 or 7 p.m. closing.

Park-opening procedures at Animal Kingdom vary. Sometimes guests arriving prior to the official opening time are admitted to The Oasis and Discovery Island. The remainder of the park is roped off until official opening time. The rest of the time, those arriving early are held at the entrance turnstiles.

During the financial turmoil of the last few years, Disney laid off a number of cast members and trotted out several cost-cutting initiatives. One of these is to delay the daily opening of Kali River Rapids in Asia, as well as the Boneyard playground, the Wildlife Express train, and Conservation Station until 30 minutes or so after the rest of the park opens.

On holidays and other days of projected heavy attendance, Disney will open the park 30–60 minutes early.

Many guests wrap up their tour and leave by 3:30 or 4 p.m. Lines for the major rides and the 3-D movie in The Tree of Life will usually thin appreciably between 4 p.m. and closing time. If you arrive at 2 p.m. and take in a couple of

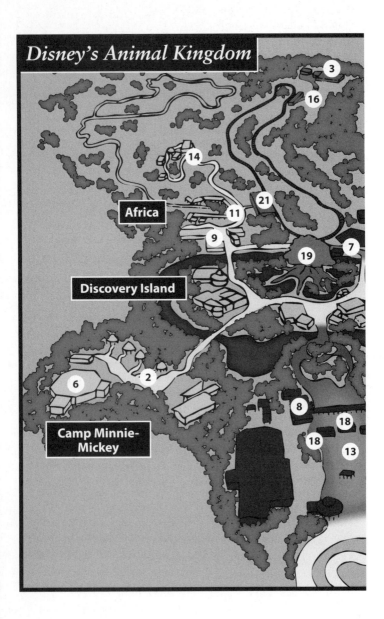

Disney's Animal Kingdom

Africa

Discovery Island

Camp Minnie-Mickey

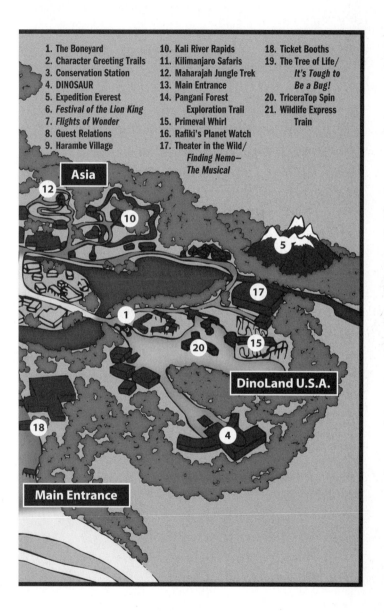

1. The Boneyard
2. Character Greeting Trails
3. Conservation Station
4. DINOSAUR
5. Expedition Everest
6. *Festival of the Lion King*
7. *Flights of Wonder*
8. Guest Relations
9. Harambe Village
10. Kali River Rapids
11. Kilimanjaro Safaris
12. Maharajah Jungle Trek
13. Main Entrance
14. Pangani Forest
    Exploration Trail
15. Primeval Whirl
16. Rafiki's Planet Watch
17. Theater in the Wild/
    *Finding Nemo—
    The Musical*
18. Ticket Booths
19. The Tree of Life/
    *It's Tough to
    Be a Bug!*
20. TriceraTop Spin
21. Wildlife Express
    Train

Asia

DinoLand U.S.A.

Main Entrance

unofficial **TIP**
Our advice is to arrive, admission in hand, 30 minutes before official opening during the summer and holiday periods, and 20 minutes before official opening the rest of the year.

stage shows (described later), waits should be tolerable by the time you hit The Tree of Life and the rides. As an added bonus for late-afternoon touring, the animals tend to be more active.

Animal Kingdom has joined the other three major theme parks in the Extra Magic Hours early-entry program. Even with Expedition Everest open, getting up early to participate in the program doesn't really save you any time standing in line. Our testing has shown that the additional attendance on early-entry days totally nullifies any advantage associated with being admitted an hour early. The time required to see the same set of attractions surpasses the time required on a non-early-entry day.

In early 2011, Disney quietly changed Animal Kingdom's schedule so that it no longer includes evening Extra Magic Hours. As we went to press, no evening hours were scheduled for March–October 2011, including holidays and other days of peak attendance. We're not sure whether this is a temporary cost-cutting move or a permanent change.

DISNEY'S ANIMAL KINGDOM SERVICES

Most of the park's service facilities are located inside the main entrance and on Discovery Island as follows:

Baby Care Center On Discovery Island, behind Creature Comforts

Banking Services ATMs at the main entrance, by the turnstiles, and near DINOSAUR in DinoLand U.S.A.

Film and Cameras Inside the main entrance at Garden Gate Gifts, in Africa at Duka La Filimu and Mombasa Marketplace, and at other retail shops throughout the park

First Aid On Discovery Island, next to Creature Comforts

Guest Relations/Information Inside the main entrance to the left

Live Entertainment/Parade Information Included in the park guide map, available free at Guest Relations

Lost and Found Inside the main entrance to the left

Lost Persons Can be reported at Guest Relations and at the Baby Care Center on Discovery Island

Storage Lockers Inside the main entrance to the left

Wheelchair, ECV, and Stroller Rentals Inside the main entrance to the right

Africa	Kilimanjaro Safaris
Asia	Expedition Everest
Camp Minnie-Mickey	*Festival of the Lion King*
DinoLand U.S.A.	DINOSAUR, *Finding Nemo—The Musical*
Discovery Island	*It's Tough to Be a Bug!*

GETTING ORIENTED

AT THE ENTRANCE PLAZA ARE TICKET KIOSKS fronting the main entrance. To your right, before the turnstiles, is an ATM. After you pass through the turnstiles, wheelchair and stroller rentals are to your right. Guest Relations—the park headquarters for information, handout park maps, entertainment schedules (*Times Guide*s), missing persons, and lost and found—is to the left. Nearby are restrooms, public phones, and rental lockers. Beyond the entrance plaza, you enter **The Oasis,** a lushly vegetated network of converging pathways winding through a landscape punctuated with streams, waterfalls, and misty glades and inhabited by what Disney calls "colorful and unusual animals."

The park is arranged somewhat like the Magic Kingdom, in a hub-and-spoke configuration. The lush, tropical Oasis serves as Main Street, funneling visitors to **Discovery Island** at the center of the park. Dominated by the park's central icon, the 14-story hand-carved **Tree of Life,** Discovery Island is the park's retail and dining center. From Discovery Island, guests can access the respective themed areas, known as **Africa, Camp Minnie-Mickey, Asia,** and **DinoLand U.S.A.** Discovery Island additionally hosts a theater attraction in The Tree of Life, and a number of short nature trails.

THE OASIS

THOUGH THE FUNCTIONAL PURPOSE of The Oasis is the same as that of Main Street in the Magic Kingdom (that is, to funnel guests to the center of the park), it also serves as what Disney calls a "transitional experience." In plain English, this means that it sets the stage and gets you into the right mood to enjoy Animal Kingdom. You will know the minute you pass through the turnstiles that this is not just another Main Street. Where Main Street, Hollywood Boulevard, and the

unofficial **TIP**
The Oasis's exhibits are designed for the animals' comfort, so you need to be patient and look closely if you want to see these creatures.

Epcot entrance plaza direct you like an arrow straight into the heart of the respective parks, The Oasis immediately envelops you in an environment that is replete with choices. There is not one broad thoroughfare, but rather multiple paths. Each will deliver you to Discovery Island at the center of the park, but which path you choose and what you see along the way is up to you. There is nothing obvious about where you are going, no Cinderella Castle or giant golf ball to beckon you. There is instead a lush, green, canopied landscape with streams, grottos, and waterfalls, an environment that promises adventure without revealing its nature.

The natural-habitat zoological exhibits in The Oasis are representative of the ones throughout the park. Although extraordinarily lush and beautiful, the exhibits are primarily designed for the comfort and well-being of the animals. A sign will identify the animal(s) in each exhibit, but there's no guarantee the animals will be immediately visible. Because most habitats are large and provide ample terrain for the occupants to hide, you must linger and concentrate, looking for small movements in the vegetation. When you do spot the animal, you may only make out a shadowy figure, or perhaps only a leg or a tail will be visible. In any event, don't expect the animals to stand out like a lump of coal in the snow. Animal watching Disney-style requires a sharp eye and a bit of effort.

TOURING TIPS The Oasis is a place to linger and appreciate, and although this is exactly what the designers intended, it will be largely lost on Disney-conditioned guests who blitz through at warp speed to queue up for the big attractions. If you are a blitzer in the morning, plan to spend some time in The Oasis on your way out of the park. The Oasis usually opens 30 minutes before and closes 30–60 minutes after the rest of the park.

DISCOVERY ISLAND

DISCOVERY ISLAND IS AN ISLAND OF tropical greenery and whimsical equatorial African architecture, executed in vibrant hues of teal, yellow, red, and blue. Connected to the other lands by bridges, the island is the hub from which guests can access the park's various themed areas. A village is arrayed in a crescent around the base of Animal Kingdom's signature landmark, **The Tree of Life.** Towering 14 stories above the village, The Tree of Life is this park's version of Cinderella Castle or Spaceship Earth. Flanked by pools, meadows, and exotic gardens populated by a diversity of birds and animals, The Tree of Life houses a theater attraction inspired by the Disney/Pixar film *A Bug's Life.*

As you enter Discovery Island via the bridge from The Oasis and the main entrance, you will see The Tree of Life directly ahead at the 12 o'clock position, with the village at its base in a semicircle. The bridge to Asia is to the right of the tree at the 2 o'clock position, with the bridge to DinoLand U.S.A. at roughly 4 o'clock. The bridge connecting The Oasis to Discovery Island is at the 6 o'clock position; the bridge to Camp Minnie-Mickey is at 8 o'clock; and the bridge to Africa is at 11 o'clock.

unofficial **TIP** It is here, in Discovery Island, that you will find the First Aid and Baby Care centers.

Discovery Island is the park's central shopping, dining, and services headquarters. **Island Mercantile** has the best selection of Disney-trademark merchandise. Counter-service food and snacks are available, but there are no full-service restaurants on Discovery Island (the three full-service restaurants in the park are the **Rainforest Cafe,** to the left of the main entrance; **Tusker House,** in Africa; and **Yak & Yeti Restaurant,** in Asia).

The Tree of Life/*It's Tough to Be a Bug!* ★★★★

APPEAL BY AGE	PRESCHOOL ★★★	GRADE SCHOOL ★★★★	TEENS ★★★★
YOUNG ADULTS ★★★★	OVER 30 ★★★★		SENIORS ★★★★

What it is 3-D theater show. **Scope and scale** Major attraction. **When to go** Before 10:30 a.m., after 4 p.m., or use Fastpass. **Special comments** The theater is inside the tree. **Authors' rating** Zany and frenetic; ★★★★. **Duration of presentation** Approximately 7½ minutes. **When to arrive** 12–30 minutes before showtime.

DESCRIPTION AND COMMENTS The Tree of Life, apart from its size, is quite a work of art. Although from afar it is certainly magnificent and imposing, it is not until you examine the tree at close range that you truly appreciate its rich detail. What appears to be ancient gnarled bark is, in fact, hundreds of carvings that depict all manner of wildlife, each integrated seamlessly into the trunk, roots, and limbs of the tree. A stunning symbol of the interdependence of all living things, The Tree of Life is the most visually compelling structure to be found in any Disney park.

In sharp contrast to the grandeur of the tree is the subject of the attraction housed within its trunk. Called *It's Tough to Be a Bug!*, this humorous 3-D presentation is about the difficulties of being a very small creature. Contrasting with the relatively serious tone of Animal Kingdom in general, *It's Tough to Be a Bug!* stands virtually alone in providing some much needed levity and whimsy. The show is similar to *Honey, I Shrunk the Audience* at Epcot in that it combines a 3-D film with an arsenal of tactile and visual special effects. We rate *Bug* as not to be missed.

TOURING TIPS Although it's situated in the most eye-popping structure in the park, *It's Tough to Be a Bug!* is rarely crowded even on the busiest days, and Fastpass is almost never needed. We recommend going in the morning after you've experienced Kilimanjaro Safaris, Kali River Rapids, Expedition Everest, and DINOSAUR. If you miss the *Bug* in the morning, try again in the late afternoon.

Be advised that *It's Tough to Be a Bug!* is very intense and that the special effects will do a number on young children as well as anyone who is squeamish about insects.

CAMP MINNIE-MICKEY

THIS LAND IS DESIGNED TO BE THE Disney characters' Animal Kingdom headquarters. A small land, Camp Minnie-Mickey is about the size of Mickey's Toontown Fair but has a rustic and woodsy theme like a summer camp. In addition to housing a character-meeting-and-greeting area, Camp Minnie-Mickey is home to a live stage production featuring Disney characters.

Situated in a cul-de-sac, Camp Minnie-Mickey is a pedestrian's nightmare. Lines for the two stage shows and from the character-greeting areas spill out into the congested walkways, making movement almost impossible. To compound the problem, hundreds of parked strollers clog the paths, squeezing the flow of traffic to a trickle. Meanwhile, hordes of guests trying to enter Camp Minnie-Mickey collide with guests trying to exit on the bridge connecting the camp to Discovery Island. To make matters worse, Disney positions vendor carts on the approaches to the bridge. It's a planning error of the first order, one that seems totally avoidable at a theme park with as much usable acreage as Animal Kingdom's.

Character Trails

DESCRIPTION AND COMMENTS Characters can be found at the end of each of several "character trails." Each trail has its own private reception area and, of course, its own queue. A sign in front of

each queue tells you to which character the path lea_
most typical lineup has Mickey, Minnie, Goofy, and Plut__
one queue each. Other frequently seen characters include Winnie the Pooh, Eeyore, Pocahontas, Timon, and Baloo. Disney
will occasionally supplement these with characters from its latest film, if the movie has anything to do with nature, animals,
or the environment. Mickey and Minnie are constants.

TOURING TIPS Characters usually appear an hour after the rest of
the park opens. Waiting in line to see the characters can be
extremely time-consuming. We recommend visiting early in
the morning or late in the afternoon. Because there are fewer
attractions at Animal Kingdom than at the other parks, expect
to find a disproportionate number of guests in Camp Minnie-
Mickey. If the place is really mobbed, you may want to
consider meeting the characters in one of the other parks.
Ditto for the stage show.

Festival of the Lion King ★★★★

APPEAL BY AGE	PRESCHOOL ★★★★½	GRADE SCHOOL ★★★★½	TEENS ★★★★½
YOUNG ADULTS ★★★★½		OVER 30 ★★★★½	SENIORS ★★★★★

What it is Theater-in-the-round stage show. **Scope and scale** Major
attraction. **When to go** Before 11 a.m. or after 4 p.m. **Special comments** Performance times are listed in the handout park map or *Times
Guide.* **Authors' rating** Upbeat and spectacular, not to be missed;
★★★★. **Duration of presentation** 25 minutes. **Preshow entertainment** None. **When to arrive** 20–35 minutes before showtime.

DESCRIPTION AND COMMENTS This energetic production, inspired by
Disney's *Lion King* feature, is part stage show, part parade, part
circus. Guests are seated in four sets of bleachers surrounding
the stage and organized into separate cheering sections, which
are called on to make elephant, warthog, giraffe, and lion noises
(you won't be alone if you don't know how to make a giraffe or
warthog noise). There is a great deal of parading around, some
acrobatics, and a lot of singing and dancing. By our count, every
tune from *The Lion King* is belted out and reprised several times.
No joke—if you don't know the words to all the songs by the
end of the show, you must have been asleep.

TOURING TIPS This show is both popular and difficult to see. Your
best bet is to go to the first show in the morning or to one of
the last two performances in the evening. To see the show
during the more crowded middle of the day, you'll need to
queue up at least 35–45 minutes before showtime. To minimize standing in the hot sun, refrain from hopping in line until
the Disney people begin directing guests to the far-right

...e small children or short adults in your party,
...he bleachers. The first five rows in particular
...ise, making it difficult for those in rows two
...ee.

AFRICA

AFRICA IS THE LARGEST of Animal Kingdom's lands, and guests enter through Harambe, Disney's immensely sanitized version of a modern rural African town. There is a market (with modern cash registers); dining options consist of a sit-down buffet, limited counter service, and snack stands. What distinguishes Harambe is its understatement. Far from the stereotypical great-white-hunter image of an African town, Harambe is definitely (and realistically) not exotic. The buildings, while interesting, are quite plain and architecturally simple. Though it's better maintained and more idealized than the real McCoy, Disney's Harambe would be a lot more at home in Kenya than the Magic Kingdom's Main Street would be in Missouri.

Harambe serves as the gateway to the African veldt habitat, Animal Kingdom's largest and most ambitious zoological exhibit. Access to the veldt is via the **Kilimanjaro Safaris** attraction, located at the end of Harambe's main drag near the fat-trunked baobab tree. Harambe is also the departure point for the train to **Rafiki's Planet Watch** and **Conservation Station,** the park's veterinary headquarters.

Kilimanjaro Safaris (*Fastpass*) ★★★★★

APPEAL BY AGE	PRESCHOOL ★★★★½	GRADE SCHOOL ★★★★½	TEENS ★★★★½
YOUNG ADULTS ★★★★★		OVER 30 ★★★★½	SENIORS ★★★★★

What it is Truck ride through an African wildlife reservation. **Scope and scale** Super-headliner. **When to go** As soon as the park opens, in the 2 hours before closing, or use Fastpass. **Authors' rating** Truly exceptional; not to be missed; ★★★★★. **Duration of ride** About 20 minutes. **Average wait in line per 100 people ahead of you** 4 minutes. **Assumes** Full-capacity operation with 18-second dispatch interval. **Loading speed** Fast.

DESCRIPTION AND COMMENTS The park's premier zoological attraction, Kilimanjaro Safaris offers an exceptionally realistic, albeit brief, imitation of an actual African photo safari. Thirty-two guests at a time board tall, open safari vehicles and are dispatched into a simulated African veldt habitat. Animals such as zebras, wildebeests, impalas, Thomson's gazelles, giraffes, and even rhinos roam apparently free, while predators such as lions, as well as potentially dangerous large animals like hippos, are separated from both prey and guests by all-but-invisible, natural-appearing barriers. Although the animals have more than 100 acres of savanna, woodland, streams, and rocky hills to call home, careful placement of water holes, forage, and salt licks ensures that the critters are hanging out by the road when safari vehicles roll by.

A scripted narration provides a storyline about poachers in the area while an onboard guide points out and identifies the various animals encountered. Toward the end of the ride, the safari chases the poachers, who are after elephants.

Having traveled in Kenya and Tanzania, I (Bob) will tell you that Disney has done an amazing job of replicating the sub-Saharan east-African landscape. The main difference that an east African would notice is that Disney's version is greener and, generally speaking, less barren. As on a real African safari, what animals you see, and how many, is pretty much a matter of luck. We've experienced Kilimanjaro Safaris more than 100 times and had a different experience on each trip.

A minus: the rather strident narrative, which is somewhat distracting when you're trying to spot and enjoy wildlife.

In 2011 Disney introduced the **Wild Africa Trek,** a behind-the-scenes tour of the Animal Kingdom that takes you through much of the Safaris' animal enclosures (3 hours, $201 per person, guests age 8 and older). As you drive past the hippo pool or over the crocodile pool, look up for a series of rope bridges towering far above the ground. You may see Trekkers on tour.

TOURING TIPS Kilimanjaro Safaris is Animal Kingdom's number-two draw behind Expedition Everest. This is good news: by distributing guests more evenly throughout the park, Expedition Everest makes it unnecessary to run to the Kilimanjaro Safaris first thing in the morning. Our Animal Kingdom touring plan has you obtain Fastpasses for the safaris just before lunch. While your Fastpass return window approaches, you'll have plenty of time to eat and tour the rest of Africa. Before Expedition Everest, seeing the Safaris early meant backtracking to Africa later in the day to see exhibits and attractions that were not open first thing in the morning; our touring plan eliminates all of that extra walking, too.

Waits for Kilimanjaro Safaris diminish in late afternoon, sometimes as early as 3:30 p.m., but more commonly somewhat later. As noted above, Kilimanjaro Safaris is a Fastpass attraction. If the wait exceeds 30 minutes when you arrive, by all means use Fastpass. The downside to Fastpass, and the reason we prefer that you ride around lunchtime, is that there aren't many other attractions in Africa to occupy your attention while you wait for your Fastpass return time. This means you will probably be touring somewhere far removed when it's time to backtrack to Safaris.

If you want to take photos on your safari, be advised that the vehicle doesn't stop very often, so be prepared to snap while under way. Also, don't worry about the ride itself: it really isn't very rough. Finally, the only thing that a young child might find intimidating is crossing an "old bridge" that pretends to collapse under your truck.

Pangani Forest Exploration Trail ★★★

APPEAL BY AGE	PRESCHOOL ★★★★	GRADE SCHOOL ★★★★	TEENS ★★★½
YOUNG ADULTS ★★★★		OVER 30 ★★★★	SENIORS ★★★★

What it is Walk-through zoological exhibit. **Scope and scale** Major attraction. **When to go** Before 10 a.m. and after 2:30 p.m. **Authors' rating ★★★. Duration of tour** About 20–25 minutes.

DESCRIPTION AND COMMENTS Because guests disembark from the safari at the entrance to the Pangani Forest Exploration Trail, many guests try the trail immediately after the safari. Winding between the domain of two troops of lowland gorillas, it's hard to see what, if anything, separates you from the primates. Also on the trail are a hippo pool with an underwater-viewing area, and a naked-mole-rat exhibit (we promise we're not making this up). A highlight of the trail is an exotic bird aviary so craftily designed that you can barely tell you're in an enclosure.

TOURING TIPS The Pangani Forest Exploration Trail is lush, beautiful, and jammed to the gills with people much of the time. Guests exiting the safari can choose between returning to Harambe or walking the Pangani Forest Exploration Trail. Not unexpectedly, many opt for the trail. Thus, when the safari is operating at full tilt, it spews hundreds of guests every couple of minutes onto the Exploration Trail. The one-way trail in turn becomes so clogged that nobody can move or see much of anything. After a minute or two, however, you catch the feel of the mob moving forward in small lurches. From then on you shift, elbow, grunt, and wriggle your way along, every so often coming to an animal exhibit. Here you endeavor to work your way close to the rail but are opposed by people trapped against the rail who are trying to rejoin the surging crowd. The animals, as well as their natural-habitat enclosures, are pretty nifty if you can fight close enough to see them.

Clearly this attraction is either badly designed, misplaced, or both. Your only real chance for enjoying it is to walk through before 10 a.m. (i.e., before the safari hits full stride) or after 2:30 p.m.

Another strategy, especially if you're more into the wild-life than the thrill rides, is to head for Kilimanjaro Safaris as soon as the park opens and get a Fastpass instead of riding. Early in the morning, the return window will be short, just short enough, in fact, for an uncrowded, leisurely tour of the Pangani Forest Exploration Trail before you go on safari.

RAFIKI'S PLANET WATCH

THIS AREA FIRST SHOWED UP on maps of Animal King-dom in 2001. It's not a "land" and not really an attraction either. Our best guess is that Disney is using the name as an umbrella for Conservation Station, the petting zoo, and the exhibits accessible from Harambe via the Wildlife Express Train. Presumably, Disney hopes that invoking Rafiki (a beloved character from *The Lion King*) will stimulate guests to check out things in this far-flung outpost of the park.

Conservation Station and Affection Section ★★★

APPEAL BY AGE	PRESCHOOL ★★★½	GRADE SCHOOL ★★★½	TEENS ★★★
YOUNG ADULTS ★★★	OVER 30 ★★★		SENIORS ★★★

What it is Behind-the-scenes walk-through educational exhibit and petting zoo. **Scope and scale** Minor attraction. **When to go** Anytime. **Special comments** Opens 30 minutes after the rest of the park. **Authors' rating** Evolving; ★★★. **Probable waiting time** None.

DESCRIPTION AND COMMENTS Conservation Station is Animal King-dom's veterinary and conservation headquarters. Located on the perimeter of the African section of the park, Conservation Station is, strictly speaking, a backstage, working facility. Here guests can meet wildlife experts, observe some of the Station's ongoing projects, and learn about the behind-the-scenes oper-ations of the park. The Station includes, among other things, a rehabilitation area for injured animals and a nursery for recently born (or hatched) critters. Vets and other experts are on hand to answer questions.

While there are several permanent exhibits, including Affec-tion Section (an animal-petting area), what you see at Conserva-tion Station will largely depend on what's going on when you arrive. On the days we visited, there wasn't enough happening to warrant waiting in line twice (coming and going) for the train.

You can access Conservation Station by taking the Wildlife Express train directly from Harambe. To return to the center of the park, continue the loop from Conservation Station back to Harambe.

TOURING TIPS Conservation Station is interesting, but you have to invest a little effort, and it helps to be inquisitive. Because it's so removed from the rest of the park, you'll never bump into Conservation Station unless you take the train.

Habitat Habit!

Listed on the park map as an attraction is Habitat Habit!, located on the pedestrian path between the train station and Conservation Station. Habitat Habit! consists of a tiny collection of signs (about coexistence with wildlife) and a few cotton-top tamarins. To call it an attraction is absurd.

Wildlife Express Train ★★

APPEAL BY AGE	PRESCHOOL ★★★½	GRADE SCHOOL ★★★	TEENS ★★★
YOUNG ADULTS ★★½		OVER 30 ★★★	SENIORS ★★★

What it is Scenic railroad ride to Rafiki's Planet Watch and Conservation Station. **Scope and scale** Minor attraction. **When to go** Anytime. **Special comments** Opens 30 minutes after the rest of the park. **Authors' rating** Ho-hum; ★★. **Duration of ride** About 5–7 minutes one-way. **Average wait in line per 100 people ahead of you** 9 minutes. **Loading speed** Moderate.

DESCRIPTION AND COMMENTS A transportation ride that snakes behind the African wildlife reserve as it makes its loop connecting Harambe to Rafiki's Planet Watch and Conservation Station. En route, you see the nighttime enclosures for the animals that populate the Kilimanjaro Safaris. Similarly, returning to Harambe, you see the backstage areas of Asia. Regardless of the direction in which you're heading, the sights are not especially interesting.

TOURING TIPS Most guests will embark for Rafiki's *Planet Watch* and Conservation Station after experiencing the Kilimanjaro Safaris and the Pangani Forest Exploration Trail. Thus, the train begins to get crowded between 10 and 11 a.m. Though you may catch a glimpse of several species from the train, it can't compare to Kilimanjaro Safaris for seeing the animals.

ASIA

CROSSING THE ASIA BRIDGE FROM DISCOVERY ISLAND, you enter Asia through the village of Anandapur, a veritable collage of Asian themes inspired by the architecture and ruins of India, Thailand, Indonesia, and Nepal. Situated near the bank of the Chakranadi River (translation: "the river that runs in circles") and surrounded by lush vegetation, Anandapur provides access to a gibbon exhibit and to Asia's two feature attractions, the **Kali River Rapids** whitewater raft ride and **Expedition Everest.** Also in Asia is *Flights of Wonder,* an educational production about birds.

Expedition Everest—yep, another mountain, and at 200 feet, the tallest in Florida—is a super-headliner roller coaster. You board an old mountain railway destined for the foot of Mount Everest that ends up racing both forward and backward through caverns and frigid canyons en route to paying a social call on the Abominable Snowman. Expedition Everest is billed as a "family thrill ride," which means simply that it's more like Big Thunder Mountain Railroad than like the Rock 'n' Roller Coaster.

Expedition Everest (*Fastpass*)   ★★★★½

APPEAL BY AGE	PRESCHOOL ★★★	GRADE SCHOOL ★★★★½	TEENS ★★★★★
YOUNG ADULTS ★★★★★		OVER 30 ★★★★★	SENIORS ★★★★

What it is High-speed, outdoor roller coaster through Nepalese mountain village. **Scope and scale** Super-headliner. **When to go** Before 9:30 a.m. or after 3 p.m., or use Fastpass. **Special comments** 44" minimum height requirement. **Authors' rating** Contains some of the park's most stunning visual elements; not to be missed; ★★★★½. **Average wait in line per 100 people ahead of you** Just under 4 minutes; assumes 2 tracks operating. **Loading speed** Moderate–fast.

DESCRIPTION AND COMMENTS The first true roller coaster in Disney's Animal Kingdom, Expedition Everest has boasted the park's longest waits in line from the moment it opened—and for good reason. Your journey begins with an elaborate waiting area modeled after a Nepalese village. Then you board an old train headed for the top of Mount Everest and embark on a ride that results in a high-speed encounter with the Abominable Snowman himself.

   The ride consists of tight turns (some while traveling backwards), hills, and dips, but no loops or inversions. From your departure at the loading station through your first high-speed descent, you'll see some of the most spectacular panoramas available in Walt Disney World. On a clear day you'll be able to view Coronado Springs Resort, Epcot's Spaceship Earth, and possibly downtown Orlando. But look quickly, because you'll immediately be propelled, projectile-like, through the inner and outer reaches of the mountain. The final drop and last few turns are among Disney's best-designed coaster effects. A few minor criticisms: At a couple of points, your stopped while the ride's track is reconfigured, he attraction's continuity. And while the Yeti tronic is undoubtedly impressive, he breaks down a 30-year old Fiat. But don't let these small short-comings stop you from riding.

The coaster reaches a top speed of around 50 mph, just about twice that of Space Mountain, so expect to see the usual warnings for health and safety. The first few seats of these vehicles offer the best front-seat experience of any Disney coaster, indoor or out. If at all possible, ask to sit up front. Also, look for the animal droppings on display in the Fastpass return line—a deliberate attempt at verisimilitude, or did Disney run out of money for ride props and use whatever they could find? You decide.

TOURING TIPS Get Fastpasses for Everest first thing in the morning. Alternatively, ride immediately after the park opens or during evening Extra Magic Hours. If using Fastpass in the morning, try to tour DinoLand U.S.A. before you return; Kali River Rapids and *Flights of Wonder* don't usually open with the rest of Asia, so you'll backtrack less if you can get the must-see attractions in DinoLand covered early.

Flights of Wonder ★★★★

APPEAL BY AGE	PRESCHOOL ★★★★	GRADE SCHOOL ★★★★	TEENS ★★★★
YOUNG ADULTS ★★★★		OVER 30 ★★★★	SENIORS ★★★★

What it is Stadium show about birds. **Scope and scale** Major attraction. **When to go** Anytime. **Special comments** Performance times are listed in the handout park map or *Times Guide*. **Authors' rating** Unique; ★★★★. **Duration of presentation** 30 minutes. **Preshow entertainment** None. **When to arrive** 20–30 minutes before showtime.

DESCRIPTION AND COMMENTS Both interesting and fun, *Flights of Wonder* is well paced and showcases a surprising number of different bird species. The show has been rescripted, abandoning an improbable plot for a more straightforward educational presentation. The focus of *Flights of Wonder* is on the natural talents and characteristics of the various species, so don't expect to see any parrots riding bicycles. The natural behaviors, however, far surpass any tricks learned from humans. Overall, the presentation is fascinating and exceeds most guests' expectations.

TOURING TIPS *Flights of Wonder* plays at the stadium located near the Asia Bridge on the walkway into Asia. Though the stadium is covered, it's not air-conditioned; thus, early-morning and late-afternoon performances are more comfortable.

Kali River Rapids (*Fastpass*)   ★★★½

What it is Whitewater raft ride. **Scope and scale** Headliner. **When to go** Before 10:30 a.m. or after 4:30 p.m., or use Fastpass. **Special comments** You are guaranteed to get wet. Opens 30 minutes after the rest of the park. 38" minimum height requirement. Switching-off option available (see page 75). **Authors' rating** Short but scenic; ★★★½. **Duration of ride** About 5 minutes. **Average wait in line per 100 people ahead of you** 5 minutes. **Loading speed** Moderate.

DESCRIPTION AND COMMENTS Whitewater-raft rides have been a hot-weather favorite of theme park patrons for more than 20 years. The ride itself consists of an unguided trip down a man-made river in a circular rubber raft with a platform seating 12 people mounted on top. The raft essentially floats free in the current and is washed downstream through rapids and waves. Because the river is fairly wide, with numerous currents, eddies, and obstacles, there is no telling exactly where the raft will drift. Thus, each trip is different and exciting. At the end of the ride, a conveyor belt hauls the raft up to be unloaded and prepared for the next group of guests.

What distinguishes Kali River Rapids from other theme park raft rides is Disney's trademark attention to visual detail. Where many raft rides essentially plunge down a concrete ditch, Kali River Rapids flows through a dense rain forest, past waterfalls, temple ruins, and bamboo thickets, emerging into a cleared area where greedy loggers have ravaged the forest, and finally drifting back under the tropical canopy as the river cycles back to Anandapur. Along the way, your raft runs a gauntlet of raging cataracts, logjams, and other dangers.

TOURING TIPS This attraction is hugely popular on hot summer days. Ride Kali River Rapids before 11 a.m., after 4:30 p.m., or use Fastpass. You can expect to get wet and probably drenched on this ride. Our recommendation is to wear shorts to the park and bring along a jumbo-sized trash bag as well as a smaller plastic bag. Before boarding the raft, take off your socks and punch a hole in your jumbo bag for your head. Though you can also cut holes for your arms, you will probably stay drier with your arms inside the bag. Use the smaller plastic bag to wrap around your shoes. If you are worried about mussing your hairdo, bring a third bag for your head.

Other tips for staying dry (make that drier) include wearing as little as the law and Disney allow and storing a change of clothes in a park rental locker. Sandals are the perfect footwear for water rides. If you don't have sandals, try to prop your feet up above the bottom of the raft.

Maharajah Jungle Trek ★★★★

APPEAL BY AGE	PRESCHOOL ★★★★	GRADE SCHOOL ★★★★	TEENS ★★★★
YOUNG ADULTS ★★★★		OVER 30 ★★★★	SENIORS ★★★★

What it is Walk-through zoological exhibit. **Scope and scale** Headliner. **When to go** Anytime. **Special comments** Opens 30 minutes after the rest of the park. **Authors' rating** A standard-setter for natural habitat design; ★★★★. **Duration of tour** About 20–30 minutes.

DESCRIPTION AND COMMENTS The Maharajah Jungle Trek is a zoological nature walk similar to the Pangani Forest Exploration Trail, but with an Asian setting and Asian animals. You start with Komodo dragons and then work up to Malayan tapirs. Next is a cave with fruit bats. Ruins of the maharaja's palace provide the setting for Bengal tigers. From the top of a parapet in the palace you can view a herd of blackbuck antelope and Asian deer. The trek concludes with an aviary.

Labyrinthine, overgrown, and elaborately detailed, the temple ruin would be a compelling attraction even without the animals. Throw in a few bats, bucks, and Bengals and you're in for a treat.

TOURING TIPS The Jungle Trek does not get as jammed up as the Pangani Forest Exploration Trail and is a good choice for midday touring when most of the other attractions are crowded. The downside, of course, is that the exhibit showcases tigers, tapirs, and other creatures that might not be as active in the heat of the day as mad dogs and Englishmen.

▎ DINOLAND U.S.A.

THIS MOST TYPICALLY DISNEY OF ANIMAL KINGDOM'S lands is a cross between an anthropological dig and a quirky roadside attraction. Accessible via the bridge from Discovery Island, DinoLand U.S.A. is home to a children's play area, a nature trail, a 1,500-seat amphitheater, and **DINOSAUR,** one of Animal Kingdom's two thrill rides.

The Boneyard ★★★½

APPEAL BY AGE	PRESCHOOL ★★★★½	GRADE SCHOOL ★★★★	TEENS ★★
YOUNG ADULTS ★★		OVER 30 ★★½	SENIORS ★★

What it is Elaborate playground. **Scope and scale** Diversion. **When to go** Anytime. **Special comments** Opens 30 minutes after the rest

of the park. **Authors' rating** Stimulating fun for children; ★★★½.
Duration of visit Varies. **Probable waiting time** None.

DESCRIPTION AND COMMENTS This attraction is an elaborate playground, particularly appealing to kids ages 10 and younger,
but visually appealing to all ages. Arranged in the form of a
rambling open-air dig site, The Boneyard offers plenty of
opportunity for exploration and letting off steam. Playground
equipment consists of the skeletons of *Triceratops, Tyranno-
saurus rex, Brachiosaurus,* and the like, on which children can
swing, slide, and climb. In addition, there are sand pits where
little ones can scrounge around for bones and fossils.

TOURING TIPS Not the cleanest Disney attraction, but certainly
one where younger children will want to spend some time.
Aside from getting dirty, or at least sandy, be aware that The
Boneyard gets mighty hot in the Florida sun. Keep your kids
well hydrated and drag them into the shade from time to
time. If your children will let you, save the playground until
after you have experienced the main attractions. Because The
Boneyard is so close to the center of the park, it's easy to stop
in whenever your kids get itchy. While the little ones clamber
around on giant femurs and ribs, you can sip a tall cool one in
the shade (still keeping an eye on them, of course).

   Be aware that The Boneyard rambles over about a half-
acre and is multistoried. It's pretty easy to lose sight of a small
child in the playground. Fortunately, there's only one entrance
and exit.

DINOSAUR (*Fastpass*) ★★★★½

APPEAL BY AGE	PRESCHOOL ★★	GRADE SCHOOL ★★★½	TEENS ★★★★
YOUNG ADULTS ★★★★		OVER 30 ★★★★	SENIORS ★★★½

What it is Motion-simulator dark ride. **Scope and scale** Super-headliner.
When to go Before 10:30 a.m., in the hour before closing, or use Fastpass.
Special comments Must be 40" tall to ride. Switching-off option provided (see page 75). **Authors' rating** Really improved; not to be missed;
★★★★½. **Duration of ride** 3½ minutes. **Average wait in line per 100
people ahead of you** 3 minutes; assumes full-capacity operation with
18-second dispatch interval. **Loading speed** Fast.

DESCRIPTION AND COMMENTS DINOSAUR, formerly known as
Countdown to Extinction, is a combination track ride and
motion simulator. In addition to moving along a cleverly hidden track, the ride vehicle also bucks and pitches (the
simulator part) in sync with the visuals and special effects
encountered. The plot has you traveling back in time on a
mission of rescue and conservation. Your objective, believe it

or not, is to haul back a living dinosaur before the species becomes extinct. Whoever is operating the clock, however, cuts it a little close, and you arrive on the prehistoric scene just as a giant asteroid is hurling toward Earth. General mayhem ensues as you evade carnivorous predators, catch Barney, and make your escape before the asteroid hits.

Elaborate even by Disney standards, the attraction provides a tense, frenetic ride embellished by the entire Imagineering arsenal of high-tech gimmickry. Although the ride is jerky, it's not too rough for seniors. The menacing dinosaurs, however, make DINOSAUR a no-go for younger children.

DINOSAUR, to our surprise and joy, has been refined and cranked up a couple of notches on the intensity scale. The latest version is darker, more interesting, and much zippier.

TOURING TIPS We recommend that you ride early after obtaining Fastpasses for Expedition Everest. If you bump into a long line, use Fastpass. for this as well.

Primeval Whirl ★★★

APPEAL BY AGE	PRESCHOOL ★★	GRADE SCHOOL ★★★★	TEENS ★★★★
YOUNG ADULTS ★★★½		OVER 30 ★★★	SENIORS ★★½

What it is Small coaster. **Scope and scale** Minor attraction. **When to go** During the first 2 hours the park is open, in the hour before park closing, or use Fastpass. **Special comments** 48" minimum height requirement. Switching-off option provided (see page 75). **Authors' rating** "Wild mouse" on steroids; ★★★. **Duration of ride** Almost 2½ minutes. **Average wait in line per 100 people ahead of you** 4½ minutes. **Loading speed** Slow.

DESCRIPTION AND COMMENTS Primeval Whirl is a small coaster with short drops and curves, and it runs through the jaws of a dinosaur, among other things. What makes this coaster different is that the cars also spin. Because guests cannot control the spinning, the cars spin and stop spinning according to how the ride is programmed. Sometimes the spin is braked to a jarring halt after half a revolution, and sometimes it's allowed to make one or two complete turns. The complete spins are fun, but the screeching-stop half-spins are almost painful. If you subtract the time it takes to ratchet up the first hill, the actual ride time is about 90 seconds.

TOURING TIPS Like Space Mountain, the ride is duplicated side by side, but with only one queue. When it runs smoothly, about 700 people per side can whirl in an hour—a goodly number for this type of attraction, but not enough to preclude long waits on busy–moderate days. If you want to ride, try to get on before 11 a.m.

Theater in the Wild/*Finding Nemo—The Musical* ★★★★

What it is Enclosed venue for live stage shows. **Scope and scale** Major attraction. **When to go** Anytime. **Special comments** Performance times are listed in the handout park map or *Times Guide*. **Authors' rating** One of Disney's best live performances; not to be missed; ★★★★. **Duration of presentation** About 35 minutes.

DESCRIPTION AND COMMENTS Another chapter in the Pixar-ization of Disney theme parks, *Finding Nemo* is arguably the most elaborate live show in any Disney World theme park. Incorporating dancing, special effects (including trapeze), and sophisticated digital backdrops of the undersea world, it features on-stage human performers retelling Nemo's story with colorful, larger-than-life puppets. To be fair, *puppets* doesn't adequately convey the size or detail of these props, many of which are as big as a car and require two people to manipulate. An original musical score was written for the show, which is a must-see for most Animal Kingdom guests. A few scenes, such as when Nemo's mom is eaten, may be too intense for some very small children. Some of the midshow musical numbers slow the pace, so the main concern for parents is whether the kids can sit still for an entire show. With that in mind, we advise parents to catch an afternoon performance—around 3 p.m. would be great—after seeing the rest of Animal Kingdom. If the kids get restless you can either leave the show and catch the afternoon parade, or end your day at the park.

TOURING TIPS To get a seat, show up 20–25 minutes in advance for morning and late-afternoon shows, and 30–35 minutes in advance for shows scheduled between noon and 4:30 p.m. Access to the theater is via a relatively narrow pedestrian path—if you arrive as the previous show is letting out, you will feel like a salmon swimming upstream.

TriceraTop Spin   ★★

What it is Hub-and-spoke midway ride. **Scope and scale** Minor attraction. **When to go** First 90 minutes the park is open and in the hour before park closing. **Authors' rating** Dumbo's prehistoric forebear; ★★. **Duration of ride** 1½ minutes. **Average wait in line per 100 people ahead of you** 10 minutes. **Loading speed** Slow.

DESCRIPTION AND COMMENTS Another Dumbo-like ride. Here you spin around a Central Plaza until a dinosaur pops out of the

he hub. You'd think with the collective imagination of
t Disney Company, they'd come up with something a
pre creative.

s An attraction for the children, except they won't
appreciate the long wait for this slow-loading ride.

LIVE ENTERTAINMENT *in* DISNEY'S ANIMAL KINGDOM

AFTERNOON PARADE Mickey's Jammin' Jungle Parade is comparable to the parades at the other parks, complete with floats, Disney characters (especially those from the *Lion King, Jungle Book, Tarzan,* and *Pocahontas*), skaters, acrobats, and stilt walkers.

unofficial **TIP**
During the afternoon parade, avoid anything in Harambe around the bridge.

Though subject to change, the parade starts in Africa, crosses the bridge to Discovery Island, proceeds counterclockwise around the island, and then crosses the bridge to Asia. In Asia, the parade turns left and follows the walkway paralleling the river back to Africa. The walking path between Africa and Asia has several small cutouts that offer good views of the parade and excellent sun protection. As it's used mainly as a walkway, the path is also relatively uncrowded. (*Note:* The paths on Discovery Island get very crowded, making it easy to lose members of your party.)

ANIMAL ENCOUNTERS Throughout the day, knowledgeable Disney staff conduct impromptu short lectures on specific animals at the park. Look for a cast member in safari garb holding a bird, reptile, or small mammal.

GOODWILL AMBASSADORS A number of Asian and African natives are on-hand throughout the park. Both gracious and knowledgeable, they are delighted to discuss their country and its wildlife. Look for them in Harambe and along the Pangani Forest Exploration Trail in Africa, and in Anandapur and along the Maharajah Jungle Trek in Asia. They can also be found near the main entrance and at The Oasis.

KIDS' DISCOVERY CLUB Informal, creative activity stations offer kids ages 4–8 a structured learning experience as they tour Animal Kingdom. Set up along walkways in six themed areas, Discovery Club stations are manned by cast members who supervise a different activity at each station. A souvenir logbook, available free, is stamped at each station when the child completes the craft or exercise. Children enjoy collecting the stamps and noodling the puzzles in the logbook while in attraction lines.

STAGE SHOWS These are performed daily at the Lion King Theater in Camp Minnie-Mickey, at the Theater in the Wild in DinoLand U.S.A., and at the stadium in Asia. Shows at Camp Minnie-Mickey and DinoLand U.S.A. feature the Disney/Pixar characters.

STREET PERFORMERS These can be found most of the time at Discovery Island, at Harambe in Africa, at Anandapur in Asia, and in DinoLand U.S.A.

DISNEY'S ANIMAL KINGDOM TOURING PLANS

TOURING ANIMAL KINGDOM IS not as complicated as touring the other parks because it has fewer attractions. Also, most Animal Kingdom rides, shows, and zoological exhibits are oriented to the entire family, thus eliminating differences of opinion regarding how to spend the day. At Animal Kingdom, the whole family can pretty much see and enjoy everything together.

Since there are fewer attractions than at the other parks, expect the crowds at Animal Kingdom to be more concentrated. If a line seems unusually long, ask an Animal Kingdom cast member what the estimated wait is. If the wait exceeds your tolerance, try the same attraction again after 3 p.m., while a show is in progress at the Theater in the Wild in DinoLand U.S.A., or while some special event is going on.

"NOT A TOURING PLAN" TOURING PLANS

FOR THE TYPE B READER, these touring plans avoid detailed, step-by-step strategies for saving every last minute in line. Use these guidelines to avoid the longest waits in line while having maximum flexibility to see whatever interests you in a particular part of the park.

FOR PARENTS AND ADULTS ARRIVING AT PARK OPENING Obtain Fastpasses for Expedition Everest in Asia, then begin a land-by-land counterclockwise tour of park starting in Dinoland U.S.A. Work in shows as you near them, but leave *Finding Nemo—The Musical* for last.

FOR PARENTS AND ADULTS ARRIVING LATE MORNING Obtain Fastpasses for Kilimanjaro Safaris, then begin counterclockwise tour of park starting in Africa. Save Kali River Rapids and Expedition Everest for last; you'll get soaked on Kali, and the waits for Everest drop significantly after the parade.

BEFORE YOU GO

1. Call ☎ 407-824-4321 before you go to learn the park's hours of operation.
2. Purchase your admission prior to arrival.

Disney's Animal Kingdom One-day Touring Plan

The Animal Kingdom One-day Touring Plan assumes a willingness to experience all major rides and shows. Be forewarned that DINOSAUR, Primeval Whirl, and Kali River Rapids are sometimes frightening to children under age 8. Similarly, the theater attraction at The Tree of Life might be too intense for some preschoolers. When following the touring plan, simply skip any attraction you do not wish to experience.

unofficial **TIP**
For the time being, the limited number of attractions in Animal Kingdom can work to your advantage.

1. Arrive 40 minutes prior to opening.
2. Send one member of your party to get Fastpasses for Expedition Everest in Asia. The group should meet up at TriceraTop Spin in DinoLand U.S.A.
3. If you have small children, ride TriceraTop Spin.
4. Ride Primeval Whirl.
5. Follow the signs to DINOSAUR, and ride.
6. In Asia, ride Kali River Rapids.
7. See *Flights of Wonder.* If wait exceeds 20 minutes, walk the Maharajah Jungle Trek first, then see the show.
8. Walk the Maharajah Jungle Trek if you have not already done so.
9. Return to Expedition Everest and ride.
10. Visit Africa, and send one member of your party to obtain Fastpasses for Kilimanjaro Safaris.
11. Eat lunch.
12. Take the Wildlife Express Train from Africa to Conservation Station/Rafiki's Planet Watch. Tour the exhibits, and take the train back to Africa.
13. Walk the Pangani Forest Exploration Trail.

14. Experience Kilimanjaro Safaris using the Fastpasses obtained in Step 10.

15. In Camp Minnie-Mickey, see *Festival of the Lion King*.

16. See *Finding Nemo—The Musical* at Theater in the Wild in DinoLand if the next show is within 25 minutes. Otherwise, see *It's Tough to Be a Bug!* on Discovery Island. Also check out exhibits at The Tree of Life.

17. If you have the time and interest (and small children), check out The Boneyard in DinoLand.

18. If you've not already done so, see *It's Tough to Be a Bug!* and the exhibits at The Tree of Life on Discovery Island.

19. Shop, snack, or repeat any attractions you especially enjoyed.

20. Visit the zoological exhibits in The Oasis.

PART TWELVE

DISNEY'S HOLLYWOOD STUDIOS

DISNEY'S HOLLYWOOD STUDIOS IS ABOUT THE SIZE of the Magic Kingdom and about half as large as the sprawling Epcot. Unlike the other parks, Disney's Hollywood Studios was conceived as a working motion-picture and television production facility when it opened in 1989. Though this is no longer the case today, the Studios still draws its theme and inspiration from film and TV.

When Epcot opened in 1982, Disney patrons expected a futuristic version of the Magic Kingdom. What they got was humanistic inspiration and a creative educational experience. Remembering the occasional disappointment of those early Epcot guests, Disney fortified the Studios with action, suspense, surprise, and, of course, special effects. If you wanted to learn about the history and technology of movies and television, Disney's Hollywood Studios would teach you plenty. If you just wanted to be entertained, you wouldn't leave disappointed.

Alas, what DHS does best these days is promote. Whereas self-promotion of Disney films and products was once subtle and in context, it is now blatant, inescapable, and detracting. Although most visitors are willing to forgive Disney its excesses, Studios veterans will lament the changes and remember how good it was when education was the goal instead of the medium.

It's impossible to see all of Epcot or the Magic Kingdom in one day. Disney's Hollywood Studios, however, is more manageable: attractions are concentrated in an area about the size of Main Street, Tomorrowland, and Frontierland combined. Someday, no doubt, as Disney's Hollywood Studios develops

NOT TO BE MISSED AT DISNEY'S HOLLYWOOD STUDIOS
Fantasmic!
Jim Henson's Muppet-Vision 3-D
Rock 'n' Roller Coaster
Star Tours—The Adventures Continue
Studio Backlot Tour
Toy Story Mania!
The Twilight Zone Tower of Terror
Voyage of the Little Mermaid

and grows, you'll need more than a day to see everything. For now, the Studios is a nice one-day outing.

Because the Studios is relatively small, it's more affected by large crowds. Our touring plans will help you stay a step ahead of the mob and minimize waiting in line. Even when the park is crowded, however, you can still see almost everything in a day.

unofficial **TIP**
After 5 p.m. or so, the lines for most attractions are manageable, and the park is cooler and more comfortable.

Because Disney's Hollywood Studios can be seen in three-fourths of a day, many guests who arrive early in the morning run out of things to do by late afternoon and leave the park. Their departure greatly thins the crowd and makes the Studios ideal for evening touring. The *Indiana Jones Epic Stunt Spectacular!* and productions at other outdoor theaters are infinitely more enjoyable during the evening than in the sweltering heat of the day.

In 1998, the Studios launched *Fantasmic!* (see page 238), arguably the most spectacular nighttime-entertainment event in the entire Disney repertoire. Staged twice weekly, weather permitting (three to seven times a week during busier times), in its own theater behind the Tower of Terror, *Fantasmic!* is rated as not to be missed. Unfortunately, evening crowds have increased substantially at the Studios because of *Fantasmic!* Some guests stay longer at DHS, and others arrive after dinner from other parks expressly to see the show. Although the crowds thin in the late afternoon, they start building again as performance time approaches, making *Fantasmic!* a challenge to get into. Also adversely affected are the Tower of Terror and the Rock 'n' Roller Coaster, both situated near the entrance to *Fantasmic!* Crowd levels throughout the remainder of the park, however, are generally light.

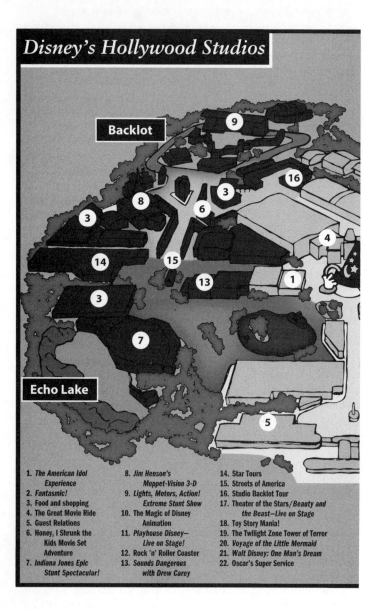

Disney's Hollywood Studios

Backlot

Echo Lake

1. *The American Idol Experience*
2. *Fantasmic!*
3. Food and shopping
4. *The Great Movie Ride*
5. Guest Relations
6. *Honey, I Shrunk the Kids Movie Set Adventure*
7. *Indiana Jones Epic Stunt Spectacular!*
8. *Jim Henson's Muppet-Vision 3-D*
9. *Lights, Motors, Action! Extreme Stunt Show*
10. *The Magic of Disney Animation*
11. *Playhouse Disney—Live on Stage!*
12. *Rock 'n' Roller Coaster*
13. *Sounds Dangerous with Drew Carey*
14. Star Tours
15. Streets of America
16. Studio Backlot Tour
17. Theater of the Stars/*Beauty and the Beast—Live on Stage*
18. *Toy Story Mania!*
19. *The Twilight Zone Tower of Terror*
20. *Voyage of the Little Mermaid*
21. *Walt Disney: One Man's Dream*
22. Oscar's Super Service

Pixar Place & Mickey Avenue

Animation Courtyard

Hollywood & Sunset Boulevards

ARRIVING

DISNEY'S HOLLYWOOD STUDIOS has its own pay-parking lot and is served by the Disney transportation system. Most larger hotels outside the World shuttle guests to the Studios. If you drive, Disney's ubiquitous trams will transport you to the ticketing area and entrance gate.

GETTING ORIENTED

GUEST SERVICES, ON YOUR LEFT as you enter, serves as the park headquarters and information center, similar to City Hall in the Magic Kingdom and Guest Relations at Epcot and Disney's Animal Kingdom. Go there for a schedule of live performances, lost persons, Package Pick-Up, lost and found (on the right side of the entrance), general information, or in an emergency. If you haven't received a map of the Studios, get one here. To the right of the entrance are locker, stroller, and wheelchair rentals.

About one-half of the complex is set up as a theme park. As at the Magic Kingdom, you enter the park and pass down a main street, only this time it's **Hollywood Boulevard** of the 1930s and 1940s. At the end of Hollywood Boulevard is a replica of Hollywood's famous Chinese Theater. Lording over the plaza in front of the theater is a 122-foot-tall replica of the sorcerer hat Mickey Mouse wore in the animated classic *Fantasia*. Besides providing photo ops, the hat is the park's most central landmark, making it a good meeting place if your group becomes separated. (In case you were wondering, Mickey would have to be 350 feet tall to wear the hat.)

Though modest in size, the open-access areas of the Studios are confusingly arranged. As you face the hat, two guest areas—**Sunset Boulevard** and the **Animation Courtyard**—branch off Hollywood Boulevard to the right. Branching left off Hollywood Boulevard is the **Echo Lake** area. The open-access **Streets of America** wraps around the back of **Echo Lake,** while **Pixar Place**'s attractions are behind the Chinese Theater and to the left of the Animation Courtyard. Between Pixar Place and the Animation Courtyard are the two minor attractions of **Mickey Avenue.** You can experience all attractions here and in the other open-access sections of the park according to your tastes and time. Still farther to the rear is a limited-access area consisting of soundstages, technical facilities, wardrobe shops, administrative offices, and sets.

Most of the park's service facilities are on Hollywood Boulevard, including:

Baby Care Center At Guest Services; baby food and other necessities available at Oscar's Super Service

Banking Services ATM outside the park to the right of the turnstiles and on Streets of America near Pizza Planet restaurant

Film At The Darkroom on the right side of Hollywood Boulevard as you enter the park, just beyond Oscar's Super Service

First Aid At Guest Relations

Live Entertainment, Parade, and Character Information Available free at Guest Relations and elsewhere in the park

Lost and Found At Package Pick-Up, to the right of the entrance

Lost Persons Report at Guest Relations

Storage Lockers Rental lockers are to the right of the main entrance, to the left of Oscar's Super Service

Walt Disney World and Local Attraction Information At Guest Relations

Wheelchair, ECV, and Stroller Rentals To the right of the entrance, at Oscar's Super Service

ATTRACTIONS

HOLLYWOOD BOULEVARD

HOLLYWOOD BOULEVARD is a palm-lined re-creation of Tinseltown's main drag during the district's golden age. The architecture is streamline moderne with Art Deco embellishments. Most service facilities are here, interspersed with eateries and shops. Merchandise includes Disney-trademark items, Hollywood and movie-related souvenirs, and one-of-a-kind collectibles found at studio auctions and estate sales. Hollywood characters and roving performers entertain on the boulevard, and daily parades and other happenings pass this way.

The Great Movie Ride   ★★★½

APPEAL BY AGE	PRESCHOOL ★★★	GRADE SCHOOL ★★★½	TEENS ★★★½
YOUNG ADULTS ★★★½	OVER 30 ★★★★		SENIORS ★★★★

What it is Movie-history indoor adventure ride. **Scope and scale** Headliner. **When to go** Before 11 a.m. or after 4:30 p.m. **Special**

comments Elaborate, with several surprises. **Authors' rating** Unique; ★★★½. **Duration of ride** About 19 minutes. **Average wait in line per 100 people ahead of you** 2 minutes; assumes all trains operating. **Loading speed** Fast.

DESCRIPTION AND COMMENTS Entering through a re-creation of Hollywood's Chinese Theater, guests board vehicles for a fast-paced tour through soundstage sets from classic films including *Casablanca, Tarzan, The Wizard of Oz, Aliens,* and *Raiders of the Lost Ark.* Each set is populated with audioanimatronic characters, as well as an occasional human, all augmented by sound and lighting effects. One of Disney's larger and more ambitious dark rides, The Great Movie Ride encompasses 95,000 square feet and showcases some of the most famous scenes in filmmaking. Life-sized audio-animatronic sculptures of stars, including Gene Kelly, John Wayne, James Cagney, and Julie Andrews, inhabit some of the largest sets ever constructed for a Disney ride.

TOURING TIPS The Great Movie Ride draws large crowds (and lines) from midmorning on. As an interval-loading, high-capacity ride, lines disappear quickly. Even so, waits can exceed an hour after midmorning. (Actual waits usually run about one-third shorter than the time posted.)

SUNSET BOULEVARD

EVOKING THE 1940s, Sunset Boulevard is a major addition to Disney's Hollywood Studios. The first right off of Hollywood Boulevard, Sunset Boulevard provides another venue for dining, shopping, and street entertainment.

Fantasmic! ★★★★★

APPEAL BY AGE	PRESCHOOL ★★★★	GRADE SCHOOL ★★★★½	TEENS ★★★★½
YOUNG ADULTS ★★★★★		OVER 30 ★★★★½	SENIORS ★★★★½

What it is Mixed-media nighttime spectacular. **Scope and scale** Super-headliner. **When to go** Staged 2–7 nights a week depending on the season. **Special comments** Disney's very best nighttime event. **Authors' rating** Not to be missed; ★★★★★. **Duration of presentation** 25 minutes. **Probable waiting time** 50–90 minutes for a seat, 35–40 minutes for standing room.

DESCRIPTION AND COMMENTS *Fantasmic!* is presented one or more times each evening when the park is open late. Off Sunset Boulevard behind the Tower of Terror, this mixed-media show is staged on an island opposite the 6,900-seat Hollywood Hills Amphitheater. By far the largest theater facility ever created by Disney, the amphitheater can accommodate an additional 3,000 standing guests for an audience of nearly 10,000.

Fantasmic! is far and away the most innovative outdoor spectacle ever attempted at any theme park. Starring Mickey Mouse in his role as the Sorcerer's Apprentice from *Fantasia,* the production uses lasers, images projected on a shroud of mist, fireworks, lighting effects, and music in combinations so stunning you can scarcely believe what you're seeing. The plot is simple: good versus evil. The story gets lost in all the special effects at times, but the spectacle is what's so powerful.

We don't receive many reports of young children being terrified by *Fantasmic!;* nonetheless, prepare your kids for what they'l see. You can mitigate the fright factor somewhat by sitting back a bit. Also, hang on to your kids after the show and give them instructions for regrouping should you get separated.

TOURING TIPS *Fantasmic!* provides a whole different dimension to nighttime at Disney's Hollywood Studios. As a day-capping event, it is to the Studios what *IllumiNations* is to Epcot. While it's hard to imagine running out of space in a 10,000-person stadium, it happens almost every performance. On evenings when there are two performances, the second show will always be less crowded. If you attend the first (or only) scheduled performance, show up at least an hour in advance. If you opt for the second show, arrive 50 minutes early.

Rainy and windy conditions sometimes cause *Fantasmic!* to be cancelled. Unfortunately, Disney officials usually don't make a final decision about whether to proceed or cancel until just before showtime. We have seen guests wait stoically for over an hour with no assurance that their patience and sacrifice would be rewarded. We don't recommend arriving more than 20 minutes before showtime on rainy or especially windy nights.

Rock 'n' Roller Coaster (*Fastpass*) ★★★★

APPEAL BY AGE	PRESCHOOL ★	GRADE SCHOOL ★★★★½	TEENS ★★★★★
YOUNG ADULTS ★★★★★	OVER 30 ★★★★★		SENIORS ★★★

What it is Rock-music-themed roller coaster. **Scope and scale** Headliner. **When to go** Before 10 a.m., in the hour before closing, or use Fastpass. **Special comments** Must be 48" tall to ride; children younger than age 7 must ride with an adult. Switching-off option provided (see page 75). Note that there is a single-rider line for this attraction. **Authors' rating** Disney's wildest American coaster; not to be missed; ★★★★. **Duration of ride** Almost 1½ minutes. **Average wait in line per 100 people ahead of you** 2½ minutes; assumes all trains operating. **Loading speed** Moderate–fast.

Motion Sickness

DESCRIPTION AND COMMENTS This is Disney's answer to the roller-coaster proliferation at Universal's Islands of Adventure and Busch Gardens theme parks. Exponentially wilder than Space Mountain or Big Thunder

Mountain in the Magic Kingdom, the Rock 'n' Roller Coaster is an attraction for fans of cutting-edge thrill rides. Although the rock icons and synchronized music add measurably to the experience, the ride itself, as opposed to sights and sounds along the way, is the focus. The Rock 'n' Roller Coaster offers loops, corkscrews, and drops that make Space Mountain seem like the Jungle Cruise. What really makes this metal coaster unusual, however, is that first, it's in the dark (like Space Mountain, only with Southern California nighttime scenes instead of space), and second, you're launched up the first hill like a jet off a carrier deck. By the time you crest the hill, you'll have gone from 0 to 57 mph in less than 3 seconds. When you enter the first loop, you'll be pulling five g's. By comparison, that's two more g's than astronauts experience at lift-off on a space shuttle.

TOURING TIPS This ride is not for everyone. If Space Mountain or Big Thunder pushes your limits, stay away from the Rock 'n' Roller Coaster. It's eye-catching, and it's definitely a zippy, albeit deafening, ride. Expect long lines except in the first 30 minutes after opening and during the late-evening performance of *Fantasmic!* Ride first thing in the morning or use Fastpass.

If you're on hand when the park opens, position yourself on the far left side of Sunset Boulevard as close to the rope barrier as possible. If there's already a crowd at the rope, you can usually work yourself forward by snaking along the wall of the Beverly Sunset Shop. Once in position, wait for the rope drop. When the park opens, cast members will walk the rope up the street toward Rock 'n' Roller Coaster and Tower of Terror. Stay on the far left sidewalk and you'll be among the first to make the left turn to the entrance of the coaster. Usually the Disney people get out of the way and allow you to run the last 100 feet or so.

A good strategy for riding both Tower of Terror and Rock 'n' Roller Coaster with minimum waits is to rush first thing after opening to Rock 'n' Roller Coaster and obtain Fastpasses, then line up for the Tower of Terror. Most days, by the time you finish experiencing the Tower of Terror, it will be time to use your Fastpass for Rock 'n' Roller Coaster. If the Tower of Terror, the Rock 'n' Roller Coaster, and Toy Story Mania! are all must-sees for you, turn to page 249.

Theater of the Stars/
Beauty and the Beast—Live on Stage ★★★★

APPEAL BY AGE	PRESCHOOL ★★★★½	GRADE SCHOOL ★★★★	TEENS ★★★★
YOUNG ADULTS ★★★★		OVER 30 ★★★★	SENIORS ★★★★½

What it is Live Hollywood-style musical, usually featuring Disney characters; performed in an open-air theater. **Scope and scale** Major attraction. **When to go** Anytime, though evenings are cooler. **Special comments** Performances are listed in the daily *Times Guide*. **Authors' rating** Excellent; ★★★★. **Duration of presentation** 25 minutes. **Preshow entertainment** None. **When to arrive** 20–30 minutes before showtime.

DESCRIPTION AND COMMENTS The Theater of the Stars combines Disney characters with singers and dancers in upbeat and humorous Hollywood musicals. The *Beauty and the Beast* show, in particular, is outstanding. The theater offers a clear field of vision from almost every seat. Best, a canopy protects the audience from the Florida sun (or rain). The theater still gets mighty hot in the summer, but you should make it through a performance without suffering heatstroke.

TOURING TIPS Unless you visit during the cooler months, see this show in the late afternoon or the evening. The production is so popular that you should show up 20–30 minutes early to get a seat.

The Twilight Zone Tower of Terror (*Fastpass*)   ★★★★★

APPEAL BY AGE	PRESCHOOL ★★½	GRADE SCHOOL ★★★★	TEENS ★★★★★
YOUNG ADULTS ★★★★★		OVER 30 ★★★★★	SENIORS ★★★★

What it is Sci-fi–themed indoor thrill ride. **Scope and scale** Super-headliner. **When to go** Before 9:30 a.m., after 6 p.m., or use Fastpass. **Special comments** Must be 40" tall to ride; switching-off option offered (see page 75). **Authors' rating** Walt Disney World's best attraction; not to be missed; ★★★★★. **Duration of ride** About 4 minutes plus pre-show. **Average wait in line per 100 people ahead of you** 4 minutes; assumes all elevators operating. **Loading speed** Moderate.

DESCRIPTION AND COMMENTS The Tower of Terror is a different species of Disney thrill ride, though it borrows elements of The Haunted Mansion at the Magic Kingdom. The story is that you're touring a once-famous Hollywood hotel gone to ruin. As at Star Tours, the queuing area immerses guests in the adventure as they pass through the hotel's once-opulent public rooms. From the lobby, guests are escorted into the hotel's library, where Rod Serling, speaking from an old black-and-white television, greets the guests and introduces the plot.

The Tower of Terror is a whopper at 13-plus stories tall. Breaking tradition in terms of visually isolating themed areas, you can see the entire Studios from atop the tower . . . but you have to look quick.

The ride vehicle, one of the hotel's service elevators, takes guests to see the haunted hostelry. The tour begins innocuously, but at about the fifth floor things get pretty weird. Guests are subjected to a full range of eerie effects as they cross into the Twilight Zone. The climax of the adventure occurs when the elevator reaches the top floor (the 13th, of course) and the cable snaps.

The Tower has great potential for terrifying young children and rattling more-mature visitors. If you have teenagers in your party, use them as experimental probes. If they report back that they really, really liked the Tower of Terror, run as fast as you can in the opposite direction.

TOURING TIPS The Tower is a veritable beacon, visible from outside the park and luring curious guests as soon as they enter. Because of its popularity with schoolkids, teens, and young adults, you can count on a footrace to the attraction, as well as to the nearby Rock 'n' Roller Coaster and Toy Story Mania!, when the park opens. Expect the Tower to be mobbed most of the day. Experience it as early as possible in the morning, in the evening before the park closes, or use Fastpass.

If you're on hand when the park opens and you want to ride Tower of Terror first, position yourself on the far right side of Sunset Boulevard as close to the rope barrier as possible. Once in position, wait for the rope to drop. When the park opens, cast members will walk the rope up the street toward Rock 'n' Roller Coaster and Tower of Terror. Just stay on the far right sidewalk and you'll be among the first to make the right turn to the entrance of the tower. Usually the Disney people get out of the way and allow you to run the last 100 feet or so. Also, be aware that about 65% of the folks waiting for the rope walk will head for Rock 'n' Roller Coaster. If you are not positioned on the far right, it will be almost impossible to move through the throng of coaster enthusiasts to make a right turn into Tower of Terror.

When you enter the library waiting area, stand in the far back corner across from the door where you entered and at the opposite end of the room from the TV. When the doors to the loading area open, you'll be one of the first admitted.

If you have young children (or anyone) who are apprehensive about this attraction, ask the attendant about switching off (page 75).

A good strategy for riding both Tower of Terror and Rock 'n' Roller Coaster with minimum waits is to rush first thing after opening to Rock 'n' Roller Coaster and obtain Fastpasses, then line up for the Tower of Terror. Most days, by the time you finish experiencing the Tower of Terror, it will be time to use your Fastpass for Rock 'n' Roller Coaster.

ECHO LAKE

AN ACTUAL MINIATURE LAKE near the middle of the Studios, to the left of Hollywood Boulevard, Echo Lake pays homage to its real-life California counterpart, which served as the backdrop to many of Hollywood's early films. Echo Lake also serves as the architectural transition from Hollywood Boulevard's retro theming to Streets of America's film-set ambience.

The American Idol Experience ★★★★

| APPEAL BY AGE | PRESCHOOL ★★★ | GRADE SCHOOL ★★★★ | TEENS ★★★★ |
| YOUNG ADULTS ★★★★ | | OVER 30 ★★★★ | SENIORS ★★★ |

What it is Theme park version of the TV show. **Scope and scale** Major attraction. **When to go** Anytime. **Special comments** Guests must be at least age 14 to perform. **Author's rating** Even if you don't watch the show, you'll find someone to cheer for; ★★★★. **Duration of presentation** 20 minutes for daytime preliminary shows, 40 minutes for the nighttime finale. **When to arrive** 20–30 minutes before showtime.

DESCRIPTION AND COMMENTS Based on the wildly popular TV talent search, *The American Idol Experience* has guests audition a cappella in front of a judge, just as in *American Idol*'s first shows of the season. Those who make the cut move on to a second audition and sing, karaoke-style, to a prerecorded track. The judges' picks from this round get to perform in one of the attraction's preliminary shows, held several times a day.

During the preliminaries, each contestant repeats his or her song from the second audition in front of a live audience of theme park guests. As with *Idol,* three judges—in this case, Disney cast members—provide feedback. Audience members decide the preliminary winners, who meet for one last showdown at night. The winner of the finale receives a "Dream Ticket"—a front-of-the-line pass to try out for *American Idol* in his or her hometown.

TOURING TIPS The last show of the day offers (ostensibly) the best talent but runs twice as long as the daytime shows. If you have dinner reservations or are lining up early for *Fantasmic!* (see page 238), see one of the daytime shows.

Indiana Jones Epic Stunt Spectacular! ★★★★

| APPEAL BY AGE | PRESCHOOL ★★★ ½ | GRADE SCHOOL ★★★★ | TEENS ★★★★ |
| YOUNG ADULTS ★★★★ | | OVER 30 ★★★★ | SENIORS ★★★★ |

What it is Movie-stunt demonstration and action show. **Scope and scale** Headliner. **When to go** First 3 morning shows or last evening show. **Special comments** Performance times posted on a sign at the entrance to the theate; Fastpasses available seasonally. **Authors'**

rating Done on a grand scale; ★★★★. **Duration of presentation** 30 minutes. **Preshow entertainment** Selection of "extras" from audience. **When to arrive** 20–30 minutes before showtime.

DESCRIPTION AND COMMENTS Coherent and educational, though somewhat unevenly paced, the popular production showcases professional stunt men and women who demonstrate dangerous stunts with a behind-the-scenes look at how it's done. Sets, props, and special effects are very elaborate.

TOURING TIPS The Stunt Theater holds 2,000 people; capacity audiences are common. If the first show is at 9:30 a.m. or earlier, you can usually walk in, even if you arrive 5 minutes late. If the first show is scheduled for 9:45 a.m. or later, arrive 20 or so minutes early. For the second performance, show up about 20–35 minutes ahead of time. For the third and subsequent shows, arrive 30–45 minutes early. If you plan to tour during late afternoon and evening, attend the last scheduled performance. If you want to beat the crowd out of the stadium, sit on the far right (as you face the staging area) and near the top.

Jedi Training Academy ★★★★

APPEAL BY AGE	PRESCHOOL ★★★★	GRADE SCHOOL ★★★★	TEENS ★★★★
YOUNG ADULTS ★★★★	OVER 30 ★★★★		SENIORS ★★★★

What it is Outdoor stage show. **Scope and scale** Minor attraction. **When to go** First 2 shows of the day. **Special comments** Volunteers from the audience are chosen to go on stage to fight Darth Vader. **Authors' rating** A treat for young *Star Wars* lovers; ★★★★. **Duration of show** About 15 minutes. **When to arrive** 15 minutes before showtime.

DESCRIPTION AND COMMENTS *Jedi Training Academy* is staged several times daily to the left of the Star Tours building entrance, opposite Backlot Express. Young Skywalkers-in-training are selected from the audience to train in the ways of The Force and do battle against Darth Vader. If all this sounds too intense, it's not—Storm Troopers provide comic relief and, just as in the movies, the Jedi always win.

TOURING TIPS Surprisingly popular, given that Disney hasn't promoted it to the same level of hype as other shows. If you happen to have a brown robe similar to Obi-Wan's, bringing it along might boost your young one's chances of getting picked.

Sounds Dangerous with Drew Carey ★★★

APPEAL BY AGE	PRESCHOOL ★½	GRADE SCHOOL ★★	TEENS ★★★
YOUNG ADULTS ★★	OVER 30 ★★		SENIORS ★★

What it is Show demonstrating sound effects. **Scope and scale** Minor attraction. **When to go** Before 11 a.m. or after 4 p.m. **Authors' rating** Funny and informative; ★★★. **Duration of presentation** 12 minutes. **Preshow entertainment** Video introduction to sound effects. **Probable waiting time** 15–30 minutes.

DESCRIPTION AND COMMENTS *Sounds Dangerous,* a film presentation starring Drew Carey as a blundering detective, is the vehicle for a crash course on movie and TV sound effects. While the film itself is funny and well paced and (for once) doesn't hawk some Disney flick or product, time has not been kind to the attraction. Earphones, worn throughout the show, often don't work properly, and the theater itself seems run-down.

TOURING TIPS *Sounds Dangerous* is periodically inundated by guests coming from a just-concluded performance of the *Indiana Jones Epic Stunt Spectacular!* This is not the time to get in line. Wait at least 30 minutes and try again.

Star Tours—The Adventures Continue (*Fastpass*) ★★★★

APPEAL BY AGE	PRESCHOOL ★★★★	GRADE SCHOOL ★★★★	TEENS ★★★★
YOUNG ADULTS ★★★★		OVER 30 ★★★★	SENIORS ★★★★

What it is Indoor space flight–simulation ride. **Scope and scale** Headliner. **When to go** First 90 minutes after opening. **Special comments** Expectant mothers and anyone prone to motion sickness are advised against riding. Too intense for many children younger than age 8. Must be 40" tall to ride. **Authors' rating** A classic adventure; ★★★★. **Duration of ride** About 7 minutes. **Average wait in line per 100 people ahead of you** 5 minutes; assumes all simulators operating. **Loading speed** Moderate–fast.

Motion Sickness

DESCRIPTION AND COMMENTS Based on the *Star Wars* movie series, this was Disney's first modern simulator ride. Star Tours completed its first major overhaul in decades in 2011, with a new story based on the "pod racing" scene from *Star Wars Episode 1: The Phantom Menace.* The new version has lots of dips, turns, twists, and climbs as your vehicle goes through an intergalactic version of the chariot race in *Ben-Hur.* The new ride film is projected in high-definition 3-D and has more than 50 combinations of opening and ending scenes.

An interactive show, *Jedi Training Academy,* is staged several times daily to the left of the Star Tours building entrance, opposite Backlot Express. See previous page for details.

TOURING TIPS Expect waits not to exceed 35–45 minutes except on unusually busy days. For the first couple of hours the park is open, expect a wait of 25 minutes or less. Even so, ride before 11 a.m., or use Fastpass. If you have young children (or anyone) who are apprehensive about this attraction, ask the attendant about switching off (see page 75). Watch for throngs arriving from performances of the *Indiana Jones Epic Stunt Spectacular!* If you encounter a long line, try again later.

STREETS OF AMERICA

FORMERLY A WALK-THROUGH back-lot movie set, Streets of America is now a designated themed area, or "land," that is home to four attractions. The back-lot street sets remain intact and serve as the primary pedestrian thoroughfare.

Honey, I Shrunk the Kids Movie Set Adventure ★★½

APPEAL BY AGE	PRESCHOOL ★★★★½	GRADE SCHOOL ★★★★	TEENS ★★★
YOUNG ADULTS ★★	OVER 30 ★★½		SENIORS ★★★

What it is Small but elaborate playground. **Scope and scale** Diversion. **When to go** Before 11 a.m. or after dark. **Special comments** Opens an hour later than the rest of the park. **Authors' rating** Great for young children, more of a curiosity for adults; ★★½. **Duration of presentation** Varies. **Average wait in line per 100 people ahead of you** 20 minutes.

DESCRIPTION AND COMMENTS This elaborate playground appeals particularly to kids age 11 and younger. The story is that you have been "miniaturized" and have to make your way through a yard full of 20-foot-tall blades of grass, giant ants, dog poop (just kidding), lawn sprinklers, and other oversized features.

TOURING TIPS This imaginative playground has tunnels, slides, rope ladders, and a variety of oversized props. All surface areas are padded, and Disney personnel are on hand to help keep children in some semblance of control.

Unfortunately, the attraction has problems that are hard to "miniaturize." First, it isn't large enough to accommodate the children who would like to play. Only 240 people are allowed "on the set" at a time, and many of these are supervising parents or curious adults who hopped in line without knowing what they were waiting for. Frequently by 10:30 or 11 a.m., the playground is full, with dozens waiting outside.

Also, kids get to play as long as parents allow. This creates uneven traffic flow and unpredictable waits. If it weren't for the third flaw, that the attraction is poorly ventilated (as hot and sticky as an Everglades swamp), there's no telling when anyone would leave.

If you visit during warmer months and want your children to experience the playground, get them in and out before 11 a.m. By late morning, this attraction is way too hot and crowded for anyone to enjoy. Access the playground via the Streets of America, or via Mickey Avenue.

Jim Henson's Muppet-Vision 3-D ★★★★½

APPEAL BY AGE	PRESCHOOL ★★★★	GRADE SCHOOL ★★★★	TEENS ★★★★
YOUNG ADULTS ★★★★		OVER 30 ★★★★	SENIORS ★★★★

What it is 3-D movie starring the Muppets. **Scope and scale** Major attraction. **When to go** Before 11 a.m. or after 3 p.m. **Authors' rating** Uproarious; not to be missed; ★★★★½. **Duration of presentation** 17 minutes. **Preshow entertainment** Muppets on television. **Probable waiting time** 12 minutes.

DESCRIPTION AND COMMENTS *Muppet-Vision 3-D* provides a total sensory experience, with wild 3-D action augmented by auditory, visual, and tactile special effects. If you're tired and hot, this zany presentation will make you feel brand new. Arrive early and enjoy the hilarious video preshow.

TOURING TIPS This production is very popular. Before noon, waits peak at about 20 minutes. Also, watch for throngs arriving from just-concluded performances of the *Indiana Jones Epic Stunt Spectacular!* If you encounter a long line, try again later.

Lights, Motors, Action! Extreme Stunt Show ★★★½

APPEAL BY AGE	PRESCHOOL ★★★½	GRADE SCHOOL ★★★★½	TEENS ★★★★½
YOUNG ADULTS ★★★★		OVER 30 ★★★★	SENIORS ★★★★

What it is Auto stunt show. **Scope and scale** Headliner. **When to go** First show of the day or after 4 p.m. **Authors' rating** Good stunt work, slow pace; ★★★½. **Duration of presentation** 25–30 minutes. **Preshow entertainment** Selection of audience "volunteers." **When to arrive** 20–30 minutes before showtime.

DESCRIPTION AND COMMENTS This show, which originated at Disneyland Paris, features cars and motorcycles in a blur of chases, crashes, jumps, and explosions. The secrets behind the special effects are explained after each stunt sequence, with replays and different camera views shown on an enormous movie screen; the replays also serve to pass the time needed in placing the next stunt's props into position. While the stunt driving is excellent, the show plods along between tricks, and you will probably have had your fill by the time the last stunt ends. Expect about 6–8 minutes of real action in a show that runs 25–30 minutes.

TOURING TIPS The auto stunt show, at the end of the Streets of America, presents two to five performances daily. It's popular, but its remote location (the most distant attraction from the park entrance) helps distribute and moderate the crowds.

Seating is in a 3,000-person stadium, so it's not difficult to find a seat except on the busiest days.

Studio Backlot Tour ★★★★

APPEAL BY AGE	PRESCHOOL ★★★ ½	GRADE SCHOOL ★★★★ ½	TEENS ★★★★
YOUNG ADULTS ★★★★	OVER 30 ★★★★		SENIORS ★★★★

What it is Combination tram and walking tour of modern film and video production. **Scope and scale** Headliner. **When to go** Anytime. **Authors' rating** Educational and fun, not to be missed; ★★★★. **Duration of presentation** About 30 minutes. **Special comments** Visit the restroom before getting in line. **Preshow entertainment** A video before the special-effects segment and another video in the tram boarding area.

DESCRIPTION AND COMMENTS Much of the Studios actually used to *be* studios, but little actual film or TV production takes place these days. Nonetheless, visitors can take a backstage tour to learn about production methods and technologies.

The tour begins on the edge of the backlot with the special-effects walking segment, then continues with the tram segment. To reach the tour, turn right off Hollywood Boulevard through the Studio Arch into the Animation Courtyard. Bear left at the corner where *Voyage of the Little Mermaid* is situated. Follow the street until you see a redbrick warehouse on your right. Go through the door and up the ramp.

The first stop is a special-effects water tank where technicians explain the mechanical and optical tricks that "turn the seemingly impossible into on-screen reality." Included are rain effects and a naval battle.

A prop room separates the special-effects tank and the tram tour. Trams depart about once every 4 minutes on busy days, winding among production and shop buildings. The tour continues through the back lot, where western desert canyons exist side-by-side with New York City brownstones. The tour's highlight is Catastrophe Canyon, an elaborate special-effects movie set where a thunderstorm, earthquake, oil-field fire, and flash flood are simulated.

TOURING TIPS Because the Backlot Tour is one of Disney's most efficient attractions, you will rarely wait more than 15 minutes (usually less than 10). Take the tour at your convenience.

PIXAR PLACE

THE WALKWAY BETWEEN *Voyage of the Little Mermaid* and the Studio Backlot Tour holds the popular Toy Story Mania! attraction. To emphasize the importance of the *Toy Story* franchise, this section of the park is called Pixar Place.

Toy Story Mania! (*Fastpass*) ★★★★½

APPEAL BY AGE PRESCHOOL ★★★★★ GRADE SCHOOL ★★★★★ TEENS ★★★★★
YOUNG ADULTS ★★★★★ OVER 30 ★★★★★ SENIORS ★★★★½

What it is 3-D ride through indoor shooting gallery. **Scope and scale** Headliner. **When to go** Before 10:30 a.m., after 6 p.m., or use Fastpass (if available). **Authors' rating** ★★★★½. **Duration of ride** About 6½ minutes. **Average wait in line per 100 people ahead of you** 4½ minutes. **Loading speed** Fast.

DESCRIPTION AND COMMENTS Toy Story Mania! ushers in a whole new generation of Disney attractions: "virtual dark rides." Imagine long corridors, totally empty, covered with reflective material. There's almost nothing there … until you put on your 3-D glasses. Instantly, the corridor is full and brimming with color, action, and activity, thanks to projected computer-graphic (CG) images.

Conceptually, this is an interactive shooting gallery much like Buzz Lightyear's Space Ranger Spin (see page 146), but in Toy Story Mania!, your ride vehicle passes through a totally virtual midway, with booths offering such games as ring tossing and ball throwing. You use a cannon on your ride vehicle to play as you move along from booth to booth. Unlike the laser guns in Buzz Lightyear, however, the pull-string cannons in Toy Story Mania! take advantage of CG image technology to toss rings, shoot balls, even throw eggs and pies. Each game booth is manned by a *Toy Story* character who is right beside you in 3-D glory, cheering you on. In addition to 3-D imagery, you experience various smells, vehicle motion, wind, and water spray. The ride begins with a training round to familiarize you with the nature of the games, then continues through a number of "real" games in which you compete against your riding mate. The technology has the ability to self-adjust the level of difficulty, and there are plenty of easy targets for small children to reach. *Tip:* Let the pull-string retract all the way back into the cannon before pulling it again.

TOURING TIPS Because it's a ton of fun and it has a relatively low rider-per-hour capacity, Toy Story Mania! is the biggest bottleneck in Walt Disney World, surpassing even Test Track at Epcot. The only way to get aboard without a horrendous wait is to be one of the first through the turnstiles when the park opens and zoom to the attraction. Another alternative is to obtain Fastpasses for Toy Story Mania! as soon as the park opens and then backtrack to ride the Rock 'n' Roller Coaster and Tower of Terror. Don't think you'll have all day to procure Fastpasses, though: even on days of moderate attendance, all Fastpasses for the day are usually gone by 11 a.m. Also, expect long queues at the Fastpass kiosks.

MICKEY AVENUE

DESIGNATED AS A NEW THEMED AREA in 2011, Mickey Avenue hosts two minor attractions on the pedestrian promenade that connects Pixar Place and the Animation Courtyard.

Journey into Narnia: Prince Caspian

DESCRIPTION AND COMMENTS Disney has been using the soundstage between Walt Disney: One Man's Dream and Toy Story Mania! to promote the Chronicles of Narnia films, but to call this sparse offering an attraction is a stretch. If you're a C. S. Lewis fan, see the attraction—it has some behind-the-scenes footage and concept art from the films, new props, and costumes. Otherwise, skip it.

Walt Disney: One Man's Dream ★★★★

APPEAL BY AGE	PRESCHOOL ★★	GRADE SCHOOL ★★★	TEENS ★★★½
YOUNG ADULTS ★★★★		OVER 30 ★★★★	SENIORS ★★★★

What it is Tribute to Walt Disney. **Scope and scale** Minor attraction. **When to go** Anytime. **Authors' rating** Excellent—and about time; ★★★★. **Duration of presentation** 25 minutes. **Preshow entertainment** Disney memorabilia. **Probable waiting time** For the film, 10 minutes.

DESCRIPTION AND COMMENTS Launched in 2001 to celebrate the 100th anniversary of Walt Disney's birthday, *One Man's Dream* consists of an exhibit area showcasing Disney memorabilia and recordings, followed by a film documenting Disney's life. On display are a replica of Walt's California office, various innovations in animation developed by Disney, and early models and working plans for Walt Disney World and various Disney theme parks around the world. The film provides a personal glimpse of Disney and offers insights regarding both his successes and failures.

TOURING TIPS Give yourself some time here. Every minute spent among these extraordinary artifacts will enhance your visit, taking you back to a time when the creativity and vision that created Walt Disney World were personified by one struggling entrepreneur.

ANIMATION COURTYARD

THIS AREA IS TO THE RIGHT of the big blue sorcerer's hat in the middle of the park. It holds two large theaters used for live stage shows, plus a separate attraction focusing on Disney animation. Spend any time here, and you'll slowly realize it's just a big swath of asphalt, and in desperate need of some landscaping or a water feature.

Disney Junior—Live on Stage! ★★★★

APPEAL BY AGE	PRESCHOOL ★★★★½	GRADE SCHOOL ★★★★	TEENS ★½
YOUNG ADULTS ★★		OVER 30 ★★½	SENIORS ★★½

What it is Live show for children. **Scope and scale** Minor attraction. **When to go** Per the daily entertainment schedule. **Authors' rating** A must for families with preschoolers; ★★★★. **Duration of presentation** 20 minutes. **Special comments** Audience sits on the floor. **When to arrive** 30+ minutes before showtime.

DESCRIPTION AND COMMENTS The show features characters from the Disney Channel's *Little Einsteins, Mickey Mouse Clubhouse, Jake and the Never Land Pirates,* and *Handy Manny,* plus other characters. Reengineered in 2011, *Disney Junior* uses elaborate puppets instead of live characters on stage. A simple plot serves as the platform for singing, dancing, some great puppetry, and a great deal of audience participation. The characters, who ooze love and goodness, rally throngs of tots and preschoolers to sing and dance along with them. All the jumping, squirming, and high-stepping is facilitated by having the audience sit on the floor so that kids can spontaneously erupt into motion when the mood strikes.

TOURING TIPS The show is headquartered in what was formerly the Soundstage Restaurant located to the immediate right of the Animation Tour. Show up at least 30 minutes before showtime. Once inside, pick a spot on the floor and take a breather until the performance begins.

The Magic of Disney Animation ★★½

APPEAL BY AGE	PRESCHOOL ★★★	GRADE SCHOOL ★★★½	TEENS ★★★½
YOUNG ADULTS ★★★½		OVER 30 ★★★½	SENIORS ★★★½

What it is Overview of Disney Animation process with limited hands-on demonstrations. **Scope and scale** Minor attraction. **When to go** Before 11 a.m. or after 5 p.m. **Special comments** Opens an hour later than the rest of the park. **Authors' rating** Not as good as previous renditions; ★★½. **Duration of presentation** 30 minutes. **Preshow entertainment** Gallery of animation art in waiting area. **Average wait in line per 100 people ahead of you** 7 minutes.

DESCRIPTION AND COMMENTS The consolidation of Disney Animation at the Burbank, California, studio has left this attraction without a story to tell. Park guests can still get a general overview of the Disney animation process, but they will not see the detailed work of actual artists as was possible in previous versions.

The revamped attraction starts in a small theater, where the audience is introduced to a cast-member host and Mushu, the dragon from Mulan. Between the host's speech, Mushu's constant interruptions, and a very brief taped segment with real Disney animators, guests are hard-pressed to learn anything about actual animation.

Next, the audience moves to another room with floor seating, where another cast member gives guests a verbal description of what used to be the walking tour of the actual animation studio. The cast member fields questions from the audience, but nothing truly enlightening is presented.

Afterwards, guests have the option of exiting the attraction or attending the Animation Academy (space is limited and is on a first-come, first-served basis). This is by far the most interesting segment of the attraction, but not designed for all guests. The animator works quickly, which seems to frustrate younger guests who need more time or assistance to get their drawing right.

TOURING TIPS Some days, the animation tour doesn't open until 10 or 11 a.m., by which time the park is pretty full. The tour is a relatively small-volume attraction, and lines can build on busy days by mid- to late morning.

Voyage of the Little Mermaid (Fastpass) ★★★★

APPEAL BY AGE	PRESCHOOL ★★★★	GRADE SCHOOL ★★★★	TEENS ★★★
YOUNG ADULTS ★★★½		OVER 30 ★★★★	SENIORS ★★★★

What it is Musical stage show featuring characters from the Disney movie *The Little Mermaid*. **Scope and scale** Major attraction. **When to go** Before 9:45 a.m., just before closing, or use Fastpass. **Authors' rating** Romantic, lovable, and humorous in the best Disney tradition; not to be missed; ★★★★. **Duration of presentation** 15 minutes. **Pre-show entertainment** Taped ramblings about the decor in the pre-show holding area. **Probable waiting time** Before 9:30 a.m., 10–30 minutes; after 9:30 a.m., 35–70 minutes.

DESCRIPTION AND COMMENTS *Voyage of the Little Mermaid* is a winner, appealing to every age. Cute without being silly or saccharine, and infinitely lovable, the *Little Mermaid* show is the most tender and romantic entertainment offered anywhere in Walt Disney World. The story is simple and engaging, the special effects impressive, and the Disney characters memorable.

TOURING TIPS Located at a busy pedestrian intersection, *Voyage of the Little Mermaid* plays to capacity crowds all day. Half of each audience is drawn from the standby line. As a rough approximation, guests in the front third of the queuing area will usually make it into the next performance, and quite often folks in the front half of the queuing area will be admitted. Those in the back half of the queuing area will probably have to wait through two showings before being admitted.

LIVE ENTERTAINMENT *at* DISNEY'S HOLLYWOOD STUDIOS

WHEN THE STUDIOS OPENED, live entertainment, parades, and special events weren't as fully developed or elaborate as those at the Magic Kingdom or Epcot. With the introduction of an afternoon parade and elaborate shows at **Theater of the Stars,** the Studios joined the big leagues. In 1998, DHS launched a new edition of *Fantasmic!* (see page 238), a water, fireworks, and laser show that draws rave reviews.

AFTERNOON PARADE Staged once a day, the parade begins near the park's entrance, continues down Hollywood Boulevard, and circles in front of the giant hat. From there, it passes in front of *Sounds Dangerous with Drew Carey* and ends by Star Tours. An alternate route begins at the far end of Sunset Boulevard and turns right, onto Hollywood Boulevard. The Studios' latest parade, **Pixar Pals Countdown to Fun,** features floats and characters from Pixar's films including *Toy Story, A Bug's Life, The Incredibles, Ratatouille, Monsters, Inc.* and *Up.*

DISNEY CHANNEL ROCKS! We can't fault Disney for trying to cash in on the success of its movie franchises, including *High School Musical,* The Cheetah Girls, and Camp Rock. The performers sing and dance their way through songs from Disney's original movies and TV shows with an enthusiasm suggesting they all had Mountain Dew for breakfast (and we mean that in a good way). Problem is, Disney doesn't give them anything in the way of a venue or script to work with. Their stage is essentially a repurposed parade float on which the old *High School Musical Pep Rally* show was shown, with new logos. The performers' singing and dancing are wasted on the show designer's lack of creativity.

DISNEY CHARACTERS Find characters in front of the Sorcerer's Hat, in front of the Magic of Disney Animation building, at the *Cars* Meet and Greet (near Mama Melrose's in Streets of America), in the Animation Courtyard, along Pixar Place, and in parades. Characters from *Monsters, Inc.* can sometimes be found near the Studio Backlot Tour. Times and locations for character appearances are listed in the complimentary *Times Guide.*

STREET ENTERTAINMENT The Studios has one of the best collections of roving street performers in all of Walt Disney World. Appearing primarily on Hollywood and Sunset boulevards, the cast of characters includes Hollywood stars and wannabes, their agents, directors, and gossip columnists. If you're looking for a spot to rest and a bit of entertainment, grab a drink and seek out these performers. Just keep in mind that they aren't shy about asking you to join their antics.

DISNEY'S HOLLYWOOD STUDIOS TOURING PLANS

TOURING THE STUDIOS CENTERS primarily around Toy Story Mania! and the fact that it simply cannot handle the number of guests who want to ride. A wonderful attraction for small children, it's therefore the first choice for families with young kids.

"NOT A TOURING PLAN" TOURING PLANS

FOR THE TYPE B READER, these touring plans avoid detailed, step-by-step strategies for saving every last minute in line. Use these guidelines to avoid the longest waits in line while having maximum flexibility to see whatever interests you in a particular part of the park.

FOR PARENTS ARRIVING AT PARK OPENING Ride *Toy Story* Mania!, then head to Animation Courtyard to begin a counterclockwise tour of the park starting with *Voyage of the Little Mermaid.* Work in other shows as you near them. End day on Sunset Boulevard for *Fantasmic!*

FOR ADULTS ARRIVING AT PARK OPENING See Rock 'n' Roller Coaster, Tower of Terror, and then begin a counterclockwise tour of the park with Toy Story Mania! and The Great Movie Ride. End in Animation Courtyard for *Voyage of the Little Mermaid* and The Magic of Disney Animation. Work in other shows as you near them. End day on Sunset Boulevard for *Fantasmic!*

FOR PARENTS AND ADULTS ARRIVING LATE MORNING Try to get Fastpasses for Rock 'n' Roller Coaster or Tower of Terror (in that order). Start clockwise tour of park with Studio Backlot Tour, working in shows as you near them. Save Toy Story Mania! for last, grab a bite to eat, and see *Fantasmic!*

BEFORE YOU GO

1. Call ☎ 407-824-4321 to verify the park's hours.
2. Buy your admission before arriving.

3. Make lunch and dinner Advance Reservations, or reserve the *Fantasmic!* dinner package (if desired) before you arrive, by calling ☎ 407-WDW-DINE.

4. Review the handout daily *Times Guide* to get a fairly clear picture of your options.

Disney's Hollywood Studios One-day Touring Plan

1. Arrive at the park 30–40 minutes before official opening time. Obtain a park map and daily entertainment schedule.

2. As soon as the park opens, ride Toy Story Mania!

3. Ride Rock 'n' Roller Coaster.

4. Ride the Tower of Terror. Use Fastpass if wait exceeds 30 minutes.

5. Ride The Great Movie Ride.

6. Obtain Fastpasses for *Voyage of the Little Mermaid.*

7. Take the Studio Backlot Tour.

8. If your Fastpass showtimes for *Voyage of the Little Mermaid* are soon, return for your performance. Disney rarely enforces the return times on Fastpasses, so you could also skip to Step 9 and return to *Mermaid* after seeing *Walt Disney: One Man's Dream* in Step 16.

9. Check your entertainment schedule for the next performance of the *Lights, Motors, Action!* show. See the show or eat lunch.

10. See *Lights, Motors, Action!* if you haven't already.

11. Explore the Streets of America on the way to *Muppet-Vision 3-D.*

12. See *Muppet-Vision 3-D.*

13. Head toward Echo Lake. If you have small children, check the daily entertainment schedule for the next performance of *Jedi Training Academy* and work Star Tours in around that show. Use Fastpass for Star Tours if wait exceeds 20 minutes.

14. Check your entertainment schedule for the next *Indiana Jones* show. If it's within 25 minutes, get in line now.

15. See *Walt Disney: One Man's Dream.*

16. Check your entertainment schedule for the next performance of *The American Idol Experience.*

17. Tour The Magic of Disney Animation. If time is short and you have small children, choose between this and *Disney Junior–Live on Stage!*

18. Work in *Disney Junior–Live on Stage!* if you have small children.

19. See *Beauty and the Beast.*

20. Tour Hollywood and Sunset boulevards.

21. Enjoy *Fantasmic!,* if it's playing.

DISNEY HAS TWO SWIMMING THEME PARKS, and two independent water parks are in the area. At Disney World, **Typhoon Lagoon** is the most diverse Disney splash pad, while **Blizzard Beach** takes the prize for the most slides and most bizarre theme. Outside the World, find **Wet 'n Wild** on International Drive and **Aquatica by SeaWorld.**

At all Disney water parks, the following rules and prices apply: one cooler per family or group is allowed, but no glass and no alcoholic beverages; towels are $2; lockers are $13 small, $15 large (includes $5 refundable deposit); life jackets are available at no cost. Admission to both parks, including tax, is $49 a day for adults and $43 a day for children ages 3–9. Children younger than age 3 are admitted free. For more information, call ☎ 407-939-6244.

BLIZZARD BEACH

BLIZZARD BEACH IS DISNEY'S MOST EXOTIC water adventure park and, like Typhoon Lagoon, it arrived with its own legend. This time, the story goes, an entrepreneur tried to open a ski resort in Florida during a particularly savage winter. Alas, the snow melted; the palm trees grew back; and all that remained of the ski resort was its Alpine lodge, the ski lifts, and, of course, the mountain. Plunging off the mountain are ski slopes and bobsled runs transformed into waterslides. Visitors to Blizzard Beach catch the thaw: icicles drip and patches of snow remain. The melting snow has formed a lagoon (the wave pool), fed by gushing mountain streams.

In addition to the wave pool, there are 17 slides (2 of which are quite long), a children's swimming area, and a tranquil stream for tubing. Picnic areas and sunbathing beaches dot the park. **Summit Plummet,** one of the world's longest speed slides, begins with a steep 120-foot descent. The **Teamboat Springs** slide is 1,200 feet long.

TYPHOON LAGOON

TYPHOON LAGOON IS COMPARABLE in size to Blizzard Beach. Eleven waterslides and streams, some as long as 400 feet, drop from the top of a 100-foot-tall, man-made mountain. Landscaping and an "aftermath-of-a-typhoon" theme add adventure to the wet rides.

Typhoon Lagoon provides water adventure for all ages. Activity pools for young children and families feature geysers, tame slides, bubble jets, and fountains. For the older and more adventurous are the enclosed **Humunga Kowabunga** speed slides, corkscrew storm slides, and three whitewater-raft rides (plus a children's rapids ride) plopping off **Mount Mayday.** Slower metabolisms will enjoy the scenic, meandering 2,100-foot-long stream that floats tubers through a hidden grotto and rain forest. And, of course, the sedentary will usually find plenty of sun to sleep in. Typhoon Lagoon's **surf pool** and **Shark Reef** are unique, and the wave pool is the world's largest inland surf facility, with waves up to 6 feet high. Shark Reef is a saltwater snorkeling pool where guests can swim among real fish.

WHEN *to* GO

THE BEST WAY TO AVOID STANDING IN LINES is to visit the water parks when they're less crowded. Our research indicates that tourists, not locals, are the majority of water-park visitors on any given day. And because weekends are popular travel days, the water parks tend to be less crowded then. In fact, of the weekend days we evaluated, the parks never reached full capacity; during the week, conversely, one or both parks closed every Thursday we monitored, and both closed at least once every other weekday. If you're a Disney resort guest, by all means use your morning Extra Magic Hours privileges; otherwise we recommend going on a weekend. If you too are traveling over the weekend, go on a Monday or Friday.

unofficial **TIP**
Fridays are good
because people
traveling by car
commonly use
this day to start
home. Sunday
morning also has
lighter crowds.

If your schedule is flexible, a good time to visit the swimming parks is midafternoon to late in the day when the weather has cleared after a storm. The parks usually close during bad weather. If the storm is prolonged, most guests leave for their hotels. When Typhoon Lagoon or Blizzard Beach reopen after inclement weather has passed, you almost have a whole park to yourself.

PART FOURTEEN

BEYOND *the* PARKS

DOWNTOWN DISNEY

DOWNTOWN DISNEY IS A SHOPPING, DINING, AND entertainment development strung out along the banks of Lake Buena Vista. On the far right is the **Downtown Disney Marketplace;** on the far left is **Downtown Disney West Side.**

DOWNTOWN DISNEY MARKETPLACE

ALTHOUGH THE MARKETPLACE OFFERS interactive fountains, a couple of playgrounds, a lakeside amphitheater, and watercraft rentals, it is primarily a shopping and dining venue. The centerpiece of shopping is the 50,000-square-foot **World of Disney,** the largest store in the world that sells Disney-trademark merchandise.

At **Disney's Design-a-Tee** you can create customized T-shirts, and **Mickey's Pantry** offers Disney home and kitchen products. Another noteworthy retailer is the **LEGO Imagination Center,** showcasing a number of huge and unbelievable sculptures made entirely of LEGO "bricks." Spaceships, sea serpents, sleeping tourists, and dinosaurs are just a few of the sculptures on display. **Once Upon a Toy** is a toys, games, and collectibles superstore. Rounding out the selection are stores specializing in resort wear, athletic attire and gear, Christmas decorations, Disney art and collectibles, and handmade craft items. Most retail establishments are open from 9:30 a.m. until 11:30 p.m.

Rainforest Cafe and **T-REX** are the headliner restaurants at the Marketplace. The others are **Pollo Campero,** a Latin chicken eatery; **Cap'n Jack's Restaurant; Earl of Sandwich; Wolfgang Puck Express Cafe;** and **Ghirardelli Soda Fountain & Chocolate Shop.**

DOWNTOWN DISNEY WEST SIDE

THE WEST SIDE IS THE NEWEST ADDITION to Downtown Disney and offers a broad range of entertainment, dining, and shopping. Restaurants include the **House of Blues,** which serves Cajun specialties; **Planet Hollywood,** offering movie memorabilia and basic American fare; **Bongos Cuban Cafe,** serving Cuban favorites; and **Wolfgang Puck Grand Cafe,** featuring California cuisine. West Side shopping is some of the most interesting in Disney World. For instance, there's **Pop Gallery,** selling high-end paintings and sculptures, and **D-Street,** offering "cutting edge" (read: bizarre) apparel and Vinylmation figurines. Other shops include a cigar shop, a magic shop, and a designer-sunglasses studio.

In the entertainment department, there is **DisneyQuest,** an interactive theme park contained in a building; the **House of Blues,** a concert and dining venue; and a 24-screen **AMC** movie theater. The West Side is also home to **Cirque du Soleil La Nouba,** a not-to-be-missed production show with a cast of more than 70 performers and musicians.

DISNEYQUEST

DISNEYQUEST, IN CONCEPT AND ATTRACTION mix, is aimed at a youthful audience, say, 8–35 years of age, though younger and older patrons will enjoy much of what it offers. The feel is dynamic, bustling, and noisy. Those who haunt the video arcades at shopping malls will feel most at home at DisneyQuest. And like most malls, when late afternoon turns to evening, the median age at DisneyQuest rises with the arrival of adolescents and teens who have been released from parental supervision for a while.

You begin your experience in the **Departure Lobby,** adjacent to admission sales. From the Departure Lobby you enter a "Cyberlator," a "transitional attraction" (read: elevator) hosted by the Genie from *Aladdin,* that delivers you to an entrance plaza called **Ventureport.** From here you can enter the four zones. As in the larger parks, each zone is distinctively themed. Some zones cover more than one floor, so, looking around, you can see things going on both above and below you. The four zones, in no particular order, are **Explore Zone, Score Zone, Create Zone,** and **Replay Zone.**

Though most kids and adolescents aren't going to care, the zone layout at DisneyQuest may confuse adults trying to orient themselves. Don't count on trapping certain kids in certain zones either, or planning a rendezvous inside one without designating a specific location. Each zone spreads out over multiple levels, with stairways, elevators, slides, and walkways linking them in a variety of ways. Still, as we said, the labyrinthine design of the place won't bother most youngsters, who are usually happy just to wander (or dash madly) between games and rides.

ESPN WIDE WORLD *of* SPORTS COMPLEX

THIS 220-ACRE, STATE-OF-THE-ART competition and training center consists of a 9,500-seat ballpark, a fieldhouse, and dedicated venues for baseball, softball, tennis, track and field, beach volleyball, and 27 other sports. From Little League Baseball to rugby to beach volleyball, the complex hosts a mind-boggling calendar of professional and amateur competitions.

Counter-service and full-service dining are available at the sports complex, but there's no on-site lodging. Disney's Wide World of Sports is off Osceola Parkway, between World Drive and where the parkway crosses Interstate 4 (no interstate access). The complex has its own parking lot and is accessible via the Disney Transportation System.

The DISNEY WILDERNESS PRESERVE

LOCATED ABOUT 40–60 MINUTES SOUTH of Walt Disney World is the Disney Wilderness Preserve, a wetlands-restoration area operated by The Nature Conservancy in partnership with Disney. At 12,000 acres, this is as real as Disney gets. There are hiking trails and an interpretive center. Trails wind through grassy savannas, beneath ancient cypress trees, and along the banks of pristine Lake Russell. More than 1,000 species of plants and animals call the preserve home. Birds include the bald eagle, red-cockaded woodpecker, Florida scrub-jay, wood stork, sandhill crane, northern harrier, and crested caracara. Other wildlife includes the southeastern big-eared bat, Sherman's fox squirrel, eastern indigo snake, and gopher tortoise. The Florida panther has been spotted here as well. The preserve is open Monday–Friday from 9 a.m. to 5 p.m.; admission is free, though donations are welcome. For more information and directions, call ☎ 407-935-0002.

WALT DISNEY WORLD SPEEDWAY

ADJACENT TO THE TRANSPORTATION and ticket center parking lot sits the Walt Disney World Speedway, a 1-mile tri-oval course. If you're a NASCAR fan, check out the **Richard Petty Driving Experience,** where you can ride in a two-seater stock car for $105.44 (3 laps) or learn to drive one for $478.18 (8 laps), $904.19 (18 laps), or $1,383.44 (30 laps). (Prices include tax.) For information call ☎ 800-BE-PETTY (237-3889) or check out **drivepetty.com.**

Also at the speedway is the **Indy Racing Experience.** Usually starting in the afternoon when the Richard Petty folks have finished, this experience features sleeker, faster open-wheeled cars like those seen in the Indianapolis 500. You can ride in a modified two-seat Indy car or drive one of the single-seat cars. Cost is $109 to ride (3 laps) or $399 to drive (8 laps). For information call ☎ 317-243-7171, ext. 106, or 888-357-5002, ext. 106, or visit **indyracingexperience.com.**

WALT DISNEY WORLD RECREATION

MOST WALT DISNEY WORLD GUESTS never make it beyond the theme parks, the water parks, and Downtown Disney. Those who do, however, discover an extraordinary selection of recreational opportunities ranging from guided fishing adventures and water-skiing outings to hayrides, horseback riding, fitness-center workouts, and miniature golf. If it's something you can do at a resort, it's probably available at Walt Disney World.

Boat, bike, and fishing-equipment rentals are handled on an hourly basis. Just show up at the rental office during operating hours and they'll fix you up. The same goes for various fitness centers in the resort hotels. Golf, tennis, fishing expeditions, water-ski excursions, hayrides, trail rides, and most spa services must be scheduled in advance. Though every resort features an extensive selection of recreational options, those resorts located on a navigable body of water offer the greatest variety. Also, the more upscale a resort, the more likely it is to have such amenities as a fitness center and spa. In addition, you can rent boats and other recreational equipment at the Downtown Disney Marketplace.

WALT DISNEY WORLD GOLF

WALT DISNEY WORLD HAS FIVE GOLF COURSES, all expertly designed and meticulously maintained. The **Magnolia, Palm,** and **Oak trails** are across Floridian Way from the Polynesian Resort. They envelop the Shades of Green recreational complex; the pro shops and support facilities adjoin the Shades of Green hotel. **Lake Buena Vista Golf Course** is at the Saratoga Springs Resort, near Walt Disney World Village and across the lake from the former Pleasure Island. The **Osprey Ridge** course is adjacent to Fort Wilderness Campground. In addition to the golf courses, there are driving ranges and putting greens at each location.

Oak Trail is a nine-hole course for beginners. The other five courses are designed for the midhandicap player and, while interesting, are quite forgiving. All courses are popular, with morning tee times at a premium, especially January through April. (*Note:* Osprey Ridge is slated to be replaced by a new course that will anchor a golf community of private homes. It was originally scheduled to close in mid-2010, but with the economy having put a damper on the real estate project, the course is now expected to remain open until 2012 at the earliest.)

Peak season for all courses is January–May, and off-season is May–October; however, summer is peak season for the non-golf parts of Walt Disney World, including the hotels. Off-season and afternoon twilight rates are available. Carts are required (except at Oak Trail) and are included in the greens fee. Tee times may be reserved 90 days in advance by Disney resort guests and 60 days in advance by day guests with a credit card. Proper golf attire, including spikeless shoes, is required. A collared shirt and Bermuda-length shorts or slacks meet the requirements.

Besides the ability to book tee times further in advance, guests of Walt Disney World–owned resorts get other benefits that may sway a golfer's lodging decision. These include discounted greens fees, free club rental, and charge privileges. The single most important, and least known, benefit is the provision of free round-trip taxi transportation between the golf courses and your hotel, which lets you avoid moving your car or dragging your clubs on Disney buses. The cabs, which make access to the courses much simpler, are paid by vouchers happily supplied to hotel guests.

unofficial **TIP**
To avoid the crowds, play on a Monday, Tuesday, or Wednesday and sign up for a late-afternoon tee time.

For more information, call ☎ 407-938-GOLF (4653) or visit **disneyworld.disney.go.com/golf/course-rates**.

MINIATURE GOLF

FANTASIA GARDENS MINIATURE GOLF is an 11-acre complex with two 18-hole dink-and-putt golf courses. One course is an "adventure" course, themed after Disney's animated film *Fantasia*. The other course, geared more toward older children and adults, is an innovative approach-and-putt course with sand traps and water hazards.

Fantasia Gardens is on Epcot Resorts Boulevard, across the street from the Walt Disney World Swan; it's open daily, 10 a.m.–11 p.m. To reach the course via Disney transportation, take a bus or boat to the Swan resort. The cost to putt, including tax, is $12.78 for adults and $10 .65 for children ages 3–9. In case you arrive hungry or naked, Fantasia Gardens has a snack bar and gift shop. For more information, call ☎ 407-WDW-PLAY (939-7529).

In 1999, Disney opened **Winter Summerland,** a second mini-golf facility, located next to Blizzard Beach water park. Winter Summerland offers two 18-hole courses—one has a blizzard-in-Florida theme, the other a tropical-holiday theme. It's open daily, 10 a.m.–11 p.m., and the cost is the same as for Fantasia Gardens.

unofficial **TIP**
The Winter Summerland courses are much easier than the Fantasia courses, making them a better choice for families with preteen children.

PART FIFTEEN

NIGHTLIFE *in* WALT DISNEY WORLD

WALT DISNEY WORLD *at* NIGHT

IN THE THEME PARKS

EPCOT'S MAJOR EVENING EVENT IS *IllumiNations,* a laser and fireworks show at World Showcase Lagoon. Showtimes are listed in the daily entertainment schedule (*Times Guide*).

In the Magic Kingdom are the popular evening parade(s) and *Wishes* fireworks show. Consult the *Times Guide* for performances.

On selected nights when the park is open late, Disney's Hollywood Studios features a fireworks presentation called *Fantasmic!,* a laser, special-effects, and water spectacular; the *Times Guide* lists showtimes.

At present there is no nighttime entertainment at Disney's Animal Kingdom.

AT THE HOTELS

A SORT OF MAIN STREET ELECTRICAL PARADE on barges, the **Floating Electrical Pageant** stars creatures of the sea. This nightly spectacle, with background music played on a doozy of a synthesizer, is one of our favorite Disney productions. The first performance of the short but captivating show is at 9 p.m. off the Polynesian Resort docks. From there, it circles around and repeats at the Grand Floridian Resort & Spa at 9:15 p.m., heading afterward to Fort Wilderness resort & Campground, Wilderness Lodge & Villas, and the Contemporary Resort–Bay Lake Tower.

For something more elaborate, consider a dinner theater. If you want to go honky-tonkin', the Buena Vista Palace, Hilton, and Royal Plaza hotels at the Downtown Disney Resort Area have lively (all right, all right, *relatively* lively) bars.

AT FORT WILDERNESS CAMPGROUND

THE NIGHTLY CAMPFIRE PROGRAM AT Fort Wilderness Campground begins with a sing-along led by Disney characters Chip 'n' Dale and progresses to cartoons and a Disney movie. Only Disney lodging guests may attend. There's no charge.

AT DISNEY'S BOARDWALK

THE BOARDWALK'S **Jellyrolls** features dueling pianos and sing-alongs. The BoardWalk also has Disney's first and only brewpub. An ESPN sports bar; the **Atlantic Dance Hall,** an upscale and largely deserted dance club; and several restaurants complete the BoardWalk's entertainment mix. Access is by foot from Epcot, by launch from Disney's Hollywood Studios, and by bus from other Disney World locations. The *Unofficial Guide* research team rates Jellyrolls as its second favorite of all Disney nightspots (**Raglan Road** at Downtown Disney is our top pick). It's raucous, frequently hilarious, and positively rejuvenating. The piano players are outstanding. Best of all, it's strictly for adults.

AT CORONADO SPRINGS RESORT

PERHAPS DISNEY'S HIPPEST NIGHTSPOT is the 5,000-square-foot **Rix Lounge,** a Vegas-ultralounge clone. DJs spin Top 40 tracks from 9 p.m. to 2 a.m.; a percussion band performs on select evenings. Few locals or resort guests have discovered Rix, so the place is frequently dead unless there's a big meeting or trade show at Coronado Springs. Also at this resort is the **Laguna Bar,** a romantic outdoor-terrace affair arrayed alongside the lake.

AT DOWNTOWN DISNEY

PLEASURE ISLAND Disney World's nighttime-entertainment complex cashed in its chips in the fall of 2008. Gone are the BET Soundstage Club, Mannequins Dance Palace, Motion, 8 TRAX, the Comedy Warehouse, and the much-loved Adventurers Club. This last so exemplified Disney whimsy that everyone thought it would surely escape the ax. No such luck. All the Pleasure Island restaurants survived, though, as did a few shops. For now, the only live-music venue is

Raglan Road, an Irish pub and restaurant. The site is being redeveloped into a dining and shopping district called **Hyperion Wharf.**

DOWNTOWN DISNEY MARKETPLACE It's flog your wallet each night at the Marketplace, with shops open until 11:30 p.m.

DOWNTOWN DISNEY WEST SIDE This is a 70-acre shopping, restaurant, and nightlife complex situated to the left of what once was Pleasure Island. The West Side features a 24-screen **AMC** movie complex, the **DisneyQuest** pay-for-play indoor theme park (see page 260), a permanent showplace for the extraordinary **Cirque du Soleil,** and a 2,000-capacity **House of Blues** concert hall. The dining options include **Planet Hollywood,** a 450-seat Cajun restaurant at **House of Blues, Wolfgang Puck** (serving California fare), and **Bongos Cuban Cafe,** owned by Gloria and Emilio Estefan. The West Side can be accessed via Disney buses from most Disney World locations.

Cirque du Soleil *La Nouba*

APPEAL BY AGE	UNDER 21 ★★★★	21–37 ★★★★★	38–50 ★★★★★
51 AND UP ★★★★½			

Type of show Circus as theater. **Tickets and information** ☎ 407-939-7600; cirquedusoleil.com/lanouba. **Admission cost** *Category Front & Center:* $132.06 adults, $105.44 children ages 3–9; *Category 1:* $116.09 adults, $92.66 children; *Category 2:* $92.66 adults, $74.55 children; *Category 3:* $75.62 adults, $60.71 children. *Category 4:* $60.71 adults and children. All prices include tax. **Cast size** 72. **Night of lowest attendance** Thursday. **Usual showtimes** Tuesday–Saturday, 6 p.m. and 9 p.m. **Authors' rating** ★★★★★. **Duration of presentation** 1 hour, 45 minutes (no intermission) plus preshow.

DESCRIPTION AND COMMENTS *La Nouba* is a far cry from a traditional circus but retains all the fun and excitement. It is whimsical, mystical, and sophisticated, yet pleasing to all ages. The action takes place on an elaborate stage that incorporates almost every part of the theater.

TOURING TIPS Be forewarned that the audience is an integral part of *La Nouba* and that at almost any time you might be plucked from your seat to participate. Our advice is to loosen up and roll with it. If you are too rigid, repressed, hungover, or whatever to get involved, politely but firmly decline to be conscripted. Then fix a death grip on the arms of your chair. Tickets for reserved seats can be purchased in advance at the Cirque box

unofficial **TIP** Unless you cancel your tickets at least 48 hours before your reservation time, your credit card will still be charged the full amount.

office or over the phone, using your credit card. Oh yeah, don't wait until the last minute; book well in advance from home.

House of Blues

Type of show Live concerts with an emphasis on rock and blues. **Tickets and information** ☎ 407-934-2222; **hob.com. Admission cost with taxes** About $8–$95, depending on who's performing. **Nights of lowest attendance** Monday and Tuesday. **Usual showtimes** Varies between 7 p.m. and 9:30 p.m. depending on who's performing.

DESCRIPTION AND COMMENTS The House of Blues, developed by original Blues Brother Dan Aykroyd, features a restaurant and blues bar, as well as the concert hall. The restaurant serves Thursday–Saturday from 11 a.m. until 1:30 a.m., which makes it one of the few late-night-dining options in Walt Disney World. Live music cranks up every night at 10:30 p.m. in the restaurant–blues bar, but even before then, the joint is way beyond 110 decibels. The music hall next door features concerts by an eclectic array of musicians and groups. During one visit, the show bill listed gospel, blues, funk, ska, dance, salsa, rap, zydeco, hard rock, groove rock, and reggae groups over a two-week period.

TOURING TIPS Prices vary from night to night according to the fame and drawing power of the featured band. Tickets ranged from $8 to $62 during our visits but go higher when a really big name is scheduled.

The music hall is set up like a nightclub, with tables and bar stools for only about 150 people and standing room for a whopping 1,850 people. Folks dance when there's room and sometimes when there isn't. The tables and stools are first-come, first-served, with doors opening an hour before showtime on weekdays and 90 minutes before showtime on weekends. Acoustics are good, and the showroom is small enough to provide a relatively intimate concert experience. All shows are all ages unless otherwise indicated.

WALT DISNEY WORLD DINNER THEATERS

SEVERAL DINNER-THEATER SHOWS play each night at Walt Disney World, and unlike other Disney dining venues, they make hard reservations instead of Advance Reservations, meaning you must guarantee your reservation ahead of time with a credit card. You'll receive a confirmation number and be told to pick up your tickets at a Disney-hotel Guest Relations desk. Unless you cancel your tickets at least 48 hours before your reservation time, your credit card will still be charged the full amount. Dinner-show reservations can be made 180 days in advance; call ☎ 407-939-3463. While getting reservations for the *Spirit of Aloha Dinner Show* isn't terribly tough, booking the *Hoop-Dee-Doo Musical Revue* is a trick of the first order.

1. Call ☎ 407-939-3463 at 9 a.m. each morning while you're at Disney World to make a same-day reservation. There are three performances each night, and for all three combined, only 3–24 people total will be admitted with same-day reservations.

2. Arrive at the show of your choice 45 minutes before showtime (early and late shows are your best bets) and put your name on the standby list. If someone with reservations fails to show, you may be admitted.

Hoop-Dee-Doo Musical Revue

Pioneer Hall, Fort Wilderness Campground ☎ 407-939-3463. **Showtimes** 5, 7:15, and 9:30 p.m. nightly. **Cost** $59–$68 adults, $30–$35 children ages 3–9. Prices include tax and gratuity. **Discounts** Seasonal. **Type of seating** Tables of various sizes to fit the number in each party, set in an Old West–style dance hall. **Menu** All-you-can-eat barbecue ribs, fried chicken, corn, and strawberry shortcake. **Vegetarian alternative** On request (at least 24 hours in advance). **Beverages** Unlimited beer, wine, sangria, and soft drinks.

DESCRIPTION AND COMMENTS Six Wild West performers arrive by stagecoach (sound effects only) to entertain the crowd inside Pioneer Hall. There isn't much plot, just corny jokes interspersed with song or dance. The humor is of the *Hee-Haw* ilk but is presented enthusiastically.

Audience participation includes sing-alongs, hand-clapping, and a finale that uses volunteers to play parts onstage. Performers are accompanied by a banjo player and pianist who also play quietly while the food is being served. The fried chicken and corn-on-the-cob are good, the ribs a bit tough though tasty. With the all-you-can-eat policy, at least you can get your money's worth by stuffing yourself silly.

Mickey's Backyard BBQ

Fort Wilderness Campground ☎ 407-939-3463. **Showtimes** March–December, Thursday and Saturday, 6:30 p.m. **Cost** $47.91 adults, $28.74 children ages 3–9. Prices include tax. **Special comments** Operates seasonally. **Type of seating** Picnic tables. **Menu** Baked chicken, barbecued pork ribs, burgers, hot dogs, corn, beans, mac-and-cheese, salads and slaw, bread, and watermelon and ice-cream bars for dessert. **Vegetarian alternatives** On request. **Beverages** Unlimited beer, wine, lemonade, and iced tea.

DESCRIPTION AND COMMENTS Situated along Bay Lake and held in a covered pavilion next to the now-closed River Country swimming park, *Mickey's Backyard BBQ* features Mickey, Minnie, Chip 'n' Dale, and Goofy, along with a live country band and line dancing. Though the pavilion gets some breeze off Bay Lake, we recommend going during the spring or fall if possible. The food is pretty good, as is, fortunately, the insect control.

Because the barbecue is seasonal, dates are usually not entered into the WDW-DINE reservations system until late February or early March. Once the dates are in the system, you can make an advance reservation for anytime during the dinner show's 10-month season.

The easiest way to get to the barbecue is to take a boat from the Magic Kingdom or from one of the resorts on the Magic Kingdom monorail. Though getting to the barbecue is not nearly as difficult as commuting to the *Hoop-Dee-Doo Revue,* give yourself at least 45 minutes if you plan to arrive by boat.

Spirit of Aloha Dinner Show

Disney's Polynesian Resort ☎ 407-939-3463. **Showtimes** Tuesday–Saturday, 5:15 and 8 p.m. **Cost** $59–$68 adults, $30–$35 children ages 3–9. Prices include tax and gratuity. **Discounts** Seasonal. **Type of seating** Long rows of tables, with some separation between individual parties. The show is performed on an outdoor stage, but all seating is covered. Ceiling fans provide some air movement, but it can get warm, especially at the early show. **Menu** Tropical fruit, roasted chicken, island pork ribs, mixed vegetables, rice, and pineapple bread; chicken tenders, PB&J sandwich, mac-and-cheese, and hot dogs are also available for children. **Vegetarian alternative** On request. **Beverages** Beer, wine, and soft drinks.

DESCRIPTION AND COMMENTS Formerly the *Polynesian Luau,* this show features native dancing followed by a "Polynesian-style" all-you-can-eat meal. The dancing is interesting and largely authentic, and the dancers are attractive though definitely PG-rated in the Disney tradition. We think the show has its moments and the meal is adequate, but neither is particularly special.

APPENDIX

Disney-speak Pocket Translator

Although it may come as a surprise to many, Walt Disney World has its own somewhat peculiar language. Here are some terms you are likely to bump into:

DISNEYSPEAK	ENGLISH DEFINITION
Adventure	Ride
Attraction	Ride or theater show
Attraction host	Ride operator
Audience	Crowd
Backstage	Behind the scenes, out of view of customers
Bull pen	Queuing area
Cast member	Employee
Character	Disney character impersonated by an employee
Costume	Work attire or uniform
Dark ride	Indoor ride
Day guest	Any customer not staying at a Disney resort
Face character	A character who does not wear a head-covering costume (such as Snow White, Cinderella, and Jasmine)
General public	Same as day guest
Greeter	Employee positioned at an attraction entrance

Disney-speak Pocket Translator (cont'd.)

DISNEYSPEAK	ENGLISH DEFINITION
Guest	Customer
Hidden Mickeys	Frontal silhouette of Mickey's head worked subtly into the design of buildings, railings, vehicles, golf greens, attractions, and the like
In rehearsal	Operating, though not officially open
Lead	Foreman or manager, the person in charge of an attraction
On stage	In full view of customers
Pre-show	Entertainment at an attraction prior to the feature presentation
Resort guest	A customer staying at a Disney resort
Role	An employee's job
Security host	Security guard
Soft opening	Opening a park or attraction before its stated opening date
Transitional experience	An element of the queuing area and/or preshow that provides a story line or information essential to understanding the attraction

ACCOMMODATIONS INDEX

RESTAURANT INDEX

SUBJECT INDEX

2011 *Unofficial Guide* Reader Survey

If you would like to express your opinion in writing about Walt Disney World or this guidebook, complete the following survey and mail it to:

Unofficial Guide Reader Survey
P.O. Box 43673
Birmingham, AL 35243

Or fill out the survey online at **touringplans.com.**
Inclusive dates of your visit: _____
Your hometown: _____
Your e-mail address: _____

Members of your party: Person 1   Person 2   Person 3   Person 4   Person 5
Gender: M   F   M   F   M   F   M   F   M   F
Age: _____   _____   _____   _____   _____

How many times have you been to Walt Disney World? _____

CAR RENTALS Did you rent a car? _____ From what company? _____ Concerning your rental car, on a scale with 5 being best and 1 worst, how would you rate: Pickup-processing efficiency? _____ Return-processing efficiency? _____ Condition of the car? _____ Cleanliness of the car? _____ Airport-shuttle efficiency? _____

LODGING On your most recent trip, where did you stay? _____
_____

Have you stayed at any other hotels in the past 12 months? Yes ___ No ___

Please indicate the hotels you have stayed at in the past year, or write in others.
☐ Ritz-Carlton ☐ Marriott Hyatt ☐ Super 8 ☐ Holiday Inn ☐ Fairfield Inn ☐ Embassy Suites ☐ Omni ☐ Ramada Inn ☐ Days Inn ☐ Hilton ☐ Drury Inn ☐ Millennium ☐ Four Seasons ☐ Radisson ☐ Best Western
Others _____

Please tell us how important the following amenities were in your selection of a Walt Disney World–area resort/hotel. Select up to five amenities, and rank them in order of importance using 1 for the most important and 5 for the least.

Cost ___ Bar ___ Distance to parks ___ In-room dining/room service ___ Food court ___ Shuttle service to parks ___ Sit-down restaurant ___ Room size ___ Fine dining ___ Multiple-bedroom suites ___ Spa/fitness center ___ In-room kitchen ___ Pool ___ Shuttle service to/from airport ___ Architecture/theme ___ Kids' activity center ___ Location inside WDW ___

On a scale with 5 being best and 1 being worst, please indicate how satisfied you were with your accommodations. Please add other items you feel are important. *When rating food services, please rate only meals eaten at your resort.*

Cleanliness of room ___ Size and layout of pool ___ Comfort of beds and pillows ___ Crowd level at the pool ___ Room size and layout ___ Cleanliness of pool area ___ Quietness of room ___ Shuttle to/from airport ___ Check-in/out process ___ Shuttle to/from parks ___ Resort staff accessibility, friendliness, and knowledge ___ Recreational amenities (marina, bikes, fitness center, etc.) ___ Overall food-court experience ___ Ability to easily find your way around ___ Overall food-court value ___ Child-care services and facilities ___ Overall experience with the full-service restaurant ___ Overall layout of the resort ___ Overall value of full-service restaurant _____

2011 *Unofficial Guide* Survey (continued)

Please check the number that best describes how satisfied you were with
your total resort experience during this trip.

1 Very dissatisfied   2 Somewhat dissatisfied   3 Neither satisfied or dissatisfied
4 Somewhat satisfied   5 Very satisfied

Would you stay at this resort again? Yes ☐ No ☐

How likely are you to recommend this resort to a friend?
☐ Will definitely recommend   ☐ May recommend   ☐ Neutral
☐ Probably won't recommend   ☐ Definitely will not recommend

DINING Concerning your dining experiences:
How many restaurant meals (including fast food) did you average per day?
_____

How much (approximately) did your party spend on meals per day?
_____

Favorite restaurant outside Walt Disney World?
_____

PARK TOURING On a scale with 5 being best and 1 being worst,
please rate how the touring plans worked:

PARK   NAME OF PLAN   RATING

Magic Kingdom _____

Epcot _____

Disney's Animal Kingdom _____

DHS _____

OTHER How did you hear about this guide? _____
What other guidebooks or websites did you use on this trip?
On the 5-as-best, 1-as-worst scale, how would you rate them?

               NAME   RATING
Guidebooks _____
_____

websites _____
_____
_____

Using the same scale, how would you rate the *Unofficial Guide*?
Have you used other *Unofficial Guides*? Which ones?
_____

Additional comments you would like to share with us about your Walt
Disney World vacation or about the *Unofficial Guide:*
_____
_____
_____
_____
_____
_____